THE
ULTIMATE KAUAI
GUIDEBOOK
Kauai Revealed

7th Edition

Andrew Doughty

WIZARD
PUBLICATIONS
INC

The Ultimate Kauai Guidebook
Kauai Revealed; 7th Edition

Published by Wizard Publications, Inc.
Post Office Box 991
Lihu'e, Hawai'i 96766–0991

ISBN 13: 978-0-9814610–1–4   3079
Library of Congress Control Number 2008929726
Printed in China

Cataloging-in-Publication Data

Doughty, Andrew
      The Ultimate Kauai guidebook : Kauai revealed / Andrew Doughty -- 7th ed.
Lihue, HI : Wizard Publications, Inc., 2009
      p. 260: col. illus., col. photos, col. maps ; 21 cm.
      Includes index.
      Summary: A complete traveler's reference to the Hawaiian island of Kauai, with
full color illustrations, maps, directions and candid advice by an author who resides in
Hawaii.
      ISBN-13: 978-0-9814610-1-4
      LCCN: 2008929726
      1. Kaua'i (Hawaii) - Guidebooks. 2. Kaua'i (Hawaii) – Description and travel.
      I. Title.

DU628.K3   919.69'41_dc22

All photographs (except the cover) taken by Andrew Doughty and Leona Boyd.
Cover imagery courtesy of NASA.
Cartography by Andrew Doughty.
All artwork and illustrations by Andrew Doughty.

Pages 2–3: Wai'ale'ale Crater, with its 3,000-foot waterfall-etched walls, was the spiritual center of the ancient Hawaiian universe.

We welcome any comments, questions, criticisms or contributions you may have, and have incorporated some of your suggestions into this edition. Please send to the address above or e-mail us at **aloha@wizardpub.com**

Check out our website at **www.wizardpub.com** for up-to-the-minute changes.

Dedicated to Sammie Dollar, who soars on the wind with the white-tailed tropic birds.

CONTENTS

ACTIVITIES
118

ISLAND DINING
202

WHERE TO STAY
232

ADVENTURES
186

INDEX
254

In a sense, this is not a guidebook, it's more of a love story. Having first seen the island as a tourist, I was immediately smitten. I had no idea that a place like this could exist anywhere in the world. Now as a resident, I marvel at its beauty every day.

Longtime locals have been stunned at some of the items in our book. We've found many special places that people born and raised here never knew about. Visitors will find this book as valuable as having a friend living on the island.

Kaua'i is a unique place. People who visit here recognize this immediately. There are plenty of places in the world featuring sun and sea, but no other place offers the incomparable beauty, lushness and serenity of Kaua'i. Living here, we get to see first-time visitors driving around with their jaws open, shaking their heads in disbelief at what they see. Without a doubt, you will never see more smiles than during your visit to Kaua'i.

Our objective at Wizard Publications is to assist you in finding the bliss that can accompany a Kaua'i visit. We recognize the effort people go through to visit here, and our goal is to expose you to every option imaginable so you can decide what you want to see and do.

We took great pains to structure this book in such a way that it will be fun, easy reading and loaded with useful information. This book is not a bland regurgitation of facts arranged in textbook fashion. We feel strongly that guidebooks should present information so that you don't have to read through every page every time you want to find something. If you're here on vacation, your time is extremely precious. You worked all year to get here, and you don't want to spend all your time flipping through a book looking for some-thing. You want to be able to locate what you want when you want it. You want to be able to access a comprehensive index, a thorough table of contents and refer to high-quality maps that were designed with *you* in mind. You want to know which helicopter, SCUBA, boat tour or lu'au is the best on the island. You want to be shown those things that will make this vacation the best of your life.

A quick look at this book will reveal features never before used in a guidebook. Let's start with the maps. They are more detailed than any other maps you will find, yet they omit extraneous information that can sometimes make a chore of reading a map. We know that people often have a hard time determining where they are on a map, especially here, so we have included landmarks. Most notable among these are mile markers. At every mile on main roads, the government has erected numbered markers to tell you where you are. We were the first to put these markers on a map so you can use them as reference points. We also made every effort to place north at the top of the page. It can be confusing when you see a map with south pointing up or to the right. Only a couple of trail maps deviate from this rule. Additionally, we repeatedly drove every inch of every road on the maps. This is important because *many* of the roads represented on existing maps have been shifted, moved or eliminated. You could become very frustrated trying to find certain beaches or other scenic spots using other maps. We personally check every place and often use aerial photography and a GPS to determine the best methods for getting to certain places.

Early on, I spent three days trying to find a certain secluded beach using existing maps. When I checked aerial shots, I discovered that *every single map was wrong*. Getting to the beach was a snap—if you knew where to go. Where needed, we've drawn legal public beach access in yellow, so you'll know when you are legally entitled to cross someone's land. Lastly, all the maps are 3-D. We've found that *accurate* shaded relief maps easily convey much more information to the map reader.

One of the things unique to this book is the acceptance of change. We produce brand new editions of our books every two years or so, but in the intervening time we are constantly incorporating changes into the text nearly every time we do a new printing. We also post these changes on our website. This allows us to make some modifications throughout the life of each edition. We don't have the luxury of making every change that happens on a weekly basis, but it does give us more flexibility than if we only acknowledged changes every two years.

Slick (and not so slick) free magazines and publications are strewn throughout the island. Most claim to point you to assorted wonders. There's nothing wrong with that. But the adage, "You get what you pay for," applies. Let's put it this way: If all the companies in this book were companies that we had to solicit for advertising, how much candor do you think we could provide? That's why *you* pay for the book, not the companies we describe. We're free to be as brutally honest as we want to be. Since we accept no advertisements, our allegiance is to our readers, not advertisers. Nonetheless, these free publications can be useful for the coupons that advertisers put inside.

As you read this book, you will notice that we are very candid in assessing businesses. Unlike some other guidebooks that send out questionnaires asking a business if they are any good (gee, they *all* say they're good), we've had *personal* contact with the businesses listed in this book. We accept no payment for our reviews, we make no deals with businesses for saying nice things, and again, there are *no advertisements* in our book. If we gush over a certain company, it comes from personal experience with the company. If we rail against a business, it is for the same reason. All businesses mentioned in this book are here by *our* choice. None have had any input into what we say, and we have not received a single cent from any of them for their inclusion. (In fact, some would probably pay to be left out of this book, given our comments.) We always approach businesses as *anonymous travelers* and later by phone as guidebook writers only if we need more information. This ensures that we are treated the same as you. (I was once *anonymously* reviewing a restaurant when a writer from another guidebook walked in, told the manager their identity and asked for food. Not surprisingly, the food was "great." But mine was lousy!) What you get here is our unbiased opinion on how companies operate—nothing more, nothing less.

This book is intended to bring you independence in exploring Kaua'i. We don't want to waste your precious time by giving you bad advice or bad directions. We want you to experience the best that the island has to offer. In the end, it's probably fair to say that our ultimate objective is to have you leave Kaua'i shaking your head saying, "I never knew a place like this existed."

We hope we succeed.

Andrew Doughty
Kapa'a, Hawai'i

The walls of Wai'ale'ale Crater, from which the island of Kaua'i burst forth in a fiery cataclysm, are now home to innumerable waterfalls. This part of the crater is called the Weeping Wall.

As with people, volcanic islands have a life cycle. They emerge from their sea floor womb to be greeted by the warmth of the sun. They grow and mature and eventually die before sinking forever beneath the sea.

HOW IT BEGAN

The Hawaiian Islands were born of fire thousands of feet below the surface in the icy cold waters on the Pacific Ocean floor. A rupture in the earth's crust caused a vent to spew hot magma that built upon itself as it reached upward. When it began, no one knows exactly, but the first of the still existing islands to boil to the surface was Kure. Nothing remains of that island today but its fringing coral reef, called an atoll.

As the Pacific plate shifted over the opening of the vent like steel over a cutting torch, more islands were created. Midway, French Frigate Shoal, Necker, Nihoa—all of these once-great islands were born and then mostly consumed by the angry ocean. What we call Hawai'i is just the last in a series of islands created by this vent. Someday these, too, will be nothing more than atolls, footnotes in the geologic history of the earth. But this vent isn't finished yet. The Big Island of Hawai'i is still expanding as lava from its active volcano continues even now to create additional real estate on that island. As we sit here, the future island of Lo'ihi is being created 20 miles southeast of the Big Island. Although still 3,200 feet below the surface of the ocean, in but a geologic moment, the Hawaiian volcano goddess Pele will add yet another piece of paradise to her impressive domain.

These virgin islands were barren at birth. The first life forms to appreciate these new islands of volcanic rock were marine creatures. Fish, mammals and microscopic animals discovered this new underwater haven and made homes for themselves. Coral polyps attached themselves to the lava rock and succeeding generations built upon these, creating what would become a coral reef.

Meanwhile, on land, seeds carried by the winds were struggling to colonize the rocky land, eking out a living and breaking down the lava rock. Storms brought the occasional bird, hopelessly blown off course. The lucky ones found the islands. The even luckier ones arrived with mates or had fertilized eggs when they got here. Other animals, stranded on a piece of floating debris, washed ashore against all odds and went on to colonize the islands. These introductions of new species were rare events. It took an extraordinary set of circumstances for a new species to actually make it to the islands. Single specimens were destined to live out their lives in lonely solitude. On average, a new species was successfully deposited here only once every 20,000 years.

As the plants and animals lived out their lives, they broke up the rock, forming soil and organic debris. The ocean, meanwhile, was busily working to reclaim the horizon from these interruptions of land. Waves battered unmercifully against the fragile lava rock. In this battle between titans, there can be but one winner. While the creation of land eventually ceases on an individual island, the ocean never gives up. Wave after wave eventually takes its toll.

In addition to the ocean, rain carves up the islands. As the islands thrust them-

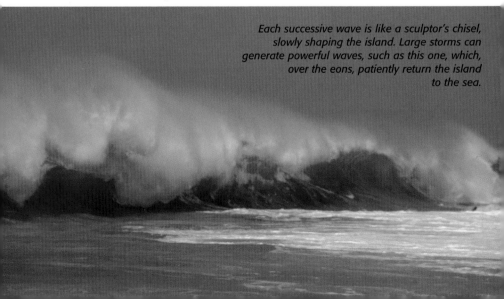

Each successive wave is like a sculptor's chisel, slowly shaping the island. Large storms can generate powerful waves, such as this one, which, over the eons, patiently return the island to the sea.

On rare occasions this ancient Hawaiian petroglyph is exposed in the mouth of the Wailua River.

selves upward into the moisture-laden trade winds, their challenge to the rain clouds is accepted. As the air encounters the slopes of these tall islands, it rises and cools, causing the air to release its humidity in the form of rain. This rain forms channels that easily carve valleys in the soft lava rock.

So what is the result of all this destruction? Paradise. Absolute paradise. There are few things more beautiful than Mother Nature reclaiming that which she gave birth to. The older the island, the more beautiful the landscape. A Hawaiian island is never more lovely than in its middle age, when the scars of constant environmental battles are carved into its face. Lush landscaped valleys, razorback ridges, long, sandy beaches—those things we cherish so much are the result of this destructive battle.

Kaua'i consists of 553 square miles of beach, rainforest, desert, mountains and plains. The island's landscape is as varied as its people. At Wai'ale'ale in the island's center, it rains nearly every day, making it the wettest place on earth. Just a few miles to the west, rain is rare, creating dry, almost arid conditions. The north shore is as lush as any place on the plan-

et. The south shore is a sunny playground. The island's first inhabitants surely must have felt blessed at the discovery of this diversity.

THE FIRST SETTLERS

Sometime around the fourth or fifth century AD, a large, double-hulled voyaging canoe, held together with flexible sennit lashings and propelled by sails made of woven pandanus, slid onto the sand on the Big Island of Hawai'i. These first intrepid adventurers encountered an island chain of unimaginable beauty.

They had left their home in the Marquesas Islands 2,500 miles away for reasons we will never know. Some say it was because of war, overpopulation, drought or just a sense of adventure. Whatever their reasons, these initial settlers took a big chance and surely must have been highly motivated. They left their homes and searched for a new world to colonize. Doubtless, most of the first groups perished at sea. There was no way for them to know that there were islands in these waters. The Hawaiian Islands are the most isolated island chain in the world. Those who did arrive brought with them food staples from home: taro, breadfruit, pigs, dogs and several types of fowl. This was a pivotal decision. These first settlers found a land that contained almost no edible plants. With no land mammals other than the Hawaiian bat, the first settlers subsisted on fish until their crops could mature. From then on, they lived largely on fish and taro. Although we associate throw-net fishing with Hawai'i, this practice was introduced by Japanese immigrants much later. The ancient Hawaiians used fishhooks and spears for the most part or drove fish into a net already placed into the water. They also had domesticated animals that were used as ritual foods or reserved for chiefs.

As the culture evolved and flourished, it developed into a hierarchical system of order. The society was governed by chiefs, called *ali'i*, who established a long list of taboos called kapu. These kapu were designed to keep order, and the penalty for breaking one was usually death by strangulation, club or fire. If the violation was serious enough, the guilty party's family might also be killed. It was kapu, for instance, for your shadow to fall across the shadow of the ali'i. It was kapu to interrupt the chief if he was speaking. It was kapu to prepare men's food in the same container used for women's food. It was kapu for women to eat pork or bananas. It was kapu for men and women to eat together. It was kapu not to observe the days designated to the gods. Certain areas were kapu for fishing if they became depleted. This allowed the area to replenish itself.

While harsh by our standards today, this system kept order. Most ali'i were sensitive to the disturbance their presence caused and often ventured outside only at night, or a scout was sent ahead to warn people that an ali'i was on his way. All commoners were required to

Who Were the Menehune?

Although the legend of Menehune exists throughout the Hawaiian Islands, the folklore is strongest on Kaua'i. Hawaiian legend speaks of a mythical race of people living in the islands before the Polynesians. Called the Menehune, these people were always referred to as small in stature. Initially referring to their social stature, the legend evolved to mean that they were physically short and lived in the woods away from the Hawaiians. (The Hawaiians avoided the woods when possible, fearing that they held evil spirits, and instead stayed on the coastal plains.) The Menehune were purported to build fabulous structures, always in one night. Their numbers were said to be vast, as many as 500,000. Today, archeologists speculate that a second wave of colonists, probably from Tahiti, may have subdued these initial inhabitants, forcing them to live in the woods. It is interesting to note that in a census taken of Kaua'i around 1800, 65 people from the upper region of the Wainiha Valley identified themselves as Menehune.

Today, Menehune are jokingly blamed for anything that goes wrong. If you lost your wallet, Menehune took it. If your car won't start, Menehune have been tinkering with it. Kaua'i residents greatly cherish their legends of the Menehune.

pay taxes to the ali'i in the form of food, labor and in other ways.

In January 1778 an event occurred that would forever change Hawai'i. Captain James Cook, who usually had a genius for predicting where to find islands, stumbled upon Hawai'i. He had not expected islands to be there. He was on his way to Alaska to search for the Northwest Passage linking the Atlantic and Pacific oceans. As Cook approached the shores of Waimea, Kaua'i, on January 19, 1778, the island's inhabitants thought they were being visited by gods. Rushing aboard to greet their visitors, the Kauaians were fascinated by what they saw: pointy-headed beings (the British wore tri-cornered hats) breathing fire (smoking pipes) and possessing a death-dealing instrument identified as a water squirter (guns). The amount of iron on the ship was incredible. (Hawaiians had only seen iron in the form of nails on driftwood but never knew the source.) Cook left Kaua'i and briefly explored Ni'ihau before heading north for his mission on February 2, 1778. When Cook returned to the Big Island of Hawai'i after failing to find the Northwest Passage, he was killed in a petty skirmish over a stolen rowboat. The Hawaiians were horrified that they had killed a man they had earlier presumed to be a god.

Just after this, Kamehameha the Great of the Big Island began consolidating his power by conquering the other islands in the chain. Kaua'i, however, presented a unique problem. Cut off from the rest of the chain by the treacherous Kaua'i Channel, Kaua'i's King Kaumuali'i had no intention of submitting himself to Kamehameha. In the spring of 1796 Kamehameha tried to invade Kaua'i. He and his fleet of 1,200 canoes carrying 10,000 soldiers left O'ahu at midnight hoping to reach Wailua, Kaua'i, by daybreak. They were in the middle of the Kaua'i Channel when the wind and seas picked up. Many of the canoes were swamped. Reluctantly, he ordered a retreat, but too late to stop some of his advance troops who were slaughtered after they arrived at the south shore beach of Maha'ulepu.

Ancient Hawaiians lived off the sea. With reefs teaming with life, Hawaiian waters have always been generous to the people of Hawai'i.

The earliest Hawaiians built elaborate terraces to grow taro, used to make poi. This one, in the Limahuli Garden, is estimated to be 700 years old.

In 1804 Kamehameha tried again. He gathered 7,000 men, all heavily armed, and prepared to set sail for Kaua'i. Just before they were to leave, typhoid struck, decimating his troops and advisers. Kamehameha himself contracted the disease but managed to pull through. Kaua'i's king must have seen the writing on the wall and agreed to give his kingdom of Kaua'i over to Kamehameha. When Kamehameha died, his son, in order to solidify his power on Kaua'i, arranged to kidnap Kaua'i's King Kaumuali'i and forced him to marry his stepmother, the powerful widow of Kamehameha. Kaua'i's last king would never return and was eventually buried on Maui.

During the 19th century, Hawai'i's character changed dramatically. Businessmen from all over the world came here to exploit Hawai'i's sandalwood, whales, land and people. Hawai'i's leaders, for their part, actively participated in these ventures and took a piece of the action for themselves. Workers were brought in from many parts of the world, changing the racial makeup of the islands. Government corruption be-

came the order of the day, and everyone seemed to be profiting except the Hawaiian commoner. By the time Queen Lili'uokalani lost her throne to a group of American businessmen in 1893, Hawai'i had become directionless. It barely resembled the Hawai'i Captain Cook had encountered in the previous century. The kapu system had been abolished by the Hawaiians shortly after the death of Kamehameha the Great. The *Great Mahele*, begun in 1848, had changed the relationship Hawaiians had with the land. Large tracts of land were sold by the Hawaiian government to royalty, government officials, commoners and foreigners, effectively stripping many Hawaiians of land they had lived on for generations.

The United States recognized the Republic of Hawai'i in 1894 with Sanford Dole as its president. It was later annexed and then became a territory in 1900. During the 19th and 20th centuries,

What's it Like in the Wettest Spot on Earth?

The center of the island is called Mount Wai'ale'ale, meaning "rippling waters." It is here that you will find the rainiest spot on the planet with an average of 440 inches of rain per year and a median of 432 inches. Rain around the rest of the island is a fraction of this (see chart on page 28). The ancient Hawaiians recognized the importance of this spot and built a temple on the summit, its remains visible to this day. The only way you will get to see Wai'ale'ale up close and personal is by air.

The top of Mount Wai'ale'ale is somewhat barren. While this might sound strange given its moniker as the wettest spot on Earth, remember that few plants in this world are genetically programmed to deal with that much rain at that altitude. Plus the ever-present rain clouds prevent sunshine from enriching the plants. The bogs on top of the mountain make for a less-than-well-defined soil base, and fungi and lichen flourish in the constant moisture. The result is few trees. Those trees that do survive are stunted by nature's over-generous gift of water.

Just below the summit—3,000 feet straight down, to be precise—exists the unimaginable lushness one would expect from abundant rain. As the clouds are forced up the walls of Wai'ale'ale Crater, they shed a portion of their moisture. With the majority of the rain

falling on the summit, the crater floor is left with just the perfect amount. With volcanically rich soil left over from the fiery eruptions, the crater floor has become a haven for

The summit of Wai'ale'ale feeds the Wailua River 3,000 feet below the sheer cliffs.

anything green. Ferns rule the crater. The ground shakes beneath your feet as your footsteps echo through generations of water-saturated fallen ferns which have created a soft underbelly to what was once a savage, lava-spewing giant.

There is a surprising lack of insect presence. And most that do live there are endemic, appearing nowhere else on earth. Aside from mosquitoes in the stream beds, we encountered almost no insects in the dense fern growth of the crater. The only exception was a single flightless grasshopper. We found some 'o'opu fish inhabiting streams between towering waterfalls. They live in these isolated pools and use their pelvic fins to actually climb the falls.

Everywhere one looks, plants have taken root. Every rock has moss, every fallen tree has other plants growing on it, every crevice has growth. Surely no other place on earth is as lush as Wai'ale'ale Crater.

sugar established itself as king. Pineapple was also heavily grown in the islands, and the entire island of Lana'i was purchased for the purpose of growing pineapple. As the 20th century rolled on, Hawaiian sugar and pineapple workers found themselves in a lofty position—they became the highest paid workers for these crops in the world. As land prices rose and competition from other parts of the world increased, sugar and pineapple became less and less profitable. Today, these crops no longer hold the position they once had. In the 1990s the "Pineapple Island" of Lana'i completely shifted away from pineapple and started luring tourists. And where dozens of sugar companies once dotted the islands, today only two remain—one here and one on Maui. Former sugar workers have moved into other vocations, usually tourist-related or farming.

The story of Hawai'i is not a story of good versus evil. Nearly everyone shares in the blame for what happened to the Hawaiian people and their culture. Nevertheless, today Hawai'i is struggling to redefine its identity. The Islands are looking back to the past for guidance. During your stay you will be exposed to a place that is attempting to recapture its cultural roots. There is more interest in Hawaiian culture and language than ever before. Sometimes it is clumsy, sometimes awkward. There is no common agreement regarding how to do it, but in the end, a reinvigoration of the Hawaiian spirit will no doubt be enjoyed by all.

NI'IHAU

No man is an island, or so they say. But in Hawai'i, one family can own one. The island of Ni'ihau is a dry, somewhat barren island of 46,000 acres located 17

On Kaua'i, the first settlers found an Eden more beautiful than any place they'd ever known.

miles to the west of Kaua'i. When Scottish-born Eliza Sinclair was sailing in the islands with her family in 1863, they were looking for land on which to settle. Having turned down offers of several tracts on O'ahu (including Waikiki, which they dismissed as showing no promise), they were about to leave for California when King Kamehameha V offered to sell them Ni'ihau. When Eliza's sons went to look at it, they found a green, wet island with abundant grass—perfect for raising cattle. What they were unaware of at the time was that Ni'ihau had experienced a *rare* rainy period and was flourishing as a result. They offered $6,000, the king countered with $10,000, and they took it.

This was 1864 and, unfortunately for the Sinclairs, the residents of Ni'ihau did not respect their ownership and resisted them. They had a further setback when an old Hawaiian showed them a deed indicating ownership to a crucial 50-acre sliver of Ni'ihau deeded to the old man by King Kamehameha III. The Sinclairs were in a bind and elicited the aid of Valdemar Knudsen to negotiate the purchase of the remaining 50 acres. He spoke fluent Hawaiian and was well known and respected by the islanders.

Knudsen went to Ni'ihau and offered $1,000 to the old man by slowly stacking the silver coins on a table while he explained how much better off the old man would be if he sold his land and lived in comfort on Kaua'i. After repeated refusals from the man, Knudsen went to take the money away when the old Hawaiian's wife grabbed the money, and the deal was consummated on the spot.

When the Sinclairs discovered that the land was actually dry and barren, unsuitable for a cattle ranch at that time, they arranged to buy 21,000 acres of West Kaua'i. (They would continue to buy land on Kaua'i, eventually acquiring 51,000 acres of the island, which they own to this day.) If you take a helicopter ride, you may see their fabulous estate nestled high in the mountains near Olokele.

Today, about 200 Hawaiians live on Ni'ihau. There is one unpaved road going halfway around the island, no telephones, except for a wireless two-way to Kaua'i and no cable TV. (Some residents tell us they've unsuccessfully tried to talk the Robinsons—the descendants of Eliza Sinclair—into getting a satellite dish so they can get CNN.) In-

So close and yet so far. This is as close as most will ever come to the "forbidden" island of Ni'ihau.

termittent power is supplied by generator and solar.

Ni'ihau's one school hosts around 40 students. The sense of family on the island is strong, and only Hawaiian is spoken in most homes. (Classes, however, are taught in English.) Ni'ihau residents are a deeply religious people, and crime against one another is almost unknown. They are intensely proud of their community and feel strongly that their people, their heritage and their way of life are special and are protected by God.

They live in one village called Pu'uwai (located in the only part of Ni'ihau where you can't see Kaua'i) and receive their mail once a week—the Post Office only delivers as far as Makaweli on Kaua'i. They shop for clothes and other durable items on Kaua'i, where most have family.

Time is fluid there. If someone says they'll see you on Wednesday, it could be any time of the day. There's no such thing as being late on Ni'ihau.

With a warehouse for staples and gardens for their fruits and vegetables, Ni'ihau islanders are reasonably self-sufficient. Travel to and from the island is via old military transport boats (like the kind in *Saving Private Ryan*), and the rough, bumpy ride takes around 3 hours each way (during which many get seasick).

Life on Ni'ihau is certainly not without problems. No drugs or alcohol are allowed on the island, and families have been banished forever from the island for growing pakalolo (marijuana). Their mortality rate is high. Virtually everyone receives welfare and/or food stamps. With no permanent streams on the island, water is sometimes scarce. Although the largest lake in the state is on Ni'ihau, it is usually only a few feet deep, muddy and generally unpleasant.

The Robinson's land is valued at well over a *billion* dollars, but crushing tax burdens and losses (from Kaua'i sugar operations) leave them relatively cash poor. Though the land has been in the family for almost a century and a half, every time a land-owning relative dies, the government takes a huge bite out of the family in massive inheritance taxes. They claim that they can only afford to go out to dinner a few times a year. (You can dry your eyes now after that one.) They warmed to the idea of using some of their Kaua'i land for tourism for a few years, then backed away. They almost allowed the federal government to install (for a fee) rocket launchers on Ni'ihau as part of an expansion of the Pacific Missile Range Facility on Kaua'i's west side. The deal fell through when the government insisted on an ethnographic survey, which the secretive Robinsons feared would be used to create precedents that would allow native Hawaiians *from Kaua'i* to visit the island (for constitutionally allowed ritual or gathering purposes). Instead, they are now contemplating a 250-room resort called Kapa-lawai on some of their west Kaua'i land and have been in talks with outsiders *for years* to convert some of the sugar cane to make ethanol. Lots of talk, lots of plans. But nothing has come of any of it.

The Robinsons claim that their unique deed to the island gives them ownership of Ni'ihau's beaches—directly in conflict with state law that proclaims that *all* beaches in Hawai'i are public beaches. To date nobody has challenged them in court. If you land on a beach on Ni'ihau, you will be asked to leave. If you refuse, a truly *gargantuan* Hawaiian gentleman will be summoned, and he will ask you a bit more firmly. This request is usually sufficient to persuade all but the most determined individuals to leave.

The bird-of-paradise is a striking flower found all over the island.

In order to get to Kaua'i, you've got to fly here. (You might be able to find a cruise to Hawai'i, but it's a pretty big and featureless piece of water to cross in a boat.)

GETTING HERE

When planning your trip, a travel agent can be helpful. Their commission has been paid directly by the travel industry, though that may change in the future. The Internet has dot.com sites such as Orbitz, Expedia, Cheaptickets, Cheapair, Pandaonline, Priceline, Travelocity, Kayak, etc. If you don't want to or can't go through these sources, there are large wholesalers that can get you airfare, hotel and a rental car, often cheaper than you can get airfare on your own. **Pleasant Holidays** (800–242–9244) provides complete package tours.

If you arrange airline tickets and hotel reservations yourself, you can often count on paying top dollar for each facet of your trip. The prices listed in the WHERE TO STAY section reflect the RACK rates, meaning the published rates before any discounts. Rates can be significantly lower if you go through a travel company.

When you pick your travel source, shop around—the differences can be dramatic. A diligent agent can make the difference between affording a *one-week* vacation and a *two-week* vacation. They don't all check the same sources for bargains; there is an art to it. Look in the Sunday travel section of your local newspaper—the bigger the paper, the better, or check online versions of major papers.

Though most visitors fly into Honolulu before arriving, there are some direct flights to Kaua'i. Not having to cool your heels while changing planes on O'ahu is a *big* plus since interisland flights aren't quite as convenient—or cheap—as they used to be. If you fly to Kaua'i from Honolulu, the best views are usually on the left side (seats with an "A"). When flying to Honolulu from the mainland, sit on the left side coming in, the right going home. Interisland flights are done by **Hawaiian** (800–367–5320), **Go!** (888–435–9462), **Island Air** (800–652–6541) and **Mokulele Airlines** (866–260–7070). Flight attendants zip up and down the aisle hurling juice at you for the short, interisland flights.

WHAT TO BRING

This list will be helpful in planning what to bring. Obviously, you won't bring everything on the list, but it might make you think of things you may otherwise overlook:

• Waterproof sunblock (SPF 15 or higher)
• Two bathing suits
• Shoes—flip-flops, trashable sneakers, reef shoes, hiking or trail shoes
• Mask, snorkel and fins
• Digital camera
• Mosquito repellent for some hikes (*Lotions,* not liquids, containing DEET seem to work longest.)
• Shorts and other cool cotton clothing
• Hat or cap for sun protection
• Light windbreaker jacket (for trip to Kalalau Lookout or helicopter trip)

• Cheap, simple backpack—you don't need to go backpacking to use one; a 10-minute trek down to a secluded beach is much easier if you bring a simple pack.
• Long, lightweight pants for hiking if you are going through jungle country.

GETTING AROUND
Rental Cars

The rental car prices in Hawai'i *can be* (but aren't always) cheaper than almost anywhere else in the country, and the competition is ferocious. Nearly every visitor to Kaua'i gets around in a rental car, and for good reason. The island's towns are separated by distances sufficient to discourage walking. Many of Kaua'i's best sights can only be reached if you have independent transportation.

At Lihu'e Airport, rental cars can easily be obtained from the booths across the street from the main terminal. It's usually a good idea to reserve your car in advance since companies can run out of cars during peak times.

Below are the companies currently operating on Kaua'i:

The Big Guys

Alamo	**(800) 327–9633**
	(808) 246–0646
Avis	**(800) 321–3712**
	(808) 245–3512
Budget	**(800) 527–0700**
	(808) 245–1901
Dollar	**(800) 800–4000**
	(866) 434–2226
Hertz	**(800) 654–3131**
	(808) 245–3356
National	**(800) 227–7368**
	(808) 245–5636
Thrifty	**(800) 367–5238**
	(866) 450–5101

The Little Guys

Island Cars **(800) 246–6009**
(808) 246–6000

Kaua'i Rent A Car
(808) 246–1881

Timeshare Auto & U-Haul
(808) 632–0741

If you're 21–24 years old, most of the companies will rent to you, but you'll pay about $25 extra *per day* for the crime of being young and reckless. If you're under 21—rent a bike or moped or take the bus. Below are a few tips to keep in mind when you rent your car on Kaua'i.

- Many **Collision Damage Waivers** will not cover vehicles on unpaved roads or beaches. Consider this when driving on dirt cane roads or at Polihale.

- **Seat belt** use and **child restraints** are required by law and police will stop you for this alone.

Car break-ins can be a problem anywhere. They seem to be more frequent in the summer due to school vacations. The places usually hit are those that require you to leave your car in a secluded place for an extended period of time. Contrary to popular belief, locals are targeted nearly as often as tourists. To protect yourself, don't leave anything valuable in the car. (Well…maybe the seats can stay.) At secluded spots that have recently been robbed, savvy locals will often leave their doors unlocked and the windows partially open to prevent having their windows smashed. If you park in a secluded spot and notice several piles of glass on the ground, leave your windows rolled down a little—broken glass is evidence that some juvenile has a new hobby. Don't kid yourself into believing that trunks are safe—they are

often easier to open than doors. One place thieves rarely look is under the hood. But don't put something there after you arrive at your destination since someone might be watching. We once drove up to the parking area at Secret Beach, and there was a suspicious looking guy there. Mr. Slick acted busy by spending considerable time checking the oil in his car—*but the rusted hulk had no wheels all the way around.* Be alert and you should be OK.

All of this is not meant to convey the impression that car break-ins are rampant. In fact, the opposite is true. You could probably spend your entire life here and never experience one. (We haven't.) But if you lose your brand new $1,000 auto-everything digital camera to some juvenile dipstick because you were one of the few…well, won't *you* feel sick?

4-Wheel Drive

With its many rugged roads, one of the best ways to see Kaua'i is by four-wheel drive. These can be difficult to come by at times. Ask if they have disabled the 4WD mechanism. If you use a gold credit card for the automatic insurance, check with the card carrier to see if you are covered when you're on unpaved roads. Another tip is to avoid deep, soft sand. Even 4WD vehicles can get stuck in sand if they have the wrong tires. If you must drive on sand, let much of the air out of the tires to get more sand traction. (We'll leave it up to you how to get the air back in.) If you already *are* stuck in sand, try pulling the carpet from the trunk and driving on it to get out. (Oh, the car companies will love us for *that* one.) Rental car companies are always changing the vehicles to keep them new. At press time, all the *big* companies we list had SUVs or other 4WD vehicles.

Hey, I Recognize That Place...

When Hollywood wants to convey the impression of beauty, lushness and the exotic, it's no contest what location they choose. Kaua'i has long been the location of choice for movie directors looking for something special. As you drive around the island, keep an eye out for the locations of scenes from some of these movies: all three Jurassic Park *movies,* Tropic Thunder, Dragonfly, To End All Wars, Six Days/Seven Nights, Mighty Joe Young, George of the Jungle, Outbreak, North, Honeymoon in Vegas, Hook, Lord of the Flies, Flight of the Intruder, Throw Momma From the Train, The Thorn Birds, Uncommon Valor, Body Heat, Raiders of the Lost Ark, Fantasy Island, King Kong, Acapulco Gold, Islands in the Stream, The Hawaiians, Lost Flight, Hawai'i, Paradise Hawaiian Style, Girls! Girls! Girls!, Donovan's Reef, Blue Hawai'i, South Pacific, Miss Sadie Thompson *and many more. Hollywood discovered Kaua'i years ago.*

Harrison Ford rehearsing at Maha'ulepu for the movie, Six days/Seven Nights.

It's cool when you literally stumble across movie props, as we did with this shipwreck from local resident Ben Stiller's film Tropic Thunder.

Even a beach with no sand can have something to offer.
Queen's Bath on the north shore is an example.

Expect to pay up to $60–$90 per day for the privilege of cheating the road builders.

Buses

Kaua'i has a bus system called the **Kaua'i Bus** (clever, eh?). It goes from Kekaha to Hanalei, and fares are $2. A monthly pass is $20, and most have bike racks. There are stops all along the main highway, but they aren't always marked as well as they should be. For a bus schedule or more information, call 241–6410.

Less Than 4 Wheels

If you really want to ham it up, try renting a HOG. (*Note:* The Supreme Court recently ruled that publishers cannot be held liable for bad puns.) **Kaua'i Harley-Davidson** on the highway in Puhi (241–7020) rents HOGs and other bikes. Good selection. Rates are $139 for 8 hours and $179 for overnight for HOGs. Expensive? You bet! But nothing else feels like a genuine Harley.

Scooters/mopeds are also available. We've seen some pretty close calls and consider them too unstable to recommend. Be *real* careful on hills and stay off the highway between Lihu'e and Kapa'a. **Kaua'i Scooter Rentals** (245–7177) have them for a confiscatory *$75* a day.

Taxis

If you want to tour the island by taxi… you have entirely too much money to burn. For those who need an occasional taxi service, you will find these available: **North Shore Cab** (639–7829), **Akiko's** (822–7588) on the east shore, or **City Cab** (245–3227) on the south shore.

Wheelchair Accessible Vans

These are available from **Wheelchair Getaways** (800–638–1912). Rates are $95 per day if you rent for a week. Don't forget to bring your placard. Also, if you're looking to rent a wheelchair, **Gammie HomeCare** (632–2333) in Lihu'e has regular and beach wheelchairs.

GETTING MARRIED ON KAUA'I

The beauty of Kaua'i has provided the backdrop for many engagements, weddings and vow renewals. And why not? It's in the air here. People are genuinely happy on Kaua'i, and the aroma of joy can make your life together even sweeter. Whether you choose a natural or man-made waterfall, a sunset on a beach, an elegant chapel, beautiful garden or an ancient Hawaiian temple, Kaua'i can create nuptial memories that will last a lifetime.

Thanks to e-mail and the Internet, you can arrange your own wedding, no matter how far away you are. All of the legal requirements, as well as possible wedding locations, are just a click away. Everything from helicopter flights landing at private waterfalls to just the two of you on a beach at sunset with a minister is available.

Some of the more popular wedding locations are at the St. Regis Princeville, Hanalei Bay Resort, Marriott, Hyatt, Sheraton and the Waimea Plantation Cottages. Many resorts have wedding coordinators and private wedding sites on property. You might also want to consider renting a private home for you and your guests. Don't let the RACK rates and wedding package prices scare you off. Nothing's carved in stone. And remember, no beach is private, and no one can charge you to use one.

The number of details in planning a wedding is dizzying, and many couples

Viewers struggle to get as close as possible to a rapidly fleeting sunset.

prefer the assistance of an independent wedding coordinator. They can be tremendously helpful in navigating the complicated waters of your marriage. (Well, the ceremony, at least. After that, you're on your own.) Don't let yourself get herded into activities (for which they get a commission), and be on the lookout for add-ons that can ratchet up the price. Be especially selective of your photographer and videographer. This is a one-time event that can't be duplicated.

Some of the more reputable companies are listed below. Unlike most activities, we can't review each in depth. It's not possible to get married a dozen times and critique the way each coordinator did their job. We have, however, anonymously contacted virtually all of the coordinators on the island (in the guise of planning a wedding) and these stood out.

Coconut Coast Weddings
   (800) 585–5595 or (808) 822–2020
Mohala Wedding Services
   (800) 800–8489

Weddings on the Beach
   (808) 742–7099
Island Weddings & Blessings
   (800) 998–1548 or (808) 828–1548

WEATHER

Kaua'i doesn't have the best weather in the state, but the best weather in the state is on Kaua'i. What do we mean by that? Well, when it's good here, it's as good as weather can get—brilliant sunshine, crystal clear air and gentle but constant breezes. That's when it's good.

Yeah, but I've heard it always rains on Kaua'i. We heard this many times before we came here for the first time. The reality of Kaua'i is that it gets more rain than the other Hawaiian islands. In fact, the rainiest spot on earth is smack dab in the middle of the island. Mount Wai-'ale'ale is the undisputed rain magnet, receiving an average of 428 inches per year (that's almost 36 *feet*). The mountain is shaped like a funnel pointing directly into the moisture-laden trade winds, which are forced to drop their precious cargo during their march up the slopes. The summit of

Waiʻaleʻale is other-worldly, with plants stunted and dwarfed by the constant inundation of rain. Moss, fungi and lichen flourish in the swamp just west of the actual peak. Alakaʻi Swamp contains flora and fauna found nowhere else in the world. On the opposite side of the mountain, the spent clouds can do no more than drift by, making the west side of the island rather arid. What rain it does get comes from the sporadic Kona winds. (Throughout the islands, Kona winds refers to winds that come from the southwest and are often associated with inclement weather.)

All that said, the odds are overwhelming that rain will *not* ruin your Kauaʻi vacation. The coast gets *far* less rain than the waterlogged central interior, and throughout Kauaʻi the lion's share of rain falls at night. When it does rain during the day, it is usually quite short-lived, often lasting a matter of a few minutes. One of the things that takes a little getting used to is the fleeting nature of the weather here. In many parts of the country, rain or sunshine are words used *by themselves* to describe the day's weather. On Kauaʻi, a warm, passing shower is to be expected and rarely signifies that a long period of rain is to follow. If you call the local telephone number for the National Weather Service (see page 28), you will probably hear something like this. "Today—mostly sunny, with a few passing windward and *mauka* (mountain) showers. Tonight—mostly fair with a few passing windward and *mauka* showers. Tomorrow—mostly sunny, with a few passing windward and *mauka* showers." So don't get bummed if it suddenly looks ominous in the sky. It'll probably pass within a few minutes, leaving happy plants in its wake.

If you want to know whether to take the top down on the convertible, look into the wind, and you'll be able to see the weather coming. Dark clouds drop rain—the darker the cloud, the harder the rain. It's as simple as that, and you will often see locals looking windward if they feel a drop on their heads. If you're inland, you will often be able to *hear* the rain approaching. When you hear the sound of a rushing river but there isn't one around, take cover until it passes. (Mango trees are ideal for this purpose and have ancillary benefits, as well.)

In planning your daily activities, a good rule of thumb is that if it is going to be a rainy day, the south shore will probably be sunny, and the west shore will almost certainly be sunny. The exception is during Kona winds when weather is the opposite of normal.

Storm systems do discover the state from time to time. Sometimes they're here for days. If one happens to hang around during your trip, don't despair. I first met Kauaʻi during one of the wettest times in decades. There was even lightning, which is rare. And it was during that stay that I fell in love with the island and vowed to make it my home. Kauaʻi in the rain is still Kauaʻi.

As far as hurricanes are concerned, don't waste your time worrying about them. It's true, we had a real ʻokole kicker back in 1992. Hurricane ʻIniki was a category 4 storm that stripped the island bare, ironically striking on Sept. 11 of that year. But after this pruning, the island recovered and became greener than ever. Hurricanes are few and far between here. The only previous hurricanes to hit the state this century were ʻIwa in 1982 and Dot in 1959. When Isabella Bird traveled here in 1873, where she penned her excellent book *Six Months in the Sandwich Isles,* she reported that "hurricanes are unknown in the islands," which means that there hadn't been one in living memory. (Of course, if one *does* strike during your stay, kindly disregard this last statement.)

As far as **temperatures** are concerned, Kaua'i is incredibly temperate. The average *high* during January is 78°, whereas our hottest time, late August/ early September, has an average *high* of 85°. With humidity percentages usually in the 60s and low 70s, Kaua'i is almost always pleasant. The exception is the extreme west side, which is about 3 degrees hotter. (That might not sound like much, but you sure do notice it.)

Kaua'i's surface **water temperatures** range from a low of 73.4° in February to a high of 80° in October. Most people find this to be an ideal water temperature range. (Ocean water near a river mouth, such as Lydgate Beach Park, can get colder—we've seen the ocean get as low as 70° there during unusually cold Februarys.)

To get current weather or ocean information, call the **National Weather Service: Weather Forecast** (245–6001) and **Hawaiian Waters Forecast** (245–3564).

Where Should I Stay?

If your decision about when to visit and where to stay takes rainfall amounts into account, the graph below should be of interest. Winter is our rainiest season. (But that's also when you will see the waterfalls at their best.) The north shore is a more popular place to stay in the summer, and the south shore is more popular in the winter due to rainfall distribution and surf.

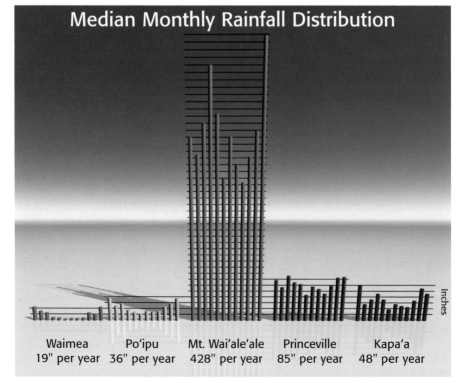

Median Monthly Rainfall Distribution

Inches

Waimea	Po'ipu	Mt. Wai'ale'ale	Princeville	Kapa'a
19" per year	36" per year	428" per year	85" per year	48" per year

GEOGRAPHY

Kaua'i is located in the tropics at 22° latitude, meaning that it receives direct sunlight twice each year three weeks before and after the summer solstice. (No part of the mainland United States ever receives direct sunshine due to its more northern location.) The island is 553 square miles, with 50 of its 113 miles of shoreline composed of sand beaches. Compared to the other Hawaiian Islands, Kaua'i and O'ahu have by far the highest proportion of sand beach shorelines. You might read in brochures about "white sand beaches." Actually, they are *golden* sand beaches, unlike the truly white sand beaches found in other parts of the world. Kaua'i is too old to have any volcanic black sand beaches since the creation of *volcanic* black sand ends when the lava flow stops. (Waimea's black sand beach is from lava flecks chipped from riverbeds and from dirt.)

Kaua'i's interior is mountainous, with deeply eroded valleys and large plains around most of the coastal areas. Its rainfall is more varied than any place in the world. The northern and eastern parts of the island (called the windward side) receive the majority of the rain, with the southern and western sections (leeward side) considerably drier. (See rain graph on facing page.)

Looking at the map on the fold-out back cover, you will notice that a highway stretches *almost* all the way around the island. This means that Ke'e is as far as you can go by car on the north shore, and Polihale or the top of Waimea Canyon Drive is as far as you can go on the west side. An attempt to link the two a few years back ended with almost comic results. (See page 92 for more on that.)

The maps in this book are unique in that they show the roadside mile markers. These correspond to the little green signs you will see along the main roads of Kaua'i. This will give you a perspective regarding distances beyond the map scales. Another feature of our maps is that north always points up. We have found that many people get confused when they try to use a map where south is pointing to where east should be, etc. The only exceptions we made were a couple trail maps that benefited from using a specific elevated perspective.

In getting around, distances are usually measured in time, rather than miles. See the back fold-out map for a chart of **driving times between towns**.

HAZARDS
The Sun

Excluding the accommodations tax, the hazard that affects by far the most people is the sun. Kaua'i's latitude means we receive sunlight that's more direct than anywhere on the mainland. (The more overhead the sunlight is, the less atmosphere it is filtered through, and it's also more concentrated than it is farther north.) If you want to enjoy your *entire* vacation, make sure that you wear a strong sunblock. We recommend a waterproof sunblock with at least an SPF of 15. **Gels** work best in the ocean, **lotions** are best if you're staying dry. Try to avoid the sun between 11 a.m. and 2 p.m. since the sun's rays are particularly strong during this time. If you are fair-skinned or unaccustomed to the sun and want to lay out, 15–20 minutes per side is all you should consider the first day. You can increase it a bit each day. *Beware of the fact that Kaua'i's ever constant trade winds will hide the symptoms of a burn until it's too late.* You may find that trying to get your tan as golden as possible isn't worth it; tropical suntans are

Watch where you choose to take a nap.

notoriously short-lived, whereas you are sure to remember a bad burn far longer.

Water Hazards

The most serious water hazard is the surf. During the winter, many beaches are not swimmable. Eastern and northern beaches are especially dangerous, and the sad fact is that more people drown in Hawai'i each year than anywhere else in the country. This isn't said to keep you from enjoying the ocean, but rather to instill in you a healthy respect for Hawaiian waters. See BEACHES chapter for more information on this.

Ocean Critters

Hawaiian marine life, for the most part, is quite friendly. There are, however, a few notable exceptions. Below is a list of those that you should be aware of. This is not mentioned to frighten you out of the water. The odds are overwhelming that you won't have any trouble with

any of the beasties listed below. But should you encounter one, this information should be of some help.

Sharks—Kaua'i does have sharks. They are mostly white-tipped reef sharks with an occasional hammerhead or tiger shark. Contrary to what most people think, sharks are in every ocean and don't pose the level of danger people attribute to them. In the past 25 years, there have been a total of 14 documented shark attacks off Kaua'i, mostly tigers attacking surfers. Considering the number of people who swam in our waters during that time, you are more likely to choke to death on a bone at a lu'au than be attacked by a shark. If you do happen to come upon a shark, however, swim away slowly. This kind of movement doesn't interest them. *Don't* splash about rapidly. By doing this you are imitating a fish in distress, and you don't want to do that. The one kind of ocean water you want to avoid is murky water, like what you'll find near river mouths. These are not interesting to swim in anyway. Most shark attacks occur in murky water at dawn or dusk since sharks are basically cowards who like to sneak up on their prey. In general, don't go around worrying about sharks. *Any* animal can be threatening, not just Jaws.

Sea Urchins—These are like living pin cushions. If you step on one or accidentally grab one, remove as much of the spine as possible with tweezers. See a physician if necessary.

Cone Shells—People tend to forget that shells are created by organisms to serve as housing. Most of these creatures are capable of protecting themselves by the use of a long stinger called a proboscis, which injects venom. You might hear that it's safer to pick up a shell by the large end. You should be aware that many shells have stingers that can reach any part of the shell and can penetrate gloves. Therefore, it is recommended that you do not pick up live shells. If you do find yourself stung, immediately apply hot water, as it breaks down the protein venom.

Portuguese Man-of-War—These are related to jellyfish but are unable to swim.

They are instead propelled by a small sail and are at the mercy of the wind. Though small, they are capable of inflicting a painful sting. This occurs when the long, trailing tentacles are touched, triggering hundreds of thousands of spring-loaded stingers, called nematocysts, which inject venom. The resulting burning sensation is usually very unpleasant but not fatal. For-

tunately, the Portuguese Man-of-War is not a common visitor to Kaua'i. When they *do* come ashore, usually during the summer on the east shore, they might do so in great numbers, jostled by a strong storm offshore. If you see them on the beach, don't go in the water. If you do get stung, immediately remove the tentacles with a gloved hand, stick or whatever is handy. Rinse thoroughly with salt or fresh water to remove any adhering nematocysts. Then apply ice for pain control. If the condition worsens, see a doctor. The folk cure is urine, and in some of us it comes in a handy applicator, but you might look pretty silly applying it.

Coral—Coral skeletons are very sharp and, since the skeleton is overlain by millions of living coral polyps, a scrape can leave proteinaceous matter in the wound, causing infection. This is why coral cuts are frustratingly slow to heal. Immediate cleansing and disinfecting of coral cuts should speed up healing time. We don't have fire coral around Kaua'i.

Sea Anemones—Related to the jellyfish, these also have stingers and are usually found attached to rocks or coral. It's best not to touch them with your bare hands. Treatment for a sting is similar to that of a Portuguese Man-of-War.

Bugs

Though devoid of the myriad of hideous buggies found in other parts of the world, there are a few evil critters brought here from elsewhere that you should know about. The worst are **centipedes**. They can get to be six or more inches long and are aggressive predators. If you do happen to get stung, you won't die (but you might wish you had). You'll probably never see one, but if you get stung, even by a baby, the pain can range from a bad bee sting to a mild gunshot blast. Some local doctors say the only cure is to stay drunk for three days. Others say to use meat tenderizer.

Cane spiders are big, dark and look horrifying, but they're not poisonous. (But they seem to *think* they are. I've had *them* chase *me* across the room when *I* had the broom in my hand.) We *don't* have no-see-ums, those irritating sand fleas common in the South Pacific and Caribbean.

Mosquitoes were unknown in the islands until the first stowaways arrived on Maui on the *Wellington* in 1826. Since then they have thrived. A good mosquito repellent containing DEET will come in handy, especially if you plan to go hiking. *Lotions* (not thin liquids) with DEET seem to work and stick best. Forget the guidebooks that tell you to take vitamin B_{12} to keep mosquitoes away; it just gives the little critters a healthier diet. If you find one dive bombing you at night in your room, turn on your overhead fan to help keep them away. Local residents and resorts often rely on genetically engineered plants such as Citrosa, which irritate mosquitoes as much as they irritate us.

Bees are more common on the drier west side of the island. Usually, the only way you'll get stung is if you run into one. If you rent a scooter, beware: I received my first bee sting while singing *Come Sail Away* on a motorcycle. A bee sting in the mouth can definitely ruin one of your precious vacation days.

Regarding **cockroaches**, there's good news and bad news. The bad news is that here, some are bigger than your thumb and can fly. The good news is that you probably won't see one. One of their predators is the **gecko**. This small, lizard-like creature makes a surprisingly loud chirp at night. They are cute and considered good luck in the islands (probably because they eat mosquitoes and roaches).

One thing nearly all visitors have heard is there are no **snakes** in Hawai'i (aside from a rare, tiny, worm-like blind burrowing snake said to be found here on occasion). There is concern that the brown tree snake *might* make its way onto the islands from Guam. Although mostly harmless to humans, these snakes can spell extinction to native birds. Guam has lost nearly all of its birds due to this egg-eating curse. Once they are fertilized, the snakes can reproduce for life from a single specimen. If there are any on Kaua'i (none are known to be on the island at this time), it would be a major disaster. Government officials aren't allowed to tell you this, but we will: If you ever see one anywhere in Hawai'i, please *kill it* and contact the **Department of Forestry and Wildlife** (274-3433). At the very least, call them immediately. The entire bird population of Hawai'i will be grateful.

Hey...what are you looking at?

Road Hazards

There are a couple things you should know about driving around Kaua'i. The speed limits here are probably slower than what you are used to, and Kaua'i police do have a few places where they regularly catch people. (That's code for speed traps.) We mention some in the tours. Also be aware that we have something on Kaua'i called **contra flow**. During commute hours, orange cones are placed on the lane divisions forcing you to drive on the wrong side of the road. The area between Lihu'e and Wailua is an example of contra flow, and it can be a bit unnerving for the uninitiated. Also, wearing **seat belts** is required by law, and police will pull you over for this alone. You should know that the Kaua'i Police Department regularly receives funds to enhance their seat belt violation enforcement, speeding enforcement and their sobriety checkpoints. So don't even think about violating these laws, or you'll likely get stung.

Lastly, even in paradise we have our **traffic**. Don't overlook the Kapa'a Bypass on the east shore, the Koloa Bypass on the south shore and the Puhi Bypass near Lihu'e. In fact, driving *south* through Kapa'a can be a pain almost *anytime* of day. If you don't take the bypass, consider taking the scenic route up 581 (at the ABC Store) to 580. Might not save any time, but it's prettier than someone else's bumper.

Dirt

Dirt? Yes dirt. Kaua'i's infamous red dirt has ruined many new pairs of Nikes in its time. If you are driving on a cane road on the west side and have your window rolled down, you will eat a lot of it. It's always best to bring some trashable sneakers if you plan to do any hiking. And leave your silk argyle socks at home. If you want to know how staining it can be, just ask the makers of *Red Dirt Shirts*. They use one bucket of Kaua'i mud to dye *five hundred* shirts.

Dehydration

Bring and drink lots of water when you are out and about, especially when you are hiking. Dehydration sneaks up on people. By the time you are thirsty, you're already dehydrated. It's a good idea to take an insulated water jug with you in the car or one of those 1½ liter bottles of water. Our weather is almost certainly different than what you left behind, and you will probably find yourself thirstier than usual. Just fill it before you leave in the morning and *suck 'em up* (as we say here) all day.

Swimming in Streams

Kaua'i offers lots of opportunities to swim in streams and sometimes under waterfalls. It's a fulfillment of a fantasy for many people. But there are several hazards you need to know about.

Leptospirosis is a bacteria that is found in some of Hawai'i's fresh water. It is transmitted from animal urine and can enter the body from open cuts, eyes and by drinking. Around 100 people a year in Hawai'i are diagnosed with the bacteria, which is treated with antibiotics if caught relatively early. You should avoid swimming in streams if you have open cuts, and treat all water found in nature with treatment pills before drinking. (Some filters are ineffective for lepto.)

Also, while swimming in freshwater streams, try to use your arms as much as possible. Kicking an unseen rock is easier than you think. Consider wearing reef shoes or, better yet, tabis, while in streams. (Tabis are sort of a fuzzy mitten for your feet that grab slippery rocks quite effectively.) You can get them at Kmart or

Wal-Mart in Lihu'e, or the Waipouli Variety Store in Waipouli Plaza in Kapa'a.

Though rare, **flash floods** can occur in any freshwater stream anywhere in the world, even paradise. Be alert for them.

Lastly, remember while lingering under waterfalls that not everything that comes over the top will be as soft as water. Rocks coming down from above could definitely ruin the moment.

Grocery Stores

Definitely a hazard. Restaurants may be expensive, but don't think you'll get off cheap in grocery stores. Though you'll certainly save money cooking your own food, a trip to the store here can be startling. Phrases like *they charge how much for milk?* echo throughout the stores. One tip: **Foodland** and **Safeway** both offer discount cards (called Maika'i Cards and Safeway Club Cards, respectively) that can bring pretty big savings off their otherwise confiscatory rates. Kapa'a's stores are easily seen along the highway; north shore has Foodland at Princeville Shopping Center and **Big Save** in Hanalei. The south shore has Big Save in Koloa on Koloa Road. If you're a **Costco** member, we have one near Kukui Grove in Lihu'e. If you're not a member and will be here awhile, consider joining as they have the best prices.

Roosters

OK, so you don't normally think of roosters as hazards. And normally they're not. These guys are wild in many parts of the island and can be charming. But our roosters have proliferated since Hurricane 'Iniki freed so many back in 1992, and they are particularly stupid here. They don't seem to know when they're supposed to crow, so they do it *all day long* just to cover themselves. (Proba-

bly for liability purposes.) If any of these two-legged alarm clocks are near where you're staying, you may find yourself waking up *real* early.

TRAVELING WITH CHILDREN (KEIKI)

Perhaps we should have put this section under HAZARDS. If you are looking for baby-sitters, nearly every lodging on the island has lists of professional services, as well as employees who baby-sit. **Babysitters of Kaua'i** (632–2252) charges $18 per hour. Some hotels, such as the **Hyatt** and the **Marriott**, offer rather elaborate services that can be a rug-rat's dream. If you are staying at a place that has no front desk, contact your rental agent for an up-to-date list of sitters.

If you need a crib, stroller, car seat and the like, **Ready Rentals** (823–8008 or 800–599–8008) from the mainland can help.

As far as swimming in the ocean with your little one, **Lydgate Beach Park** in Wailua has a boulder-enclosed keiki (kid) pond that is wildly popular. (See the aerial photo on the inside back cover.) It also has two playgrounds (Kamalani), the best on the island. Overall, it's a nice place for keiki. Also check out **Salt Pond Beach Park** in Hanapepe and **Baby Beach**, both under BEACHES. **Po'ipu Beach Park** in Po'ipu is popular with local parents, as well as visitors. These are considered the best places for children except during periods of high surf. Obviously surf and keiki don't go well together.

During calm summer surf, **Kalihiwai Beach** can be a pleasant place to bring kids. While not as protected as Lydgate or Salt Pond, it's picturesque, and your kids will make many new local friends.

Train lovers might want to check out **Kaua'i Plantation Railway** (245-7245).

Your keiki doesn't swim, you say?
No problem. Teach 'em how to boogie board
out at the dunes of Polihale.

They cruise through 2½ miles of the Kilohana Plantation in Lihu'e. You'll stop and feed pigs along the way, which the kids go crazy over.

THE PEOPLE

The people of Kaua'i are the friendliest people in the entire country. "Oh, come on!" you might say. But this is not the admittedly biased opinion of someone who lives here. This conclusion was reached by the participants in the *Condé Nast Readers' Choice Awards.* This is a sophisticated and savvy lot. *Condé Nast* is the magazine of choice for world travelers. When asked in their yearly poll, readers rate Kaua'i at or near the top of the list in friendliness nearly every year.

What does this mean? Well, you will notice that people smile here more than other places. Drivers wave at complete strangers (without any particular fingers leading the way). If you try to analyze the reason, it probably comes down to a matter of happiness. People are happy here, and happy people are friendly people. It's just that simple. Some people compare a trip to Kaua'i with a trip back in time, when smiles weren't rare, and politeness and courtesy were the order of the day.

Some Terms

If you are confused regarding terms in Hawai'i, this should help. A person of Hawaiian blood is **Hawaiian**. That is a racial term, not a geographic one, so only people of the Hawaiian race are called Hawaiian. They are also called **Kanaka Maoli**, but only another Hawaiian can use this term. Anybody who was born here, regardless of race (except whites) is called a **local**. If you were born elsewhere but have lived here a while, you are called a **kama'aina**. If you are white, you are a **haole**. It doesn't matter if you have been here a day or your family has been here for over a century, you will always be a **haole**. The term comes from the time when westerners first encountered these islands. Its precise meaning has been lost, but it is thought to refer to people with no background (since westerners could not chant the kanaenae of their ancestors).

Visitors are prohibited by law from bringing their worries to Kaua'i.

The continental United States is called the **mainland**. If you are returning home, you are not "going back to the states" (we *are* a state). When somebody leaves the island, they are **off-island**.

Ethnic Breakdown

Kaua'i has an ethnic mix that is as diversified as any you will find. Here, *everyone* is a minority; there are no majorities. The last census count revealed the ethnic makeup below.

Asian	21,042
White	17,255
Hawaiian or other Pacific Islander	5,334
Other	505
Native American or Alaska Native	212
Black	177
Mixed or didn't respond	13,938
Total	**58,463**

Hawaiian Time

One aspect of Hawaiian culture you may have heard of is Hawaiian Time. The stereotype is that everyone in Hawai'i moves just a little bit more slowly than on the mainland. We are supposed to be more laid back and don't let things get to us as easily as people on the mainland. This is the stereotype... OK, it's *not* a stereotype. It's real. During your visit, if you get in the rhythm, you'll notice that this feeling infects *you* as well. You might find yourself letting another driver cut in front of you in circumstances that would incur your wrath back home. You might find yourself willing to wait for a red light without feeling like you're going to explode. The whole reason for coming to Hawai'i is to experience beauty and a sense of peace, so let it happen. If someone else is moving a bit slower than you would like, just go with it.

THE HAWAIIAN LANGUAGE

The Hawaiian language is a beautiful, gentle and melodious language that flows smoothly off the tongue. Just the sounds of the words conjure up trees gently swaying in the breeze and the sound of the surf. Most Polynesian languages share the same roots and many have common words. Today, Hawaiian is spoken *as an everyday language* only on the privately owned island of Ni'ihau, 17 miles off the coast of Kaua'i (see INTRODUCTION chapter). Visitors are often intimidated by

Hawaiian. With a few ground rules you'll come to realize that pronunciation is not as tough as you might think.

When missionaries discovered that the Hawaiians had no written language, they sat down and created an alphabet. This Hawaiian alphabet has only 12 letters. Five vowels: A, E, I, O and U, as well as seven consonants: H, K, L, M, N, P and W.

The consonants are pronounced just as they are in English, with the exception of W. It is often pronounced as a V. Vowels are pronounced as follows:

A—pronounced as in *Ah* if stressed or *above* if not stressed.

E—pronounced as in *say* if stressed or *dent* if not stressed.

I—pronounced as in *bee*.

O—pronounced as in *no*.

U—pronounced as in *boo*.

If you examine long Hawaiian words, you will see that most have repeating syllables, making them easier to remember and pronounce.

One thing you will notice in this book are glottal stops. These are represented by an upside-down apostrophe ʻ and are meant to convey a hard stop in the pronunciation (and are quite awkward to type). So if we are talking about the type of lava called ʻaʻa, it is pronounced as two separate As (AH-AH).

Another feature you will encounter are diphthongs (no, that's not a type of bathing suit), where two letters glide together. They are ae, ai, ao, au, ei, eu, oi and ou. Unlike many English diphthongs, the second vowel is always pronounced. One word you will read in this book, referring to Hawaiian temples, is heiau (HEY-YOW). The e and i flow together as a single sound, then the a and u flow together as a single sound. The ee sound binds the two sounds, making the whole word flow together.

Let's take a word that might seem impossible to pronounce. When you see how easy this word is, the rest will seem like a snap. The Hawaiʻi state fish is the Humuhumunukunukuapuaʻa. At first glance it seems like a nightmare. But if you read the word slowly, it is pronounced just like it looks and isn't nearly as horrifying as it appears. Try it. Humu (hoo-moo) is pronounced twice. Nuku (noo-koo) is pronounced twice. A (ah) is pronounced once. Pu (poo) is pronounced once. Aʻa (ah-ah) is the ah sound pronounced twice, the glottal stop indicating a hard stop between sounds. Now you should try it again.

Humuhumunukunukuapuaʻa.

Now, wasn't that easy? OK, so it's not easy, but it's not impossible either.

Below are some words that you might hear during your visit.

ʻAina (EYE-na)—Land.

Akamai (AH-ka-MY)—Wise or shrewd.

Aliʻi (ah-LEE-ee)—A Hawaiian chief; a member of the chiefly class.

Aloha (ah-LO-ha)—Hello, goodbye or a feeling or the spirit of love, affection or kindness.

Hala (HA-la)—Pandanus tree.

Hale (HA-leh)—House or building.

Hana (HA-na)—Work.

Hana hou (HA-na-HO)—To do again.

Haole (HOW-leh)—Originally foreigner, now means Caucasian.

Heiau (HEY-YOW)—Hawaiian temple.

Hula (HOO-la)—The story-telling dance of Hawaiʻi.

Imu (EE-moo)—An underground oven.

ʻIniki (ee-NEE-key)—Sharp and piercing wind (as in Hurricane ʻIniki).

Kahuna (ka-HOO-na)—A priest or minister; someone who is an expert in a profession.

Kai (kigh)—The sea.

Kalua (KA-LOO-ah)—Cooking food underground.

Kamaʻaina (KA-ma-EYE-na)—Long-time Hawaiʻi resident.

Kane (KA-neh)—Boy or man.

Kapu (KA-poo)—Forbidden, taboo; keep out.

Keiki (KAY-key)—Child or children.

Kokua (KO-KOO-ah)—Help.

Kona (KO-na)—Leeward side of the island; wind blowing from the south, southwest direction.

Kuleana (KOO-leh-AH-na)—Concern, responsibility or jurisdiction.

Lanai (LA-NIGH)—Porch, veranda, patio.

Lani (LA-nee)—Sky or heaven.

Lei (lay)—Necklace of flowers, shells or feathers. The mokihana is the official flower of Kauaʻi.

Lilikoʻi (LEE-lee-KO-ee)—Passion fruit.

Limu (LEE-moo)—Edible seaweed.

Lomi (LOW-me)—To rub or massage; lomi salmon is raw salmon rubbed with salt and spices.

Luʻau (LOO-OW)—Hawaiian feast; literally means taro leaves.

Mahalo (ma-HA-low)—Thank you.

Makai (ma-KIGH)—Toward the sea.

Malihini (MA-lee-HEE-nee)—A newcomer, visitor or guest.

Mauka (MOW-ka)—Toward the mountain.

Moana (mo-AH-na)—Ocean.

Moʻo (MO-oh)—Lizard.

Nani (NA-nee)—Beautiful, pretty.

Nui (NEW-ee)—Big, important, great.

ʻOhana (oh-HA-na)—Family.

ʻOkole (OH-KO-leh)—Derrière.

ʻOno (OH-no)—Delicious, the best.

Pakalolo (pa-ka-LO-LO)—Marijuana.

Pali (PA-lee)—A cliff.

Paniolo (PA-nee-OH-lo)—Hawaiian cowboy.

Pau (pow)—Finish, end; *pau hana* means quitting time from work.

Poi (poy)—Pounded kalo (taro) root that forms a paste.

Pono (PO-no)—Goodness, excellence, correct, proper.

Pua (POO-ah)—Flower.

Puka (POO-ka)—Hole.

Pupu (POO-POO)—Appetizer, snacks or finger food.

Wahine (vah-HEE-neh)—Woman.

Wai (why)—Fresh water.

Wikiwiki (WEE-kee-WEE-kee)—To hurry up, very quick.

Quick Pidgin Lesson

Hawaiian pidgin is fun to listen to. It's like ear candy. It is colorful, rhythmic and sways in the wind. Below is a list of some of the words and phrases you might hear on your visit. It's tempting to read some of these and try to use them. If you do, the odds are you will simply look foolish. These words and phrases are used in certain ways and with certain inflections. People who have spent years living in the islands still feel uncomfortable using them. Thick pidgin can be incomprehensible to the untrained ear (that's the idea). If you are someplace and hear two people engaged in a discussion in pidgin, stop and eavesdrop for a bit. You won't forget it.

Pidgin Words & Phrases

An' den—And then? So?

Any kine—Anything; any kind.

Ass right—That's right.

Ass why—That's why.

Beef—Fight.

Brah—Bruddah; friend; brother.

Brok' da mouf—Delicious.

Buggah—That's the one; it is difficult.

Bus laugh—To laugh out loud.

Bus nose—How one reacts to a bad smell.

Chicken skin kine—Something that gives you goosebumps.

Choke—Plenty; a lot.

Cockaroach—Steal; rip off.

Da kine—A noun or verb used in place of whatever the speaker wishes. Heard constantly.

Fo Days—plenty; "He got hair fo days."

Geevum—Go for it! Give 'em hell!

Grind—To eat.

Grinds—Food.

Hold ass—A close call when driving your new car.

How you figga?—How do you figure that? It makes no sense.

Howzit?—How is it going? How are you? Also, Howzit o wot?

I owe you money or wot?—What to say when someone is staring at you.

Mek ass—Make a fool of yourself.

Mek house—Make yourself at home.

Mek plate—Grab some food.

Mo' bettah—This is better.

Moke—A large, tough local male. (Don't say it unless you *like beef*.)

No can—Cannot; I cannot do it.

No make lidat—Stop doing that.

No, yeah?—No, or is "no" correct?

'Okole squeezer—Something that suddenly frightens you ('okole meaning derrière).

O wot?—Or what?

Pau hana—Quit work. (A time of daily, intense celebration in the islands.)

Poi dog—A mutt.

Shahkbait—Shark bait, meaning pale, untanned people.

Shaka—Great! All right!

Shredding—Riding a gnarly wave.

Sleepahs—Flip-flops, thongs, zoris.

Stink eye—Dirty looks; facial expression denoting displeasure.

Suck rocks—Buzz off, or pound sand.

Talk stink—Speak bad about somebody.

Talk story—Shooting the breeze; to rap.

Tanks eh?—Thank you.

Tita—A female moke. Same *beef* results.

Yeah?—Used at the end of sentences.

MUSIC

Hawaiian music is far more diverse than most people think. Many often picture Hawaiian music as someone twanging away on an 'ukulele (pronounced OO-KOO-LAY-LAY, not YOU-KA-LAY-LEE) with his voice slipping and sliding all over the place, as though he has an ice cube down his back. In reality, the music here can be outstanding. There is the melodic sound of the more traditional music. There are young local bands putting out modern music with a Hawaiian beat. There is even Hawaiian reggae and hip hop. If you get a chance, stop by **Borders Books and Music** (246–0862) at Kukui Grove in Lihu'e or **Hawaiian Music Store** (826–0245) in Princeville Shopping Center. They have a good selection of Hawaiian music.

THE HULA

The hula evolved as a means of worship, later becoming a forum for telling a story with chants (called mele), hands and body movement. It can be fascinating to watch. When most people think of the hula, they picture a woman in a grass skirt swinging her hips to the strumming of an 'ukulele. But in reality there are two types of hula. The modern hula, or hula 'auana, uses musical instruments and vocals to augment the dancer. It came about after westerners first encountered the islands. Missionaries found the hula distasteful, and the old style was driven underground. The modern type came about as a form of entertainment and was practiced in places where missionaries had no influence. Ancient Hawaiians didn't even use grass skirts. They were brought in later by Gilbert Islanders.

The old style of hula is called hula kahiko (also called 'olapa). It consists of chants and is accompanied only by percussion and takes years of training. It can be exciting to watch as performers work together in synchronous harmony. Both men and women participate, with women's hula somewhat softer (though no less disciplined) and men's hula more active. This type of hula is physically demanding and requires strong concentration. Keiki (children's) hula can be charming to watch, as well.

Kaua'i was the home of the most prestigious hula school in all the islands. People came from every part of the island chain to learn the hula at the Ka-ulu-Paoa. Great discipline was required, and the teachers could be very strict. The remains of this school are still evident at a plateau above Ke'e Beach.

The lu'aus around the island usually have entertaining hula shows, though not as "authentic" as some of the festival demonstrations seen on occasion. Some resorts and shopping centers also have hula shows on occasion.

FARMER'S MARKETS

Called Sunshine Markets locally, you'll find one every day of the week and it's a great place to pick up locally grown fruits and produce. Get there before they open, because things go fast. Below is a list; each is also shown on the maps.

Monday—In Lihu'e at Kukui Grove Shopping Center off Nawiliwili Road at 3 p.m., and Koloa Ball Park on Maluhia Road at noon.

Tuesday—In Kapa'a at Wailua Homesteads Park on Kamalu Road at 3 p.m., and in Kalaheo at the Kalaheo Neighborhood Center on Papalina Road off the Hwy at 3 p.m.

Wednesday—In Kapa'a at the Kapa'a New Town Park on Kahau Street at 3 p.m.

Thursday—In Hanapepe at Hanapepe Park at 3 p.m., and in Kilauea at the Kilauea Neighborhood Center on Keneke off Lighthouse Road at 4:30 p.m.

Friday—In Lihu'e at Vidinha Stadium on Hoolako Road at 3 p.m.

Saturday—In Kekaha at Kekaha Neighborhood Center on Elepaio Road at 9 a.m.

BOOKS

There is an astonishing variety of books available about Hawai'i and Kaua'i. Everything from history, legends, geology, children's stories and just plain ol' novels. **Borders Books** (246–0862) near Kukui Grove in Lihu'e has a dazzling selection, and their people know their stuff. Walk in and lose yourself in Hawai'i's richness. In Kapa'a on the highway in Kinipopo Shopping Center just north of the Wailua River, **Tin Can Mailman** (822–3009) also has a very nice selection, as well as hard-to-find used books, as does the **Talk Story Bookstore** (335–6469) in Hanapepe. Lastly, don't forget the **Kaua'i Museum** (246–2470). They, too, have interesting and hard-to-find books.

A NOTE ON PERSONAL RESPONSIBILITY

In past editions we've had the sad task of removing places that you can no longer visit. The reason, universally cited, is *liability*. Although Hawai'i has a statute indemnifying landowners, the mere threat is often enough to get something closed. Because we, more than any other publication, have exposed heretofore unknown attractions, we feel the need to pass this along.

You need to assess what kind of traveler you are. We've been accused of leaning a bit toward the adventurous side, so you should take that into account when deciding if something's right for you. To paraphrase from the movie *Top Gun*, "Don't let your ego write checks your body can't cash."

Please remember that this isn't Disneyland—it's nature. Mother Nature is hard, slippery, sharp and unpredictable. If you go exploring and get into trouble, whether it's your ego that's bruised or something more tangible, please remember that neither the state, the private land owner nor this publication *told* you to go. You *chose* to explore, which is what life, and this book, are all about. And if you complain to or threaten someone controlling land, they'll rarely fix the problem you identified. They'll simply close it... and it will be gone for good.

Sometimes even good intentions can lead to disaster. At one adventure, a trailhead led hikers to the base of a wonderful waterfall. There was only *one* trail, to the left at the parking lot, that a person could take. Neither we, other guides nor websites ever said, "stay on the trail to the left" because at the time there was only one trail to take. The state (in their zeal to protect themselves from liability at an unmaintained trail) came along and put up a DANGER KEEP OUT sign at the trailhead. Travelers encountering the sign assumed they were on the wrong trail and started to beat a path to the right instead. But that direction started sloping downward and ended abruptly at a 150-foot-high cliff. Hikers retreated and in a short time a previously non-existent trail to the right became as prominent as the correct (and heretofore *only*) path to the left. Not long after the state's well-intentioned sign went up, an unwitting pair of hikers took the new, incorrect trail to the right and fell to their deaths. They probably died because they had been dissuaded from taking the correct trail by a state sign theoretically erected to keep people safe.

Our point is that nothing is static and nothing can take the place of your own observations and good judgment. If you're doing one of the activities you read about in our book or someplace else and your instinct tells you something is wrong, *trust your judgment* and go do another activity. There are lots of wonderful things to do on the island, and we want you safe and happy.

MISCELLANEOUS INFORMATION

Kaua'i has no distinct **visitor season**. People come here year round to enjoy the island's blessings. However, certain times of the year are more popular than others. Christmas is always a particularly busy time, and you may have trouble getting a room if you are determined to stay at a particular resort. The graph below illustrates typical visitor distribution here. The island never feels crowded the way other destinations can feel. This might sound surprising, given poll results. When pollsters ask people where they would like to go, Kaua'i is always in the top 10.

If you're looking to dump your **digital images** onto a CD, **Photo Spectrum** (245–7667) or **Wal-Mart** (246–1599) on Hwy 56 in Lihu'e have the best prices.

Travelers' checks are usually accepted, but you should be aware that some merchants might look at you like you

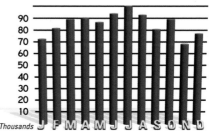

just tried to offer them Mongolian money. You should also know that the American Express Card seems to be less welcome here than at some destinations. A number of places will not accept it.

The **area code** for the entire state is 808. If you are planning to see either the **National Tropical Botanical Gardens** or the **Grove Farm Museum**, make your reservations before you get here to assure admittance. Campers should also obtain their permits before they arrive, especially for the Na Pali Coast. See CAMPING in the ACTIVITIES chapter.

If you have an **early checkout** (or **late flight**) and need a place to freshen up before your flight, consider the bathrooms at Lydgate State Park, several miles north of the airport, which have some showers. Upon entering the road to Lydgate, the showers to the right on Nehe Street are a bit more private.

If you wear **sunglasses**, *polarized* lenses are highly recommended. Not only are colors more brilliant here, but the lower latitudes of Hawai'i make polarized lenses particularly effective.

If you **lose your new wedding ring** (or anything else metallic) while frolicking at a beach, there are people for hire on the island with metal detectors. The one we recommend is **Ken** (823–6424). Ken's in his 70s and is the terror of the triathlon circuit. Good luck trying to keep up with him.

One attraction becoming more popular on Kaua'i is the NO TRESSPASSING sign. Sometimes these are sincere. Other times, they are a way for large landowners with deep pockets to avoid liability. It's sometimes tough to tell them apart. We've even had a representative of a large landowner tell us outright that they don't mind if people ignore their signs—the sign puts users on notice

The bountiful lushness of the Garden Island presents itself in many ways.

that they are on their own and not to come crying to them if they get hurt. We're *not* encouraging trespassing; we just want to tell you how some people feel here and leave it up to your own good judgment.

It is customary on Kaua'i for *everyone* to remove their shoes upon entering someone's house (sometimes their office). Kaua'i's red dirt can be particularly pernicious, and nobody wants to spend their day cleaning floors.

Daylight saving time isn't observed here.

If you are going to spend any time at the beach (and you really should), woven bamboo beach mats can be found all over the island for $1 or $2. Some roll up, some can be folded. The sand comes off these more easily than it comes off towels.

If you want to arrange a **flower lei** for you or your honey as you arrive at the airport on a direct flight (no inter-island flights), call **Greeters of Hawai'i** (800–366–8559) or **Honolulu Lei Greeting** (800–665–7959) before you arrive. For $25 and up, it's a pretty romantic way to start your trip, huh? While on island, **JC's Flowers** (240–0461) in Kapa'a has nice leis for reasonable prices. A plumeria lei is $7. (Not bad!)

THE INTERNET

Our website, **www.wizardpub.com**, has recent changes, links to cool sites, the latest satellite weather shots and more. We've posted our own aerial photos of nearly every resort on the island—so you'll *know* if oceanfront *really* means oceanfront. The site also has links to *every* company listed in the book that has a site—including those we like and those we recommend

against. For the record, we don't charge a cent for links (it would be a conflict of interest), and there are no advertisements on the site. (Well...except for our own books, of course.) Some books and magazines print all the URL addresses, but it seems pretty mean to make you type in all those long, clumsy URLs. Besides, they change too often. Posting them as links from our site allows us to keep those Internet addresses current. (And they look downright ugly in print anyway.)

In earlier editions we had a **Calendar of Events** mentioning festivals, island celebrations and special events. Waste of time! Organizers make changes so often (including days before scheduled events) that it wasn't reliable enough to continue printing it in advance. But the Internet is perfect for that. So the website has updated listings of island events.

If you're on-island and need **Web access** (to check your mail, etc.), most of the big resorts have business services available for around $20 an hour. Many other places have computers for about $6 per hour. On the north shore in Hanalei, try **Bali Hai Photo** (826–9181). On the east shore in Kapa'a, try either **Small Town Coffee** (821–1604) or **Akamai Computer** (823–0047). On the south shore, the **Koloa Public Library** (742–8455) has a 3-month visitor card available for $10 that allows you access to the computers in any library in the state.

If you're just looking for a Wi-Fi signal, try Small Town Coffee or Java Kai in Kapa'a. In Lihu'e use the lobby area of Harbor Mall or the Kukui Grove Shopping Center. Kalaheo Café is the place on the south shore.

Swimmers enjoying a giant tide-pool called Queen's Bath, a north shore gem.

Kaua'i's north shore…where lushness takes on a whole new meaning. Every shade of green imaginable is represented in its myriad plant life. Its beaches are exquisite and its mountains unmatched in their sheer majesty. After a heavy rain, you will literally be unable to count the number of waterfalls etched into the sides of north shore mountains.

For the sake of clarity, we will identify the north shore as everything north of Kapa'a. (Look at the fold-out back cover map to orient yourself.) While this description includes Anahola (which some may consider east shore), it is easier to remember it this way, and anyone driving north of Kapa'a is usually going to the north shore anyway. The main highway, which stretches around the island, occasionally changing its name, has mile markers every mile. These little green signs can be a big help in knowing where you are at any given time. Therefore, we have placed them on the maps represented as a number inside a small box 16. We will often describe a certain feature or unmarked road as being "4⁄10 miles past the 16 mile marker." We hope this helps.

Everything is either on the *mauka* side of the highway (toward the mountains) or *makai* (toward the ocean). Since people get these confused, we'll refer to them as *mauka side* and *ocean side*.

All beaches we mention are described in detail in the section on Beaches.

Driving north of Kapaʻa, you'll see **Kealia Beach** on your right, just past the 10 mile marker. This is a popular boogie boarding beach. At this beach you can often see water spitting into the air from the collision of an incoming and outgoing wave, called *clapotis* for the trivia-minded. (Doesn't that sound more like something a sailor might pick up while on shore leave?)

ANAHOLA

Next, comes the town of Anahola. This area is designated Hawaiian Homelands, meaning it is available to persons of Hawaiian descent. The spike-shaped mountain you see on the *mauka* side is **Kalalea Mountain**, also called **King Kong's Profile**. As you drive north of Anahola, look back, and you will see the striking resemblance to King Kong. To the right of the profile is a small hole in the mountain called (this is clever) **Hole-in-the-Mountain**. It used to be bigger, but a landslide in the early 1980s closed off most of it. You can see it best between the 15 and 16 mile markers. One legend says that a supernatural bird named Hulu pecked the hole in order to see Anahola on the other side. Geologists say that there was once a long lava tube stretching from Waiʻaleʻale to the sea. The mountain mass on either side of the ridge has been removed by ceaseless erosion, leaving only the ridge and its ghost of a lava tube.

Perched on a bluff overlooking the vast Pacific Ocean, the Kilauea Lighthouse stands as a silent sentry.

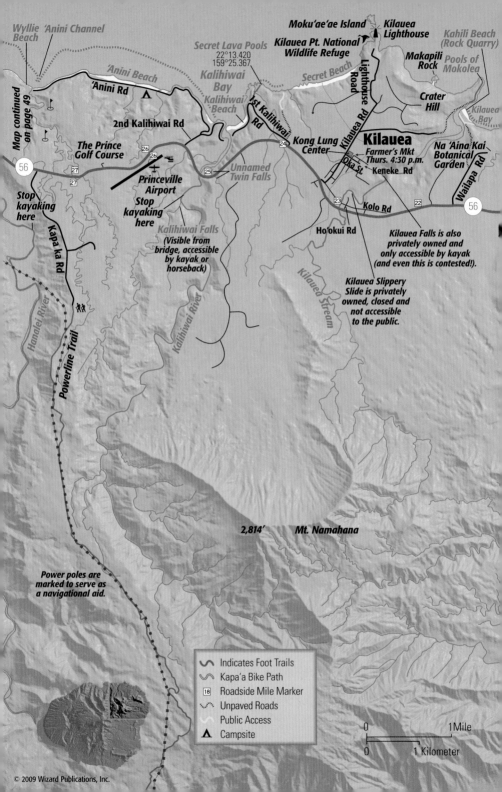

Wyllie 'Anini Channel
Beach

'Anini Beach

'Anini Rd

2nd Kalihiwai Rd

Map continued on page 49

The Prince Golf Course

Princeville Airport
Stop kayaking here

Stop kayaking here

56

27

26

25

24

23

22

Kalihiwai Bay
'Kalihiwai Beach

1st Kalihiwai Rd

Kong Lung Center

Secret Lava Pools
22°13.420
159°25.367

Secret Beach

Moku'ae'ae Island
Kilauea Pt. National Wildlife Refuge

Kilauea Lighthouse

Lighthouse Road

Kilauea Rd

Makapili Rock

Pools of Mokolea

Crater Hill

Kahili Beach (Rock Quarry)

Kilauea Bay

Kilauea
Farmer's Mkt
Thurs. 4:30 p.m.

Oka St

Keneke Rd

Kolo Rd

Ho'okui Rd

Na 'Aina Kai Botanical Garden

Wailapa Rd

56

Kapa ka Rd

Unnamed Twin Falls

Kalihiwai Falls
(Visible from bridge, accessible by kayak or horseback)

Kalihiwai River

Kilauea Stream

Kilauea Falls is also privately owned and only accessible by kayak (and even this is contested!).

Kilauea Slippery Slide is privately owned, closed and not accessible to the public.

Hanalei River

Powerline Trail

Power poles are marked to serve as a navigational aid.

2,814'   Mt. Namahana

⌇ Indicates Foot Trails
⌇ Kapa'a Bike Path
18 Roadside Mile Marker
⌇ Unpaved Roads
⌇ Public Access
▲ Campsite

0   1 Mile
0   1 Kilometer

The reef edges are denoted by ···················
and come directly from government topographic
maps. The task of verifying the precise location
of all underwater reefs would be herculean and
has not been attempted by us.

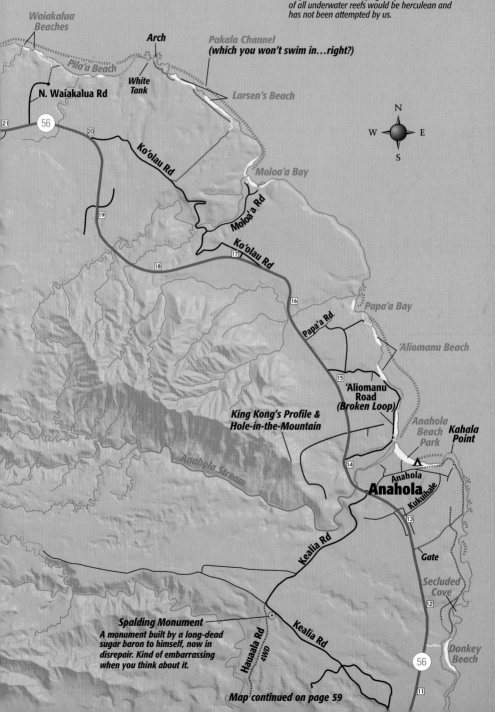

Waiakalua Beaches

Arch

Pakala Channel
(which you won't swim in...right?)

Pila'a Beach

White Tank

Larsen's Beach

N. Waiakalua Rd

21

56

20

Ko'olau Rd

Moloa'a Bay

19

Moloa'a Rd

Ko'olau Rd

18

17

16

Papa'a Bay

Papa'a Rd.

'Aliomanu Beach

15

'Aliomanu Road
(Broken Loop)

King Kong's Profile &
Hole-in-the-Mountain

Anahola
Beach
Park

Kahala
Point

Anahola Stream

14

Anahola
Anahola

Kukuihale

13

Kealia Rd

Gate

Secluded
Cove

12

Spalding Monument
A monument built by a long-dead
sugar baron to himself, now in
disrepair. Kind of embarrassing
when you think about it.

Hauaala Rd
4WD

Kealia Rd

Donkey
Beach

56

11

Map continued on page 59

N
W   E
S

Duane's Ono-Char Burger is in Anahola. This is a good place for burgers and shakes if you're hungry.

There are several secluded beaches north of Anahola that require walks of various lengths, including **Larsen's Beach** and **Waiakalua Beach**. See map on the previous page and the BEACHES chapter.

Near the 17 mile marker is the **Moloa'a Sunrise Fruit Stand**. They have one of the best selections of fruit available on the island, as well as good (if a bit pricey) sandwiches.

At the end of Wailapa Road (on the ocean side of the highway between the 21 and 22 mile markers) are the **Na 'Aina Kai Botanical Gardens** (828–0525). This is what happens when you have someone with obvious big bucks (in this case the first wife of the late *Peanuts* creator Charles Schulz) with a dream and vision to create 240 acres of tropical gardens, sculptures, a teak wood plantation, a desert garden, secluded beach and stream, all scrupulously maintained. Guided tours are expensive—$40 for the recommended 2½-hour tour—but it's such an exceptionally beautiful area that it's worth it. Arrange in advance. Other guided tours of different lengths also available.

KILAUEA

The former plantation town of **Kilauea** is just past the 23 mile marker and is accessible off Kolo Road. It is known for the **Kilauea Lighthouse** (828–1413). This is a postcard-perfect landmark perched on a bluff and represents the northernmost point of the main Hawaiian Islands. When it was built in 1913, it had the largest clamshell lens in existence and was used until the mid '70s when it was replaced by a beacon. Directly offshore is **Moku'ae'ae Island**, a bird sanctuary. Self-guided tours of the lighthouse area are available, though you can't go upstairs and visit the light itself. The view from the bluff is smashing and worth your time.

Princeville to Na Pali

Tunnels Beach

Ke'e Beach

Cannons

Ha'ena Beach Park

Kepuhi Beach

Alamoo
Alealea

Hula Heiau

Parking

10

560

9

8

Ha'ena
One One Street

Hanalei Colony Resort

Kalalau Trail map on page 190–191

Wet Caves

Limahuli Nat'l Tropical Botanical Garden

Dry Cave

Waniha Beach Park

Lumaha'i Beach

7

6

Limahuli Stream

Manoa Stream

Wainiha Power House Road

Alaeke

Double Bridges

Wainiha River

Lumaha'i River

	Indicates Foot Trails
23	Roadside Mile Marker
	Unpaved Roads
	Public Access
▲	Campsite

0 ———— 1 Mile

0 ———— 1 Kilometer

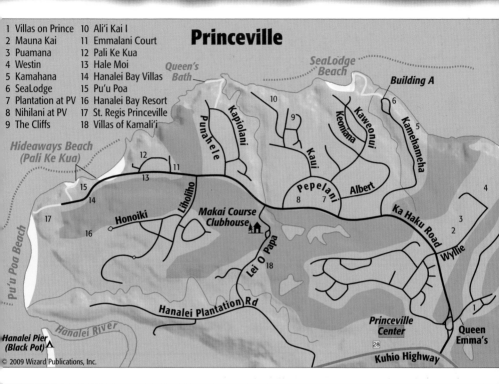

Princeville

1 Villas on Prince
2 Mauna Kai
3 Puamana
4 Westin
5 Kamahana
6 SeaLodge
7 Plantation at PV
8 Nihilani at PV
9 The Cliffs
10 Ali'i Kai I
11 Emmalani Court
12 Pali Ke Kua
13 Hale Moi
14 Hanalei Bay Villas
15 Pu'u Poa
16 Hanalei Bay Resort
17 St. Regis Princeville
18 Villas of Kamali'i

Queen's Bath
SeaLodge Beach
Building A

Hideaways Beach (Pali Ke Kua)
Pu'u Poa Beach
Honoiki
Makai Course Clubhouse
Lei O Papa

Punahele
Kapiolani
Liholiho

Keonana
Kaweonui
Kamehameha

Kaui
Pepelani
Albert
Ka Haku Road
Wyllie

Hanalei Plantation Rd
Princeville Center
Queen Emma's

Hanalei Pier (Black Pot)
Hanalei River
Kuhio Highway

© 2009 Wizard Publications, Inc.

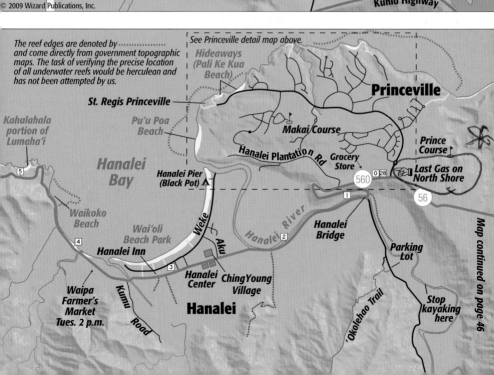

The reef edges are denoted by ·········· and come directly from government topographic maps. The task of verifying the precise location of all underwater reefs would be herculean and has not been attempted by us.

See Princeville detail map above.

Hideaways (Pali Ke Kua) Beach)

Princeville

St. Regis Princeville

Kahalahala portion of Lumaha'i

Pu'u Poa Beach

Makai Course

Prince Course

Hanalei Bay

Hanalei Plantation Rd

Grocery Store

Last Gas on North Shore

Hanalei Pier (Black Pot)

Waikoko Beach

Wai'oli Beach Park
Hanalei Inn

Weke
Aku

Hanalei River

Hanalei Bridge

Parking Lot

Hanalei Center
Ching Young Village

Hanalei

Waipa Farmer's Market Tues. 2 p.m.

Kumu Road

'Okolehao Trail

Stop kayaking here

Map continued on page 46

Open 10 a.m. to 4 p.m., it's $5 per person to get in. Take Kilauea Road.

Kilauea has also become a high-priced refuge for the super rich. Many exotic compounds are sprinkled about the area, just beyond sight.

Just north of Kilauea, on the *mauka* side, is **Banana Joe's** fruit stand. They also carry numerous locally made products. The frosties are excellent. (Frozen bananas ground through a Champion Juicer, which creates a consistency similar to ice cream.)

KALIHIWAI

After Kilauea you will notice two Kalihiwai Roads on the map. It used to be a loop connected at the bottom via a bridge. The bridge was erased by a tsunami in 1957, and the state hasn't replaced it yet. (Give 'em time; they're still debating whether computers are just another passing fad.) The first Kalihiwai Road leads to a beautiful little bay, **Kalihiwai Bay**. This is a good place to stretch your legs and enjoy the scenery. Also off the first Kalihiwai Road is a dirt road that leads to the public access of **Secret Beach** and the **Secret Lava Pools**. It requires a hike and is described under HIKING on page 151.

Back on the highway, there's a small pull-out ½ mile past the 24 mile marker. It's the only place you can park to walk to an **unnamed falls** 320 yards ahead on the left. (The falls are sometimes used by people to rinse off saltwater after they've been to **Secret Beach**.) The stream flows under the road and falls again into the valley. The long bridge past the falls has a narrow walkway. Visible on the *mauka* side is **Kalihiwai Falls**, a gorgeous, two-tiered falls. The cars on this bridge *seem* to go by at 110 mph, so be careful. You might see the remains of a vehicle turnout right at the bridge. The state closed it because of our old buddy, *liability*.

As you continue, take the second Kalihiwai Road to 'Anini Road, which leads to 'Anini Beach, where many of the rich and famous choose to build their homes. This is one of the safest places on the north shore to swim and is protected by a long, fringing reef.

PRINCEVILLE

Continuing on Highway 56, the resort area of **Princeville** beckons. It was named after Prince Albert, the visiting 2-year-old son of King Kamehameha IV. Although the young lad died two years later, the name stuck. The resort is renowned for its ocean bluff condominiums and its golf. In fact, the best course on the island (some say the best in all Hawai'i) is **The Prince Course** located on your right after the 26 mile marker. This is the sort of course that makes the non-golfer want to learn.

Past the 27 mile marker is Kapa Ka Road. The end of this road is one end of the **Powerline Trail**—10¼ miles of outstanding views. See HIKING on page 155.

Princeville's cliffs lead many to think that it has no beaches to offer. *Au contraire*, beaches don't get much better than **Hideaways**, a very pleasant little pocket of coarse sand. The catch is that you need to hike down about 5–10 minutes to it. Another gem is **Queen's Bath**. This is **A REAL GEM** a natural pool located on a lava bench. See BEACHES on page 101. The **St. Regis Princeville** is a good place to dine, shop or just gawk. If you are staying in Princeville, you may choke over the prices at Foodland or Big Save in Hanalei. Consider stocking up on food in Kapa'a where it's *somewhat* cheaper.

As you leave Princeville, note that the highway changes names again and the mile markers start at 0. The gas station here is the last place to get gas on the north shore (and they have the prices to prove it!). Across the street is the **Hanalei Lookout**. Many postcards have been sold featuring this view. This valley is where most of the taro in Hawai'i is grown. Taro corm (the root portion) is pounded to make poi. This is the stuff everyone told you not to eat when you came to Hawai'i. If you go to a lu'au, try it anyway. Then you can badmouth it with authority.

HANALEI

Going down the road, you come to the old-style **Hanalei Bridge**. Its wood planks are slippery when wet. This is a good time to tell you about Kaua'i's one-lane bridge etiquette. All vehicles (up to 7 or 8) on one side proceed, so if the car directly in front of you goes, you go. Otherwise, stop and wait for the other side to go first. All bridges from here on have one lane. Hanalei Bridge has a 15-ton weight limit, so you won't see big tour buses past this point. One bridge, called the Waipa Bridge, was built in 1912 for $4,000. It's so sturdy that it has *never* needed a major repair. The state found this intolerable and planned to replace it with a $5 million bridge that would hopefully require *lots* of maintenance. Local residents banded together in the late '90s and successfully fought 'em off.

The area around **Hanalei** (meaning wreath-shaped or crescent-shaped) **Bay** is a pretty little community. The surfing here is famous throughout the islands for its challenging nature during the winter. The entire bay is ringed by beach. A wide assortment of people live in Hanalei, including long-time locals, itinerant surfers, new age types, celebrities and every other type of individual you can imagine. You're as likely to see locals driving a Mercedes or Hummer as you are a car held together with bungee cords and duct tape.

The Hanalei Lookout is a postcard waiting to happen...

After Hanalei, you ascend the road to a turnout overlooking **Lumaha'i Beach** (if the vegetation next to the turnout is not overgrown). This is a fantastic looking beach made famous when Mitzi Gaynor washed that man right out of her hair in the classic Kaua'i-made movie *South Pacific* in 1957. (If you haven't seen the movie, that last statement must sound awfully stupid.) The eastern portion is the best but requires a hike down. Otherwise, you can walk right onto it just before the Lumaha'i Stream.

Notice how lush everything looks from here on? This part of the island gets the perfect amount of rain and sunshine, making anything green very happy.

HA'ENA

Wainiha Beach Park, past the 6 mile marker, is often a great place to beachcomb, but the swimming is not good.

One of the best **snorkel** and shore SCUBA spots on the island, **Tunnels Beach**, is past the 8 mile marker. See BEACHES chapter. Before you get to the 9 mile marker, the road dips at **Manoa Stream**. The stream flows over the road and is always creating potholes. It often creates a hole big and deep enough to pop your tire, so look for it as you cross. You are now at **Ha'ena Beach Park**. Camping is allowed with a county permit, and the beach is lovely year round (but the *swimming* isn't always lovely; see BEACHES chapter). Across the street is the **Manini-holo Dry Cave**. Manini-holo was said to be the chief fisherman for the Menehune. He and other Menehune dug the cave looking for supernatural beasts called akua who had been stealing their fish, but they didn't find *da buggah*.

Past the 9 mile marker you will come to **Limahuli Stream**. Many people (including us) use this stream to rinse off the saltwater after their day at **Ke'e Beach**, which is still ahead, or use it to rinse SCUBA gear after a dive at Tunnels.

Above Limahuli Stream is the **Limahuli Garden** (826–1053). It is part of the National Tropical Botanical Gardens. They have guided tours (by reservation

Shave Ice: An Island Delicacy

One treat everyone should try is shave ice. Lest you be confused, shave ice is not a snow cone. Snow cones are made from crushed ice with a little fruit syrup sprinkled on. True shave ice (that's shave, not shaved) uses a sharp blade to literally "shave" a large block of ice, creating an infinitely fine powder. (Keeping the blade sharp is vital.) Add to this copious amounts of exotic fruit flavors, put it all on top of a big scoop of ice cream, and you have an island delight that is truly broke da mouf. In our constant quest to provide as thorough a review as possible, we have unselfishly tried nearly every combination of shave ice. The result: We recommend the rainbow shave ice with macadamia nut ice cream. But by all means, engage in research of your own to see if you can come up with a better combination. The best shave ice on the island is at Paradise Shave Ice and Wishing Well Shave, both in Hanalei, Jo-Jo's Clubhouse in Waimea and Halo Halo Shave Ice in Lihu'e. These can be found in the ISLAND DINING chapter.

only) of the gardens for $30, self-guided tours for $15. The variety of endangered plants is refreshing. A real treat is the ancient terrace system, crafted by some of the earliest Hawaiians, estimated to be 700 years old and in fantastic condition.

Just past the Limahuli Stream are the **Wet Caves**, called **Waikapala'e Cave** (reachable by a short trail) and **Waikanaloa Cave** (right there on the road). The upper **Waikapala'e Cave** contains a clean, freshwater pool. Until a few years ago the back portion of the cave (reachable only by swimming in the cold water) hid a phenomenon called the **Blue Room** (a chamber where the light turned everything blue). But the water level is now too low, and too much light has erased the blue from the blue room. The wet and dry caves are former sea caves, gouged by waves when the sea level was higher than it is today. We were silly enough to SCUBA dive the upper cave and can report that there is not much to see, but it was kind of fun anyway (and spooky when we swam past where you could see the light entering the cave). Hawaiian legend has it that these caves were dug by the fire goddess Pele. She dug them for her lover but left them when they became filled with water.

At the 10 mile marker, you have gone as far as you can go by car. This is **Ke'e Beach**, marked by a fabulous lagoon that offers great swimming and snorkeling when it's calm. The well-known **Kalalau Trail** begins here. Eleven miles of hills and switchbacks culminate in a glorious beach setting, complete with a waterfall. The first leg of the hike leads to **Hanakapi'ai Beach** with a side trip to **Hanakapi'ai Falls**. You sure ain't gonna do this trail on a whim, so for more on the **Kalalau Trail**, see AD-VENTURES on page 190.

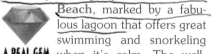

A REAL GEM

Ke'e is where **Na Pali Coast** begins. You can see its edges from here. Part of *The Thorn Birds* and numerous other movies have been filmed at this location. If you walk past Ke'e Beach on the shoreline trail beside the rocks, you'll get an enticing look at the rugged **Na Pali coastline**. Look up toward the mountains and you'll see **Bali Hai** (Hawaiian name **Makana Peak**). Clever photography turned the peak into the mystical island of Bali Hai in the movie *South Pacific*. As you stare at this peak with its incredibly steep sides, picture the following scene that took place in ancient times.

Men would climb the 1,600-foot peak carrying special spears made of hau and papala. The trail was so difficult in spots that they had to cling to the side of the mountain for dear life. When it got dark, they would light the spears and hurl them as hard as they could toward the ocean below. The spears were designed to leave a fire trail behind and were light enough to get caught in the updrafts. The light show was immensely popular.

From the end of Ke'e Beach, a trail cuts through the jungle up to the **Ka-ulu-Paoa Heiau**, still visible by the pavement of stones outlining its foundations next to a lava cliff. Other trails to the heiau may be on private property, but the shoreline trail from the beach is public. For over 1,000 years this heiau served as the most important and prestigious school for hula in the islands. Would-be students came from around the island chain to learn from the *kumu hula,* or hula master. Please don't disturb any rocks lying about. Just past the heiau a short trail leads to a small waterfall (which is merely a trickle during dry times). *Fifty* generations of hot, thirsty students came to this tiny waterfall, sat on these very rocks and talked about their lives, hopes, fears and dreams. It's humbling to share these rocks with their spirits. It's as if you can still hear

Walk the shoreline trail past Ke'e Beach for a great view of Na Pali.

Kaua'i's north shore is where the majority of the state's taro is grown. This field, in the Hanalei Valley, was planted with rice to look like Vietnam in the movie Uncommon Valor.

the echo of their lives in the sound of the gurgling water.

Just east of **Ke'e** is where the infamous **Taylor Camp** used to be. This is where Howard Taylor, brother of Elizabeth Taylor, owned a piece of land in the 1960s and encouraged other "hippies" to come and live off the land. The camp swelled to more than 100 people who mostly ended up living off residents or the government. Before the state condemned the property in 1977, camp residents began what would become the national *puka shell* craze when one of the residents fashioned a necklace of shells and gave it to Howard, who in turn gave it to his famous sister Liz.

NORTH SHORE SHOPPING

Across from mile marker 20 on the way north to Kilauea is **Hawaiian Hardwoods** for everything from boxes to tables, most following the natural forms found in the original wood. In Ki-lauea at Kong Lung Center try **Kong Lung Co**. for outstanding Japanese ceramics, housewares and other items. Also in the same building don't miss **Banana Patch Gallery** for Hawaiian style ceramics and other island items for the home. In the back is **Cake**, a women's boutique with some unique clothing and accessories. Outside at the back of the center is **Coconut Style**, if your bedding could use some bright original island batik designs. **Island Soap & Candle** has just what the name implies, all made locally. And for jewelry, stop in at **Lotus Gallery**. Next to the Center pick up some fine wines and gourmet foodstuffs at **Kilauea Town Market**.

In the Princeville Shopping Center, **Magic Dragon Toy & Art Supply** has many options to keep the young and old entertained, including books, games, puzzles and of course, dragons. **Walking in**

Paradise has all kinds of sandals from fancy to functional.

As you approach Hanalei, the north shore's shopping Mecca, stop at Hanalei Dolphin Center and have a look at Ola's for fine arts and some pretty unusual gifts. Also in the center is **Overboard** for men's and women's island fashions and **Black Pearl** for...well, pearls. On the same side of the road is the green Halele'a Building where **Titus Kinimaka Kai Kane** has some good buys on surfwear. On the main highway before Ching Young Village, don't pass up some of the shops behind the main road in Kauhale Center, such as the **The Root**, for women's clothes and **Crystals & Gems Gallery**, which has some unusual handcrafted jewelry. Next door, try Kauai Nut Roasters they use no oil to cook their nuts fresh on site. They come in exotic flavors with delicious results and give free samples. Back on the main highway **Kokonut Kids** has adorable children's island wear and some toys. Browse **Artists Gallery of Kaua'i** (aka **Evolve Love Gallery**) for art, jewelry and clothing all made by local artists. One of our favorite shops is **On The Road In Hanalei** next door for Asian-inspired housewares, pottery and jewelry.

In Ching Young Village there are many shops and places to eat. Some places are a must-see like **Hot Rocket**, where all the Hawaiian shirts are *actually* made in Hawaii. They are some of the most unusual we've seen. **Peddle 'N Paddle** has great outdoor gear for sale and rent, and if your shoes have taken a beating on your trip, this is a great place to pick up island-friendly surf and turf footwear. **Spinning Dolphin** will print Hawaiian design T-shirts while you wait. **Hanalei Music's Strings & Things** has a small selection of Hawaiian music and 'ukuleles.

Across the street in Hanalei Center be sure to walk behind the building and see **Hula Beach** for hip island clothing for the whole family. **Havaiki Oceanic and Tribal Art** has extensive and unique artworks from all over the pacific islands and is not to be missed. **Yellowfish Trading Co.** carries vintage Hawaiiana, antiques and collectables. **Tropical Tantrum** has batik print clothing; **Sand People** also has women's clothes and island-style items for your home. **Hanalei Surf Co.** has surfer gear and clothes. **Jewel of Paradise** has some unusual glass paperweights of celestial bodies that are worth a look. If you are heading up to Ha'ena, stop in at the Hanalei Colony Resort and check out **Na Pali Art Gallery & Coffee House**. The have some outstanding Hawaiian pieces of glasswork, art, jewelry and pottery.

NORTH SHORE BEST BETS

Best Beach—Ke'e or Hideaways
Best Snorkeling—Tunnels, Hideaways or Ke'e
Best Treat—Apple Cobbler at Village Snack & Bakery or any flavor at Kauai Nut Roasters
Best Lava Swimming Pool—Queen's Bath or Secret Lava Pools
Best View from a Treadmill—Prince Health Club
Best Secluded Beach—Waiakalua
Best Swimming When Calm—Ke'e
Best Shore SCUBA Dive—Tunnels Beach
Best Beachcombing—Wainiha Beach
Best Golf—The Prince Course
Best View—Sunset from Ke'e Overlooking Na Pali, or from Kalalau Trail
Best Parking Spot—One of the Few Available at Tunnels
Best Place to be Glad You're Wearing Comfortable Shoes—The End of the 11-Mile Long Kalalau Trail

Wailua is known as the coconut coast—can you guess why?

Kaua'i's east shore is where the majority of the population resides. The kings of yesteryear chose the Wailua River area to live, making it forever royal ground. All members of Kaua'i royalty were born in this area. Kuamo'o Road, designated as 580 on the maps, is also called the King's Highway. In ancient times only the king could walk along the spine of this ridge. (Kuamo'o means the lizard's spine.)

Today, the east shore is often referred to as the Coconut Coast. One drive through Wailua and it's obvious why: thousands of coconut trees planted over a century ago by an idealistic young German immigrant who

dreamed of overseeing a giant copra (dried coconut) empire. Unfortunately, nobody told him how long coconut trees took to mature, and the plantation was not economically successful, but his legacy lives on in the form of a gigantic coconut grove.

For our description, the east shore means the Wailua/Kapa'a area to Lihu'e. (Take a look at the fold-out back cover map to orient yourself.) Both areas are heavily populated. (This is a relative term; together they have about 20,000 residents.)

The same descriptive ground rules that we discussed at the beginning of NORTH SHORE SIGHTS apply here.

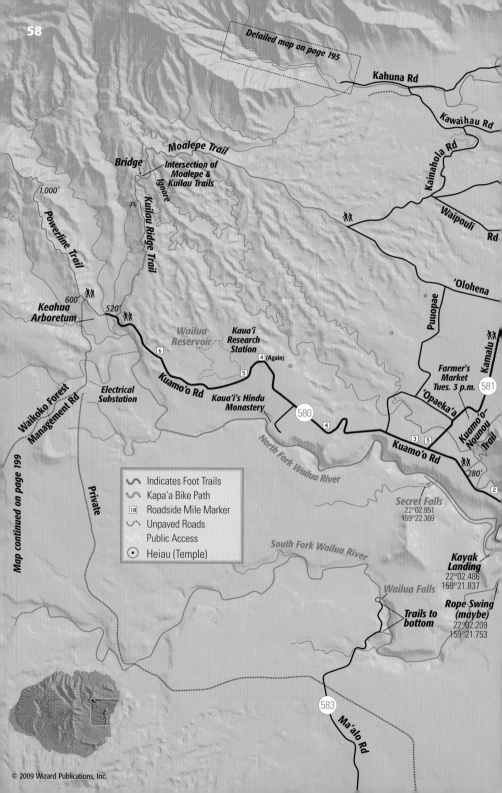

Detailed map on page 195

Kahuna Rd

Kawaihau Rd

Kainahola Rd

Waipouli Rd

Moalepe Trail

Bridge

Intersection of
Moalepe &
Kuilau Trails

Ignore

1,000'

Kuilau Ridge Trail

Powerline Trail

'Olohena

Puuopae

Kamalu

Keahua
Arboretum

600'

520'

Wailua
Reservoir

Kaua'i
Research
Station

4 (Again)

5

6

Kuamo'o Rd

Farmer's
Market
Tues. 3 p.m.

581

'Opaeka'a

Kuamo'o-
Nounou
Trail

Waikoko Forest
Management Rd

Electrical
Substation

Kaua'i's Hindu
Monastery

580

4

Kuamo'o Rd

3   5

280'

2

Map continued on page 199

North Fork Wailua River

Secret Falls
22°02.951
159°22.369

Private

Indicates Foot Trails

Kapa'a Bike Path

18   **Roadside Mile Marker**

Unpaved Roads

Public Access

Heiau (Temple)

South Fork Wailua River

Kayak
Landing
22°02.486
159°21.837

Wailua Falls

Trails to
bottom

Rope Swing
(maybe)
22°02.209
159°21.753

583

Ma'alo Rd

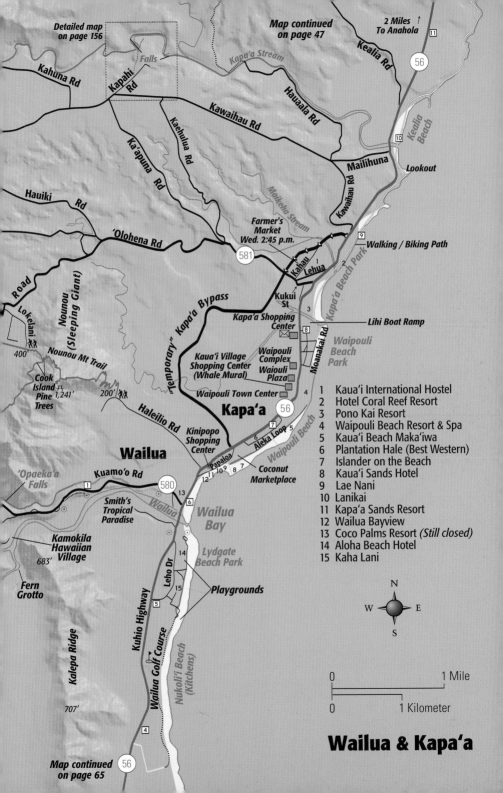

Detailed map on page 156

Map continued on page 47

2 Miles ↑ To Anahola

11

Kealia Rd

56

Kahuna Rd

Kapahi Rd

Falls

Kapa'a Stream

Hauaala Rd

Kealia Beach

10

Kawaihau Rd

Ka'apuna Rd

Kaehulua Rd

Mailihuna

Lookout

Hauiki Rd

'Olohena Rd

Moikeha Stream

Kawaihau Rd

9

Walking / Biking Path

Farmer's Market
Wed. 2:45 p.m.

581

Kahau

Lehua

Road

Lokelani

Nounou
(Sleeping Giant)

400'

Nounou Mt Trail

200'

Cook
Island
Pine 1,241'
Trees

Kukui St

Kapa'a Shopping Center

8

Lihi Boat Ramp

Kaua'i Village Shopping Center (Whale Mural)

Waipouli Complex

Waipouli Plaza

Waipouli Town Center

Kapa'a Beach Park

Waipouli Beach Park

3

Moanakai Rd

"Temporary" Kapa'a Bypass

Kapa'a

56

4

Haleilio Rd

Kinipopo Shopping Center

Aleka Loop

6

7

Waipouli Beach

Wailua

Kuamo'o Rd

580

13

Papaloa

12 11 10 9 8 7

Coconut Marketplace

'Opaeka'a Falls

1

Smith's Tropical Paradise

Wailua

6

Wailua Bay

Kamokila Hawaiian Village

683'

Lydgate Beach Park

14

Fern Grotto

Leho Dr

15

Playgrounds

Kalepa Ridge

Kuhio Highway

5

707'

Wailua Golf Course

Nukoli'i Beach (Kitchens)

1. Kaua'i International Hostel
2. Hotel Coral Reef Resort
3. Pono Kai Resort
4. Waipouli Beach Resort & Spa
5. Kaua'i Beach Maka'iwa
6. Plantation Hale (Best Western)
7. Islander on the Beach
8. Kaua'i Sands Hotel
9. Lae Nani
10. Lanikai
11. Kapa'a Sands Resort
12. Wailua Bayview
13. Coco Palms Resort *(Still closed)*
14. Aloha Beach Hotel
15. Kaha Lani

N
W E
S

0 ——————— 1 Mile
0 ——————— 1 Kilometer

Wailua & Kapa'a

4

56

Map continued on page 65

Unlike other areas of the island where a single road dominates your tour, this area has many significant sights located off the main road. Therefore, we will describe them in a more scattershot manner and generally work our way from north to south.

WAILUA/KAPA'A

In the extreme northern part of Kapa'a is a delightful waterfall called **Ho'opi'i Falls**, which you can hike to. See HIKING on page 156.

While we are up the road off the main highway, there are several hikes in this area that provide excellent views. The **Nounou Mountain Trail** (also called the **Sleeping Giant**), the **Kuilau Ridge Trail**, the **Jungle Hike** and the **Secret Tunnel to the North Shore Hike** are all located inland and all are worthy of consideration. (See HIKING in the ACTIVITIES chapter for more information.)

One aspect of ancient Hawaiian culture that can be seen to this day is the heiau, a structure carefully built from lava rocks and used for religious purposes. There are **seven heiau** stretching from the mouth of the **Wailua River** to the top of **Mount Wai'ale'ale**. All except the Wai'ale'ale heiau are marked on the map on the previous page. The mouth of the Wailua River was well known, not only throughout the Hawaiian Islands, but also in parts of central Polynesia as well. Ancient Polynesians are thought to have come all the way from Tahiti to visit it.

Wailua is also known for ghosts and spirits. It was thought that during a certain phase of the moon, spirits of those who died recently would paddle down the river in large numbers and work their way around the island to a cliff at Polihale (described on page 88) where they would leap to the next life. Known as **night marchers**, these ghosts are still believed by many Hawaiians to exist, and sightings are most prevalent along the highway between Wailua and Lihu'e. Interestingly, this stretch of road has also been responsible for many bad car accidents. Of course, police blame the wrecks on another type of spirit—the kind that comes in a bottle.

The first heiau, near the mouth of the Wailua River on the southern side, is called **Hauola, City of Refuge**. It is part of what was a larger structure called **Hikina-akala**, meaning the rising of the sun. If a person committed an offense worthy of execution (such as allowing his shadow to touch the shadow of a chief or interrupting an important person), he would attempt to elude his executioners by coming here. By staying at the site and performing certain rites prescribed by the priest, he would earn the right to leave without harm.

The second temple is on the *mauka* side of the highway between the north end of Leho Road and the road to **Smith's Tropical Paradise**. This is called **Malae** and at 273 x 324 feet, it is the largest heiau on Kaua'i. Legend states that it was built by Menehune. Although there is not a lot to see, the view from there is interesting. If you decide to visit it, be wary of your footing.

The third heiau is just up Kuamo'o Road (580) on the left side. This area had several names and several functions. The first portion that you see is called **Holoholoku**. Some archeologists say that this area was used for human sacrifice. Most of the time those sacrificed were prisoners of war. If none could be found, however, the Kahuna would select a commoner and have the executioner strangle him secretly at night. Some archaeologists find this interpretation of Hawaiian history in spiritual bad taste, given its very close proximity to the **Birthstones**,

Throw-net fishing was introduced to Hawai'i by Japanese immigrants. The native Hawaiians quickly embraced this method, and today it is considered an island tradition.

described below, and assume that the area was used for animal sacrifices. The heiau was later purposely desecrated and used as a pigpen by the wife of the last king of Kaua'i, who did so as a signal that the ancient religious ways should be abandoned in favor of Christianity.

Just a few dozen feet up the road from **Holoholoku** is the **Birthstone**. It was essential that all kings of Kaua'i be born here, even if they were not of chiefly origin. One of the two stones supported the back of the mother-to-be while the other was where she placed her legs while giving birth. The outline of stones near here indicates where a grass shack once stood, where the pregnant mother stayed until it was time to give birth. The flat slab of sandstone that you see on the ground covered the remains of a sacrificed dog, indicating that the place was kapu, or forbidden to commoners. The giant crack in the rock wall was where the umbilical cord of the newborn was placed. If a rat came and took the cord, it was a sign that the child would grow up to be a thief (or worse, a tax collector); otherwise, all was well.

Continuing up 580, a short way past the 1 mile marker, there's a dirt road angling back toward the ocean. Located at the end of the road are two large boulders. (Sometimes State Parks inexplicably lets weeds grow over them.) Though few residents are aware of it, the rocks' position is no accident and dates back over 1,000 years.

The ancient Hawaiians didn't live in a world of well-defined seasons. They didn't even measure their own lives in years, but rather stages of life. But they did need to keep track of the passage of the sun for planting and religious reasons. These two multi-ton rounded and shaped boulders are perfectly offset so that if you align yourself with them so they appear to touch with the right one closer to you, the sun will rise from the intersection on the summer solstice. (Winter solstice involves aligning the right side of the left boulder with the thumb-like hill on Sleeping Giant behind you.) Imagine the importance they must have attributed to this task by considering the difficulty of hauling these boulders up from the Wailua River, perhaps one boulder from each fork for symmetry. (Hawaiians *loved* symmetry.)

From those boulders, if you walk down the path about 100 feet past the guardrail, you will see several large stones. One of them was known as the **Bellstone** and,

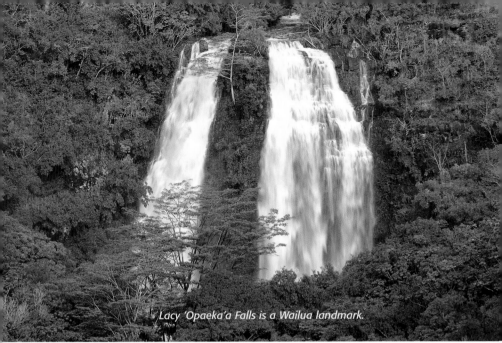

Lacy ʻOpaekaʻa Falls is a Wailua landmark.

if thwacked properly, can produce a metallic clank (not the gong we have come to expect from metal bells). This sound supposedly carried throughout the entire Wailua Valley. The stone was struck in ancient times to signal the birth of what would be a new chief.

Still on 580 just before you get to the ʻOpaekaʻa Falls turnout is the last heiau you will see. Called **Poliʻahu**, this is a rather mysterious heiau. Legend states that it was built by Menehune, the legendary people of small stature, and was devoted to the interests and activities of the gods, demigods and high aliʻi. Look for lots of native and Polynesian-introduced plant species in the area. There is also a nice **Wailua River Lookout** here.

The actual final heiau in this chain rests atop the rain-soaked plateau of **Waiʻaleʻale**. The remnants of this most sacred heiau are still visible today. Called **Kaʻawako**, the altar itself stood 2 feet high, 5 feet wide and 7 feet long. Toward the rear, standing on one end was a phallic stone. It is located on the wettest spot in the entire world. According to the USGS, this spot receives 428 inches of rain

per year. (You read a lot of numbers about the annual rainfall on **Waiʻaleʻale**—this number comes straight from the people who read the rain gauges. The original gauge is in the Kauaʻi Museum.)

The ancient Hawaiians were bothered that the small, sacred pool on top of Waiʻaleʻale didn't feed their most sacred river, the Wailua. Not to worry. In a project that would make the Army Corps of Engineers proud, they cut a trench at the top of the mountain from the small pool to the edge of the cliff so the water would add to the waterfalls that feed the Wailua River. Then they could say the most sacred pool fed the most sacred river.

While on Kuamoʻo Road *(a well-known speed trap)*, stop by the ʻOpaekaʻa Falls Lookout. These lacy 151-foot falls flow year round. Late morning light is best, around 10:30 a.m. There is another **Wailua River Lookout** across from the ʻOpaekaʻa Lookout.

NOT TO BE MISSED!

Kamokila Hawaiian Village (823–0559) is across the street from ʻOpaekaʻa

Falls. It's 3 acres of private land with numerous huts scattered about. Some might find it interesting; others might get antsy. It's not exactly lavishly maintained, but it's only $5 per person to get in and wander around. It'll probably take 40 minutes to see it, and it's certainly *not* indispensable. You can also do a canoe trip to Secret Falls from here (see KAYAKING on page 165) for $30.

Further up Kuamo'o Road, past some hairpin turns, is a road on the left called Kaholalele. At the end is **Kaua'i's Hindu Monastery** (888–735–1619). This is an *incredible* place, but they only give free tours by reservation once a week from 9 a.m. to noon. (It varies depending on the Hindu calender—call for dates.) It's set in an absolutely idyllic environment next to the Wailua River. This temple is built entirely of hand-carved stones from India. Some stones take as long as 7 years to carve, and there are 4,000 of them. (Gee, and we buy pre-sliced cheesecake because we're too impatient to cut it up.) They say it's the only pure stone temple being built anywhere in the world and should be complete by 2010. They have a strict dress code, so wear long pants and shirts with short or long sleeves. If you get a chance, a tour is highly recommended. Bring mosquito repellent.

Continuing several miles up Kuamo'o Road, the road eventually crosses *under* a stream and becomes unpaved. It occasionally flows too heavily over the road to cross in your car. See the detailed map of this area on page 199. A 4WD is a dream back here, but regular cars are often OK, depending on the maintenance cycle of the road and the weather. (Sometimes the wimpiest Neon can make it; other times pre-maintenance ruts become too much for some 4WDs.) Large puddles are usually lined with small rocks, not mud. Several trailheads are in this region.

A pretty one, before the road becomes unpaved, is the **Kuilau Ridge Trail**. The **Keahua Arboretum** is located near here, but it's been rather unkempt for years, so don't knock yourself out to see it.

The unpaved section of this road is Waikoko Forest Management Road. The area feels like a giant oxygen factory. Take a big whiff and you'll almost get a buzz from the purity of the air. The **Jungle Hike** on page 153 and the **Secret Tunnel to the North Shore** in ADVENTURES are back here, as well as stunning forests. This area is excellent for mountain biking.

Back on the main highway, you'll find that traffic in downtown Kapa'a (on the highway) can get congested at times, *especially* going south. The county opened up a "temporary" bypass road. (See map.) The "permanent" bypass road is scheduled to be completed sometime during the next ice age. All the land around the bypass area was for sale some years back. Kaua'i residents were worried that someone would buy the 1,400 acres and develop it, connecting Kapa'a to Wailua and creating a big-city feel. Entertainer Bette Midler (a part-time resident) bought it instead and promised never to put anything other than trees on it.

One of Kapa'a's notable views is the **Sleeping Giant**. The best angle is from the small turnout kitty-corner from the Chevron station (on the main highway). Look *mauka* and you will see the outline of a giant. (This is your *ink blot* test for the day.) According to legend, the giant you see (you *do* see it, don't you?) was a friendly sort who flattened areas where he sat. Local villagers liked this and also planted bananas in his footsteps. One day the chief ordered a heiau to be built. Villagers were too busy, so the giant volunteered. It took two weeks and he did a great job. Villagers threw a party to celebrate, and the giant ate a bit too much.

Lihu'e & Puhi

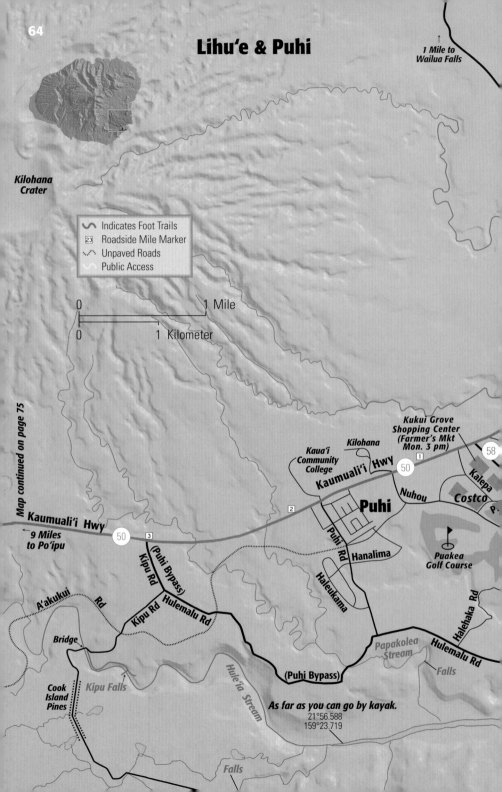

1 Mile to
Wailua Falls

Kilohana
Crater

Indicates Foot Trails
23 Roadside Mile Marker
Unpaved Roads
Public Access

0   1 Mile

0   1 Kilometer

Map continued on page 75

Kukui Grove
Shopping Center
(Farmer's Mkt
Mon. 3 pm)

Kilohana

Kaua'i
Community
College

58

Kaumuali'i Hwy

1

50

Nuhou

Costco

Kalepa

Puhi

P.

2

Puhi Rd

Hanalima

Puakea
Golf Course

Kaumuali'i Hwy

9 Miles
to Po'ipu

50

3

Haleukama

Halehaka Rd

(Puhi Bypass)

Kipu Rd

Hulemalu Rd

A'akukui Rd

Kipu Rd

Papakolea
Stream

Hulemalu Rd

Falls

Bridge

Kipu Falls

Hule'ia Stream

(Puhi Bypass)

Cook
Island
Pines

As far as you can go by kayak.
21°56.588
159°23.719

Falls

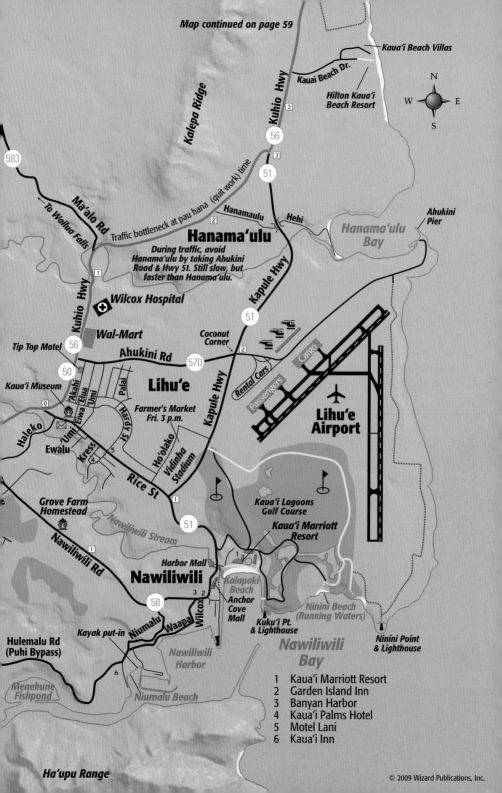

Map continued on page 59

Kaua'i Beach Villas

Kauai Beach Dr.

Kuhio Hwy

Hilton Kaua'i
Beach Resort

N
W • E
S

Kalepa Ridge

3

56

3

Ahukini
Pier

583

51

Ma'alo Rd

Traffic bottleneck at pau hana (quit work) time

Hanamaulu

Hehi

To Wailua Falls

2

Hanama'ulu

*During traffic, avoid
Hanama'ulu by taking Ahukini
Road & Hwy 51. Still slow, but
faster than Hanama'ulu.*

Hanama'ulu
Bay

Kuhio Hwy

1

Kapule Hwy

✚ **Wilcox Hospital**

51

Coconut
Corner

Tip Top Motel

Wal-Mart

56

Ahukini Rd

2

Cargo

Lihu'e Airport

50

570

Kaua'i Museum

Akahi
'Elua
'Umi

Palai

Lihu'e

Kapule Hwy

Rental Cars

Passengers

0

'Umi
Ewa

Hardy St

*Farmer's Market
Fri. 3 p.m.*

Haleko

Kress St

Ho'olako

Ewalu

4

5

Vidinha
Stadium

Rice St

1

Grove Farm
Homestead

Nawiliwili Stream

51

Kaua'i Lagoons
Golf Course

Kaua'i Marriott
Resort

Lihu'e
Airport

Nawiliwili Rd

1

Harbor Mall

Nawiliwili

1

Kalapaki
Beach

Anchor
Cove
Mall

Ninini Beach
(Running Waters)

58

3 2

Hulemalu Rd
(Puhi Bypass)

Kayak put-in

Niumalu

Waapa

Wilcox

Kuku'i Pt.
& Lighthouse

Ninini Point
& Lighthouse

*Nawiliwili
Bay*

Nawiliwili
Harbor

6

**Menehune
Fishpond**

Niumalu Beach

1 Kaua'i Marriott Resort
2 Garden Island Inn
3 Banyan Harbor
4 Kaua'i Palms Hotel
5 Motel Lani
6 Kaua'i Inn

Ha'upu Range

© 2009 Wizard Publications, Inc.

(If you've been to a lu'au, you can relate.) He fell asleep and has not been roused since, but is expected to wake up any time (maybe during your visit).

Local folklore says that if Kaua'i's people learned of an attempt to invade their island, they would light fires behind the **Sleeping Giant** in order to illuminate his profile at night. This would frighten invading warriors into thinking that Kaua'i had some really big dudes and that they should rethink their invasion plans.

While you are in Wailua, riverboat trips up the **Wailua River** can take you to the **Fern Grotto** for $20 per person. This is a natural amphitheater filled with ferns and is a popular place to hold weddings. See RIVER TRIPS in the ACTIVITIES chapter. The **Wailua River** is usually called the only navigable river in all Hawai'i, but that depends on your definition of navigable. The mouth of the river has several stones with ancient **petroglyphs** carved in them. After heavy rains, the river sometimes washes away large amounts of sand, revealing these stones for a short period of time. The mouth itself is always changing, and watching it wash over its banks after

These petroglyphs are usually submerged in the mouth of the Wailua River, but can appear after heavy rains.

a heavy rain can be wild. The river mouth can go from not flowing at all to carving up the mouth in a matter of hours.

There is a paved beachside walking path behind the Kaua'i Beach at Maka'iwa, and a longer path from Kapa'a Beach Park north to beyond Kealia Beach. They are great for a stroll or to ride a bike. A good place to take a *sandy* beach walk is from **Lydgate Beach Park** south as far as the Hilton Kaua'i. The sand is continuous almost the whole way.

Lydgate Beach Park is the best place on the island to learn snorkeling. It has a boulder-enclosed pond that allows water and fish in, but keeps out the ocean's force. See SNORKELING on page 177 and BEACHES on page 109. There is even a keiki (kid) pond, which is shallower. Add to this showers, restrooms and two playgrounds, and you have a nice little park for a day at the beach.

On the southern side of the Wailua River is **Smith's Tropical Paradise**. Here you will find a nice garden (not in the same league as other nicer island gardens) in which to stroll, filled with tropical plants and wailing peacocks (which sound like cats being tortured). Entrance is $6 per person. They also hold a pretty good lu'au here. See ISLAND DINING chapter for more information.

As you pass the **Wailua Municipal Golf Course** going south toward Lihu'e, realize that the entire coast fronting the course is a sandy beach. Called **Nukoli'i Beach**, there are rarely more than a few people on it.

LIHU'E

Coming from Kapa'a and just before you enter Lihu'e

from Highway 56, you see Maʻalo Road (583) on the *mauka* side. This leads to Wailua Falls. In ancient (and occasionally modern) times, men would jump off the top of the falls to prove their manhood (which was often left on the rocks below). This test was often fatal. Government maps list the falls' height at 80 feet. It always bothered us because it sure *looks* taller. So, a few years ago we dropped a fishing line and sinker to the bottom from the lip of the falls (boy, did *we* look stupid) and measured it. To our amazement, it was 173 feet of solid drop. (We measured it *twice* to be sure.) That's actually taller than Niagara Falls (though the latter has a tad more water flowing).

You might see people splashing about in the pool below the falls. It's a wonderful scene and lots of fun. They either took the steep trail (if it's dry) about 100 feet before the metal guard-rail ends at the lookout, or the less steep trail 3/10 mile back down the road from the end of the turn-around. (See map.) The latter requires a much longer walk, is not as steep but includes river walking. Neither are professionally maintained and both can be slippery when wet. The state also, in their paranoia about liability, has erected signs telling you not to take the trails to the bottom. They even cut the ropes once (but users keep replacing them) that had been strung to make it safer and easier. (Making it *less* safe apparently makes some bureaucrat *feel* safer.) We see people ignoring the signs, and the fences erected by the state are promptly vandalized by local residents who have played at the bottom of the falls for generations.

The falls plunge into a pool that's 33 feet deep. Why so exact? Because in one of those *just because* moods, we hiked down with some friends, hauling SCUBA gear (gee, those ropes sure did help), and SCUBA-dived the pool. There we found 14-inch long small-mouthed bass and some giant shrimp (isn't that an oxymoron?) with bodies over 8 inches long, plus arms. Lingering beneath the falls, the scene is like an upside-down battlefield with explosions of white that will cause percussive waves to sweep through your entire body, your air-filled chest shuddering from the blasts. We also found rental car keys (perhaps tossed by an irate but shortsighted spouse), bolt cutters, a cane knife and other odds and ends.

Back on the highway, if we're just trying to get *through* Lihuʻe during traffic, we usually take 51 to 570 (Ahukini Road) to Hwy 56. (See map on page 65 for this to make sense.) It bypasses Hanamaʻulu and much of Lihuʻe.

In Lihuʻe, one place worth stopping for is the **Kauaʻi Museum** (245–6931) on Rice Street. They have an interesting display of Hawaiian artifacts and a permanent display called *The Story of Kauaʻi* and other rotating displays. Their gift shop is well stocked with books, maps and assorted items. If you are looking for topographic maps of the various areas (serious hikers prefer these as traveling companions) or just an obscure book on Kauaʻi or Hawaiʻi, this is a good place to stop. This isn't exactly the Smithsonian, but admission is only $10 per person unless you are going to the gift shop, which is free.

If you need camping permits or other county or state items, their buildings are behind the museum on Eiwa Street.

While you are in the area, there is a dumpy little place on Kress Street called **Halo Halo Shave Ice** inside Hamura Saimin that serves good shave ice (when they feel like serving it). Have them put ice cream on the bottom for a real treat.

Taking Rice Street east leads you to Nawiliwili Harbor. There are two shopping centers here called **Harbor Mall** and **Anchor Cove Shopping Center**. **Kalapaki Beach**, behind Anchor Cove, is a good place to watch sailboats, outrigger canoes and cruise ships, in addition to the beach's other attributes.

On Rice Street, you will pass the main entrance to the **Kaua'i Marriott**. Its other entrance is off Kapule Highway (51) and leads through **Kaua'i Lagoons** to either **Ninini/Running Waters Beach** or the **Ninini Lighthouse**. If there is a maintenance volunteer at the lighthouse, ask if you can go to the top. The view from the 86-foot lighthouse is superb. The lighthouse uses a 4.7 million candlepower light. We remember how that sounded like *a lot* the first time we heard it, until we realized you can go to the store and buy 3 million candlepower flashlights for $30. Anyway, if you happen to be on top when a jet comes in for a landing, you'd swear you could reach up and touch it. To get to the lighthouse, you pass by two golf courses. Both were undergoing lengthy and extensive changes at press time.

Rice Street loops around and becomes Nawiliwili Road. It is here that you will find **Grove Farm Homestead Museum** (245–3202). This was the private home of George N. Wilcox and his nieces. It was turned into a museum by Mabel Wilcox shortly before her death in 1978. With 80 acres and several buildings to browse through, it is quite popular. (And they make an awesome sugar cookie here.) Groups of about six are escorted around the grounds and house for 2 hours for $10 per person. Even if this isn't normally your cup of tea, you will probably find it interesting. It's the story of an incredible family's rise to prominence in the old, sugar-dominated Kaua'i. Reservations are required. Tours on Mon., Wed. and Thur.

Off Nawiliwili Road is Wa'apa Road. Take this road to Hulemalu Road and

you will come to an overlook for the **Menehune (Alekoko) Fishpond**. This is a large, impressive fishpond adjacent to the **Hule'ia Stream**. According to legend, it was built in one night by the Menehune as a gift for a princess and her brother. Estimates of its age range as high as 1,000 years. Today, it is privately owned and has fallen into disrepair as a fishpond. Nonetheless, it is a remarkable landmark that is worth a look.

Back on the main highway (which has changed its name to Hwy 50, the Kaumuali'i Hwy), we find ourselves heading south. Before the 1 mile marker is **Kukui Grove Shopping Center**, the biggest shopping center on the island. It's more geared toward locals but might have something to offer you. Past it is our island **Costco**.

Past the 1 mile marker you will see Kilohana (245–5608) on your right. This was the home of Gaylord and Ethel Wilcox and has been lovingly restored to its former glory. Gaylord Wilcox was manager of the Grove Farm Plantation. Walk through the door of this 16,000-square-foot mansion and you get a sense of Kaua'i in days past. The furniture, fittings and motif all harken back to a simpler day when sugar was king. Inside is Gaylord's Restaurant, as well as several shops, galleries and a lu'au. They also have a train ride for $18 that kids might enjoy. See BASICS on page 34 for more.

Across from the 3 mile marker on the main highway is Kipu Road, which also acts as a bypass road. Located off this road is a glorious little hidden place you might find enchanting. If you go, do it during the week, as it's a bit less likely to be crowded. It's a small waterfall called **Kipu Falls** pouring into a deep pool,

which is ringed half-way by a 20-foot cliff. On the far side is a rope swing with a ladder leading up the side of a cliff. Get out of the pond via thick tree roots. The **A REAL GEM** entire setting is wonderful. Obviously, you need to evaluate the condition of the rope, pond and ladder yourself to determine if it's safe. People use the rope all the time (including us), but we won't vouch for its safety. Also, don't underestimate how much strength it takes to hold onto the rope. If you slide down before you're ready, it could (and has) caused serious injury to a place you *don't* want injured. Jump out, swing and *release* and hope there's only water below you.

To get to the falls, walk the trail on your left just before the bridge on Kipu Road (see map). The land was formerly used for growing sugar. Although the land company has posted No TRESPASSING signs on their land, it hasn't stopped locals—who have visited this waterfall for generations—from walking to it. In fact, according to the local newspaper, comminity activists contend that access has occurred for so long, a "perscriptive easement" exists. Regardless, we'll just tell you where it is and leave the rest to you. Maybe you can call Grove Farm and ask if you can use the trail to their waterfall. They've certainly been gracious about letting people use their private road to Maha'ulepu Beach in Po'ipu for years. You should know that the stream itself and the falls (though not the rope swing) are on *state land* and not owned by or leased to anyone. Only the surrounding land is private. As long as you're between the stream banks, you're not trespassing, according to county personnel we spoke with. Anyway, just before the trail you're walking on begins to ascend, there is a very short (but sometimes slippery) trail down to the top of the falls on your right. (The sugar cane on the main trail gets a little intrusive at times.) The entire walk takes about 5 minutes. You're on your own from here. The alternative is to walk in the stream from the bridge the whole way. That way is perfectly legal, according to the county. Remember not to leave valuables in your car; break-ins are not uncommon here.

If you were to continue on Kipu Road, you would quickly come to a magnificent strand of Cook Island pines. These trees were highly valued as ship's masts in the Age of Discovery. This entire area is called **Kipu** and is currently leased to the Rice family and the Waterhouse Trust. William Hyde Rice was a cattle rancher, and a monument to him was erected here by his Japanese workers. Behind Ha'upu mountain is the fabulous beach called **Kipu Kai**. This long crescent of sand is a beachgoer's dream. Unfortunately, the only way to reach it is by boat or over the private road owned by Kipu Ranch and the Waterhouse Trust. This road is closed to the public, though you can get a glimpse of Kipu Kai from the ATV tour on page 119. John Waterhouse ordered that the 1,096 acres of leased state land revert to the state at the time of death of the last of his four nieces and one nephew (which hasn't happened yet). We've tried walking to Kipu Kai from Ha'ula Beach. The horse path up and over the tall mountain is riddled with evil plants with thorns that turned our exposed legs to hamburger.

EAST SHORE SHOPPING

The east shore is a shopper's paradise. Starting in northern Kapa'a, there's the **Kaua'i Products Fair** Thursdays through Sundays. Most of the products, ironically, are *not* made on Kaua'i—so ask—but a few are and may be worth a look. Next door is the **Red Dirt Store**.

In downtown Kapa'a, try **Island Hemp & Cotton**, **Deja Vu** and **Tropical Tan-**

*Enchanting Kipu Falls and pool—
part of Kaua'i's hidden charm.*

trum for clothing. Look for vintage-style Hawaiian clothing and gifts at **Hula Girl**. Next door is **Jacques Amo** for custom Tahitian pearl jewelry. **Kela's a Glass Gallery** has amazing glass art and decorative items. Fantastic stuff, though ultra-pricey, but worth a look even if it's not in the budget. Across the street in Roxy Square, **The Glass Shack** has hand-blown glass you can watch being made at prices for the rest of us. Behind them, pick up some fresh bread at **Country Moon Bakery**. The **Pono Market** is a good stop for manju, plate lunches and other local foods. **Orchid Alley** will ship any of their plants to the mainland.

Continuing south just before the whale mural, **Jungle Girl** near the Lemongrass Restaurant offers some great clothing and accessories, as does **Marta's Boat** (across the street from the Foodland). Plan to shop here in the afternoons to be sure they're open.

In Kaua'i Village Shopping Center, if you enjoy making your own jewelry, visit **Divine Planet** for a huge selection of beads, as well as textiles for the home.

At Coconut Marketplace you'll find many shopping options in all price ranges. Some to note are: **Ship Store Galleries** for art and antiques *mostly* with a nautical theme. **Hot Flashes** (not the kind you're thinking of) has art glass jewelry at reasonable prices. **Jungle Rain** has a selection of island-style clothing and gifts. (Their stuffed roosters only *look* like the ones that woke you up at 4 a.m. Clap your hands and they will crow just as annoyingly.) **Palm Palm Kaua'i** has outstanding locally made jewelry and other accessories.

At Kinipopo Shopping Village across from Haleilio Road stop at **Tin Can Mailman** if you truly love books as we do and want to add some rare, out-of-print Hawai'i-related titles to your personal collection. For women's clothes in natural fabrics check out **Style World**. If Fido was hoping you'd bring him back a Hawaiian shirt or his name on a custom-made Swarovski crystal collar, stop in at **CJ's Bow Wow Boutique**.

Before or after your visit to Wailua Falls, stop by **Kapaia Stitchery**. In addition to the *unrivaled* Hawaiian print fabric selection (some of which they can make into clothing for you), they also have beautiful Japanese kimonos and everything any quilter could need. Gentlemen can relax on the lanai while their quiltress (hey, is that a real word?) checks things out. Koa wood items can be seen at **William & Zimmer Woodworkers** next door.

In Lihu'e, many visitors stop at **Wal-Mart** or **Hilo Hattie's** (on Hwy 56 near Ahukini) before that last rush to the airport. Always something here for everyone. Wal-Mart is also a good first stop on the island for tabis, water shoes and all kinds of outdoor gear (or even a nice flower lei and macadamia nuts).

Anchor Cove and Harbor Mall near Kalapaki Beach *mostly* cater to the cruise ships, but some shops are worth your time. In Anchor Cove, **Seven Seas Trading Co.** has gift items from all around the world. **Maui Divers** will let you shuck an oyster (they're seeded) for a pearl, which you get to keep, or can have it set into a ring. **Island Sandal** has a great selection of footwear.

Kukui Grove Shopping Center at the corner of Hwy 50 and Nawiliwili Road is a sprawling mall in two large sections. One section contains **Borders Books** and **Kmart**. The other portion has some good places to grab a treat or a sandwich while shopping at **Macy's**, **Sears** or any of the other specialty stores. **Kaua'i Products Store** carries only Kaua'i-made items and foodstuffs. Try their fudge. There is also a **Longs Drugs** and a **Starbucks**.

Heading south on the highway, you'll come to **Kilohana Plantation**, a former plantation manager's private home. The pottery at **Clayworks of Kilohana** (behind the main house) is worth a stop, and you or your young one can make a keepsake of your own to take home or have shipped. **Grande's Gems**, above the restaurant, has some of the most beautiful fine gemstone

jewelry on the island. There are also galleries in the main house worth a browse.

Puhi Village Plaza at the stoplight in Puhi has unusual baked goods (like crab rolls and cherry rolls) from **Hanalima Baking**. Get there before 7 a.m., or they run out of many items. Specialty wines (including Hawaiian), liquors or champagne are available at **The Wine Garden** and so are Kaua'i Cigars—at least the tobacco comes from Kaua'i. They're not bad but smoke a bit young and are pretty pricey.

If you'd like to arrange a shipment of tropical flowers or a dwarf tree grown on lava rock, try **Kaua'i Nursery & Landscape** (245–7747) on the left side as you head toward Po'ipu.

EAST SHORE BEST BETS

Best Beach Walk—Lydgate Beach Park to Hilton Kaua'i

Best View—From the Top of Sleeping Giant for Hikers; Sunrise over Lydgate for Non-Hikers

Best Place for Novice Snorkelers, Fish Feeding or to Let Children Swim— Lydgate State Park

Best Treat—Apple Turnover at Kaua'i Bakery

Best Hidden Gem—Kipu Falls or Ho'opi'i Falls

Best Uncrowded Beach—In front of Wailua Golf Course

Best Playground—Kamalani Playground at Lydgate Park

Best Boogie Boarding—Kealia Beach

Best Evening Stroll—Paved Beach Path between Kapa'a Beach Park and Kealia)

Best Lu'au—Smith's Tropical Paradise or Kalamaku at Kilohana

Best Way to Spend 7 Years—Carving One Stone for the Hindu Temple

Best Place to Make Your Pupils Big— Mile-Long Secret Tunnel to the North Shore

Semi-protected Po'ipu Beach Park is one of the many beaches that bless the south shore.

The sunny south shore... where rainfall is less frequent and sunshine is abundant. Many people prefer the sunnier quality of the south shore to the lushness of the north shore. Fortunately, you can have it all.

For the sake of this discussion, we will consider the south shore as everything past Puhi to Kalaheo. (Look at the fold-out back cover map to orient yourself.) Past Kalaheo, the character of the island changes again, and we will cover that in the WEST SHORE SIGHTS chapter.

The same descriptive ground rules that we discussed at the beginning of NORTH SHORE SIGHTS chapter apply here.

All beaches we mention are described in detail in the chapter on BEACHES.

Driving to Po'ipu from Lihu'e along the main highway, you will pass through the Knudsen Gap between the 6 and 8 mile markers. A century ago this was the scariest part of the island. The small gap between the mountains was the only route you could take to the south shore and was a perfect place for an ambush. Even the local sheriff always dreaded going through the Knudsen Gap.

Past the 6 mile marker you will come to Hwy 520, or Maluhia Road. This road to Koloa and Po'ipu is called the Tree Tunnel. When Walter Duncan

Koloa, Po'ipu & Kalaheo

1. Prince Kuhio
2. Kuhio Shores
3. Whalers Cove
4. Waikomo Stream Villas
5. Alihi Lani
6. Po'ipu Kapili
7. Sheraton Kaua'i Resort
8. Kiahuna Plantation Resort
9. Ko'a Kea Hotel & Resort
10. Marriott's Waioha'i Beach Club
11. Regency II & Villas
12. Po'ipu Kai Resort
13. Hideaway Cove Villas
14. Nihi Kai Villas
15. Honu Kai Villas
16. Po'ipu Plantation
17. Po'ipu Shores
18. Sunset Kahili
19. Po'ipu Crater Resort
20. Po'ipu Palms
21. Po'ipu Makai
22. Makahu'ena
23. Point at Po'ipu
24. Grand Hyatt

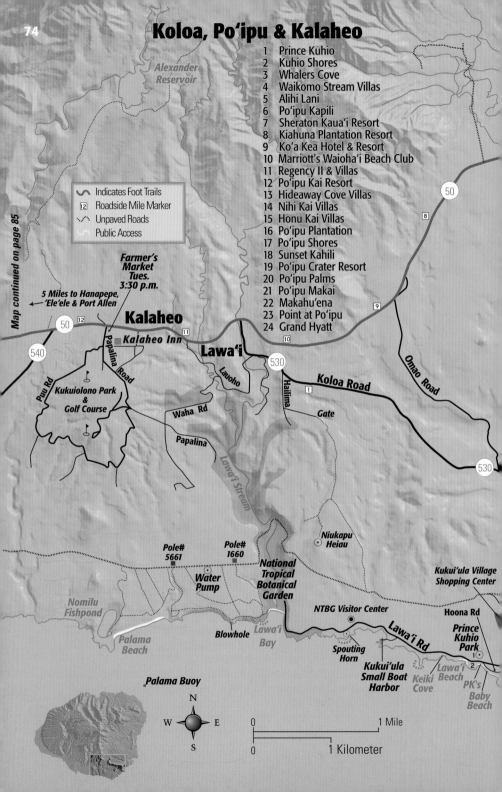

Indicates Foot Trails
⑫ Roadside Mile Marker
Unpaved Roads
Public Access

Map continued on page 85

Alexander Reservoir

Farmer's Market Tues. 3:30 p.m.

5 Miles to Hanapepe, 'Ele'ele & Port Allen

Kalaheo

Kalaheo Inn

Lawa'i

50   ⑫   50   540

Papalina Road

Puu Rd

Kukuiolono Park & Golf Course

Waha Rd

Papalina

Lauoho

Lawa'i Stream

Hailima

Koloa Road

Gate

Omao Road

530   530   1   9   10   11   8   50

Pole# 5661

Pole# 1660

Water Pump

Niukapu Heiau

National Tropical Botanical Garden

Kukui'ula Village Shopping Center

Nomilu Fishpond

NTBG Visitor Center

Hoona Rd

Palama Beach

Blowhole

Lawa'i Bay

Spouting Horn

Lawa'i Rd

Prince Kuhio Park

Palama Buoy

Kukui'ula Small Boat Harbor

Keiki Cove

Lawa'i Beach

PK's Baby Beach

1   2

N
W   E
S

0   1 Mile
0   1 Kilometer

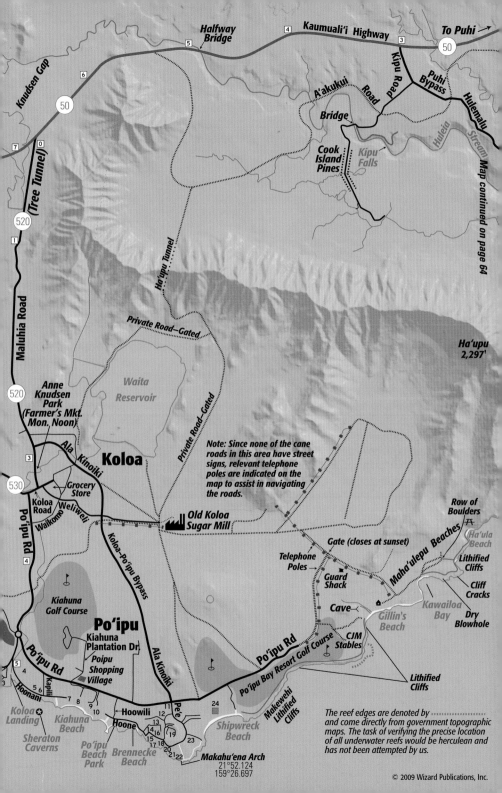

Halfway Bridge

Kaumuali'i Highway

To Puhi

Puhi Bypass

Kipu Road

A'akukui Road

Bridge

Cook Island Pines

Kipu Falls

Huleia

Hulemalu Stream

Map continued on page 64

Knudsen Gap

50

(Tree Tunnel)

520

Maluhia Road

Ha'upu Tunnel

Private Road—Gated

Waita Reservoir

Private Road—Gated

Ha'upu 2,297'

Anne Knudsen Park (Farmer's Mkt. Mon. Noon)

520

Ala Kinoiki

Koloa

Note: Since none of the cane roads in this area have street signs, relevant telephone poles are indicated on the map to assist in navigating the roads.

Grocery Store

Koloa Road

Weliweli

Waikomo

Old Koloa Sugar Mill

Koloa-Po'ipu Bypass

Telephone Poles

Gate (closes at sunset)

Guard Shack

Row of Boulders

Ha'ula Beach

Lithified Cliffs

Cliff Cracks

Maha'ulepu Beaches

Po'ipu Rd

Kiahuna Golf Course

Po'ipu

Kiahuna Plantation Dr

Poipu Shopping Village

Ala Kinoiki

Po'ipu Rd

Cave

Gillin's Beach

Kawailoa Bay

Dry Blowhole

CJM Stables

Po'ipu Bay Resort Golf Course

Lithified Cliffs

Po'ipu Rd

Hoonani

Kapili

Koloa Landing

Kiahuna Beach

Po'ipu Beach Park

Hoowili

Hoone

Brennecke Beach

Pe'e

Shipwreck Beach

Makewehi Lithified Cliffs

Sheraton Caverns

Makahu'ena Arch
21°52.124
159°26.697

The reef edges are denoted by ⋯⋯⋯⋯ and come directly from government topographic maps. The task of verifying the precise location of all underwater reefs would be herculean and has not been attempted by us.

Move over sugar—coffee is the new cash crop of the south shore.

McBryde was landscaping his home in the early 1900s, he found that he had over 500 eucalyptus trees *left over*. He donated these trees, called swamp mahogany, to the county. Many residents showed up to help plant the trees. The result is the Tree Tunnel. (Part of it was torn down in the '50s when they rerouted the highway.) Today it should more aptly be called the "tree corridor." Though still beautiful, the trees don't intertwine at the top the way they did before either Hurricane 'Iwa in 1982 or 'Iniki on Sept. 11, 1992.

KOLOA

Driving down Hwy 520 you come to the town of Koloa, sometimes called Old Koloa Town. This was the first sugar plantation town in all the islands when Kamehameha III leased the land to Ladd and Company in 1835. The town has much charm and is worth a stop. Next to Crazy Shirts Store there is a marvelous monkeypod tree whose branches seem to meander forever. In Koloa you'll find Lappert's Ice Cream, which is made here on Kaua'i. It's still good but has been slipping lately. It's also getting pretty darned expensive. Two people can easily spend $10 for one scoop each with cone. (The scoops should be bigger for that.) They also have locally roasted coffee, but it's unremarkable.

Across the street (kitty-corner) from the shops are the remnants of an old sugar mill built 150 years ago. There you will also find a plaque dedicated to the sugar plantation workers and a good (if somewhat dated) synopsis of sugar history on the island.

Looking at the map, you will see a dirt road leading to Waita Reservoir and Ha'upu Range Tunnel. They are gated and not available to visit unless you book an ATV tour. We used to think these gates were a relatively modern annoyance until we stumbled across an old local newspaper from 1934. In a letter to the editor the writer warned people not to accept an invitation from a well-known plantation manager when he said he "wanted to show you something interesting." Apparently the crafty manager did this whenever he had a long way to drive and wanted to have somebody along to open and close all the gates.

PO'IPU

Continuing to Po'ipu on Hwy 520 and doglegging onto Po'ipu Road, watch your speed. This is a notorious speed trap and sobriety checkpoint area, and the limit is 25 mph, 15 mph near the school. (The Po'ipu Bypass shown on the map is an even more effective speed trap because you are easily lulled into going over 35 mph.)

Past the 4 mile marker as you approach Po'ipu, the road forks. If you take the right fork, you come to **Prince Kuhio Park**. There you will find a monument to Prince Kuhio, the last royally designated heir to the Hawaiian throne. He went on to become a delegate to Congress until the early 1920s. In this park you will also find the **Ho'ai Heiau**, impressive in its perfection and almost chiseled appearance. The entrance is toward the rear on the left side.

Continuing along Lawa'i Road, you will come to **Spouting Horn Beach Park**. This wonderful delight is a small

NOT TO BE MISSED!

lava shelf where water from waves is thrust through an opening, causing water and air to squirt out a blowhole. This particular site distinguishes itself from other blowholes around Hawai'i in that it has an additional hole that blows only air, causing a loud moaning and gasping sound. Legend has it that the entire coastline in this area was once guarded by a giant female lizard called a mo'o. She would eat anyone who tried to swim or fish in the area. One day a man named Liko went fishing. The mo'o went to attack Liko, who threw a spear into the mo'o's mouth. The angry mo'o chased Liko into the lava tube. Liko escaped, but the mo'o became trapped in what we now call Spouting Horn, where its cries of hunger and pain can be heard to this day.

The Spouting Horn was formerly dwarfed by an adjacent blowhole called the Kukui'ula Seaplume. That seaplume would shoot much higher—as high as

Spouting Horn is often more dramatic at high tide.

Watch your step around these ficus roots at the Allerton Garden in Lawa'i. This tree is where they found the dinosaur eggs in the movie Jurassic Park.

200 feet into the air. But on an early Sunday morning back in the 1920s a sugar company manager ordered one of his workers to drop blasting powder into the hole to widen it so the plume wouldn't shoot into the air. The reason? The salt spray from the geyser was stunting the growth of 10 acres of cane (among the company's many thousands of acres), and the manager would not stand for that. From down on the lava shelf you can see its remains in the form of a large rectangular aperture to the left of the current blowhole opening.

The view from the guard-rail is quite interesting. Many people walk down and view the Horn and some of the other delightful offerings from the lava area itself. The power and forces in this area can only be experienced from this vantage point. Be forewarned, however, that while the experience is far more rewarding than the view from the guard-rails, it can be dangerous. There have been incidents where people have been swept to their deaths into the Horn. Unexpectedly large waves can even wash over the entire shelf, dragging you into the hole or over the edge into the open ocean.

There may be signs suggesting that you not go down, although county personnel we spoke with said it wasn't illegal. Use caution and common sense. If you go onto the bench, you do so at your own risk. (For some odd reason, tour bus drivers sometimes authoritatively yell at people on the bench, but hey…they're just tour bus drivers.) In any event, *never* stand between the hole and the ocean. A very large wave would have no difficulty dragging you in. A while back two visitors from San Francisco were knocked in while they stood between the hole and the ocean. One was *on crutches* at the time. They were lucky—rather than being crushed inside the hole, they were immediately sucked out of the blowhole and into the open ocean where they were rescued by some phone workers on their break.

The vendors you see there selling cheap jewelry and such have been evicted by the county, and have until 2013 to leave. (Hey, at least they can't complain that they weren't given adequate notice.)

Just before Spouting Horn is the entrance to the National Tropical Botanical Gardens. This incredibly beautiful garden consists of 252 acres called the McBryde Garden and 100 acres called the Allerton Garden (742–2623). Even if you normally wouldn't visit a garden, you'll probably like this one. Rich and lush with remarkably varied plants and abundant birds, tours here are guided and last about two hours. The fee for the tour is $20 per person (self-guided) for McBryde, $45 for the more desirable Allerton. Reservations are required. Kids must be at least 10 years old on the Allerton tour.

Going back the way you came, just before the fork is a road leading to Koloa Landing. This is a popular SCUBA shore dive. Until the 1900s this was Kaua'i's main port. Whaling ships used to winter here, and all goods brought to Kaua'i came through either Koloa Landing or Waimea.

Going to the fork again, take the left (eastern) fork. (Or, as Yogi Berra used to say, "If you come to a fork in the road, *take it*.") Po'ipu is turtle country. Look out at the water for any reasonable length of time, and you'll see green sea turtles swimming nearby. This area was developed in the '70s and '80s and has become a much sought-after visitor destination. Swanky hotels and condominium resorts line the road. (See

WHERE TO STAY chapter for more information.) The beaches in this area are fantastic, with the best of the best located past

A REAL GEM

the resorts at a place called Maha'ulepu. This beach (see BEACHES chapter) sports lots of places to walk and some incredible sandstone cliffs. The dirt roads around here can be good places to ride mountain bikes. Horseback riding, windsurfing, snorkeling, fishing and more are all available in this area. The lithified cliffs from Maha'ulepu to Shipwreck Beach offer delicious shoreline hikes. See HIKING in the ACTIVITIES chapter for information.

One thing that totally escaped our attention until an alert reader pointed it out

These lithified sand dunes of Maha'ulepu are a stunning testament to the power of the ocean.

to us was the presence of a cool-looking lava arch at the shoreline between the Point at Po'ipu Resort and Makahu'ena at the southern tip of the island. Park at the Point and walk along the shoreline until you see a light beacon. The chain link fence from Makahu'ena points toward the arch. Don't let the ocean smack you around here.

There's lots of cactus along this part of the island. It was imported in the 1800s because it made a perfect natural cattle fence—and you don't even need to repair it.

KALAHEO

After Lawa'i comes Kalaheo (which has the best pizza on the island—see ISLAND DINING). One of Kalaheo's lesser known gems is the Kukuiolono Park and Golf Course (see GOLFING in the ACTIVITIES chapter). This is the private course and garden donated by Walter McBryde to the people of Kaua'i. If you want to try your hand at golf, this is the place to learn. The price is $9 *per day*. The small Japanese garden located on the course was Mr. McBryde's pride and joy. This is where he chose to be buried, near the 8th tee.

Although it was sugar that drove the economy along here for over a century, it was phased out in the 1990s to grow coffee, on the assumption it would be more profitable. (So far it hasn't been.) The Kaua'i Coffee Company, has 3,100 acres under cultivation. To be honest, it's not very good coffee. Most of the trees

The alien landscape of the tortured sandstone cliffs between Maha'ulepu and the Hyatt.

are an unimpressive breed called *yellow catuai.* Don't confuse it with the *far* superior coffee grown on the Kona coast of the Big Island where the coffee-growing environment is ideal. Also, Kaua'i coffee is machine picked, so that beans slightly under and over their peak get picked in the process. Kaua'i Coffee has smaller fields of *blue mountain,* which is better, but it's expensive, and we've only found this coffee at their visitor center located on Hwy 540 just past the 12 mile marker on Hwy 50. That 4-mile-long road, sometimes called the Coffee Highway, cuts through much of the coffee plantation. The visitor center is popular with tour buses but is only marginally interesting, and their museum is particularly scant. Only for the hard-core coffee groupies.

Incidentally, any fixed-wing pilot on the island will tell you they *love* coffee trees. Their leaves are dark and dense, which capture the sun and heat the air around them. This makes them exceptional generators of thermal currents, providing free lift when the heated air rises.

Just after the 14 mile marker you will come to the Hanapepe Valley Lookout. As you gaze over the peaceful vista, it's hard to believe that this was the scene of the bloodiest and most savage battle known to have taken place on Kaua'i. The embittered son of Kaua'i's last king started a revolt against government rule. Remember that Kaua'i had never been conquered by Kamehameha the Great. Both of his invasion attempts had been costly in terms of men, and neither had even reached Kaua'i in large numbers. Even though Kaua'i's last king voluntarily accepted Kamehameha's rule, it forever stuck in the royal craw that Kaua'i had not been *forced* into submission. So when this revolt occurred, it was a perfect excuse to send Hawai'i troops over to show those Kauaians who was boss. Government troops sent to put down the revolt were unimaginably brutal, and their methods were reviled even among their supporters. Men, women and children were needlessly slaughtered, and the wanton killing continued for 10 days.

Everything past here is covered in the WEST SHORE SIGHTS chapter.

SOUTH SHORE SHOPPING

In Kalaheo, if you have decided to take up the 'ukulele, hit Scotty's Music on the main highway. Just off Highway 50 in Lawa'i on Koloa Road is Hawaiian Trading Post, which has the largest selection of Ni'ihau shell leis and Tahitian Black Pearls on the island, as well as other jewelry and gift items.

Following Koloa Road will take you right into Koloa Town, where there are many shops and galleries to browse. Among the more interesting, starting from the east end of Koloa Road, is The Wine Shop, which has a great selection of wines, spirits and gourmet foodstuffs. At Island Soap & Candle Works, you can watch the items for sale being made. The many scents can become overwhelming, but small bowls of coffee beans placed around the store will help your nasal palate stay clear. Behind their store is Discount Variety for reasonably priced beach mats, etc. Jungle Girl carries some funky island fashions for women. In the courtyard is James Hoyle Gallery whose work reminds us of a modern day Van Gogh. On down Poipu Road Pohaku T's carries only locally made items and has a huge selection of T-shirts, all designed and printed on Kaua'i.

Continuing on Poipu Road toward Po'ipu, the place to shop is Poipu

Shopping Village. You will find many boutique fashions from $3 flip-flops to $30,000 pearl necklaces and, of course, a Starbucks. If you forget your swimsuit or just want to look more island-style, try Making Waves for women and keiki or Overboard for men. For kids' fashions, you can't beat Blue Ginger or Sand Kids, where they also have lots of toys to entertain your keiki. Po'ipu Fine Arts is one of the better art galleries. Black Pearls Kaua'i has stunning pearls (not just black ones).

SOUTH SHORE BEST BETS

Best Strolling Beach—Maha'ulepu

Best Short Cliff Stroll—To the Left of Shipwreck Beach near Hyatt

Best Snorkeling—Around the sandy island at Po'ipu Beach Park

Best Sunset View—At Spouting Horn

Best Hot Dog—Puka Dogs

Best Treat—Baked Chocolate Soufflé at Roy's Po'ipu Bar & Grill

Best Place To Watch Fools Jump Off A Cliff—Shipwreck Beach in Front of the Hyatt Po'ipu

Best Secluded Beach—Ha'ula Beach

Best Swimming—Po'ipu Beach Park

Best Pizza—Brick Oven Pizza

Best Beachcombing—Kawailoa Bay

Best Golf—Po'ipu Bay Resort

Best Hotel Grounds—Hyatt

Best Chance of Seeing a Beached Monk Seal—Po'ipu Beach Park

Best Lasagna—Pomodoro

Best Romantic Restaurant—Tidepools at Hyatt or Beach House at Sunset

Best Place for a Sunset Cocktail—The Sheraton Kaua'i Resort

Ni'ihau Shell Leis

The women of Ni'ihau carry on a tradition dating back centuries. With indescribable patience, they collect tiny Ni'ihau shells, then clean, drill, string and pack them with fiber, creating fabulous leis. This is no easy task. An entire day's labor often reaps only four or five useable shells. And it requires thousands of shells to make a lei. Some women only search for shells at night, believing that the sunlight dulls the shell's luster. While costing from several hundred to several thousand dollars each, this is a relative bargain given the amount of labor that goes into one. It can take several years to complete the more ornate leis. The result is a perfect, handcrafted and tightly packed lei representing one of the last truly Hawaiian art forms. There are fewer and fewer people on Ni'ihau who are willing to participate in this process, and many consider it a matter of time before this art form will be lost.

If you purchase one, the best selection on the island is at the Hawaiian Trading Post on the corner of Highways 50 and 530 (Koloa Road) in Lawa'i. Make sure it was actually made on Ni'ihau, and not a copycat made on Kaua'i.

One last caveat: If you buy one, do it for yourself. It would be crushing to spend all that money only to show your lei to someone and have 'em say, "Oh, yeah, I got one for free at Hilo Hattie's." While Ni'ihau shell leis are infinitely more beautiful, some might not appreciate the difference.

Polihale is where the Na Pali coastline gives way to 17 miles of uninterrupted sand beach.

If the south shore is called the sunny south shore, western Kaua'i should be called the *very* sunny west shore. That's because rain is very scant indeed, and the temperature is 3 to 4 degrees hotter than most of the rest of the island. The first two things visitors notice on this side of the island are the relative aridity of the land and the deep red color of the soil. Trade winds coming from the northeast lose the bulk of their rain on Mount Wai'ale'ale, creating a rain shadow on the west side. Unless there are Kona winds (meaning from the south or west), you can pretty much be assured that it will be dry and sunny on the west side.

This part of the island is dominated by two attractions: the 17-mile-long sand beach stretching from Waimea to Polihale and the incredible Waimea Canyon in the interior.

HANAPEPE

As you drive along the main highway leaving Kalaheo, you will come to the **Hanapepe Valley Lookout**, described in SOUTH SHORE SIGHTS chapter. After you go through 'Ele'ele (where many of the boat tours leave from), you come to Hanapepe. Called Kaua'i's "Biggest Little Town," Hanapepe is but a shadow of its former self. It was founded by Chinese rice farmers in the mid to late 1800s. They were opium-smoking

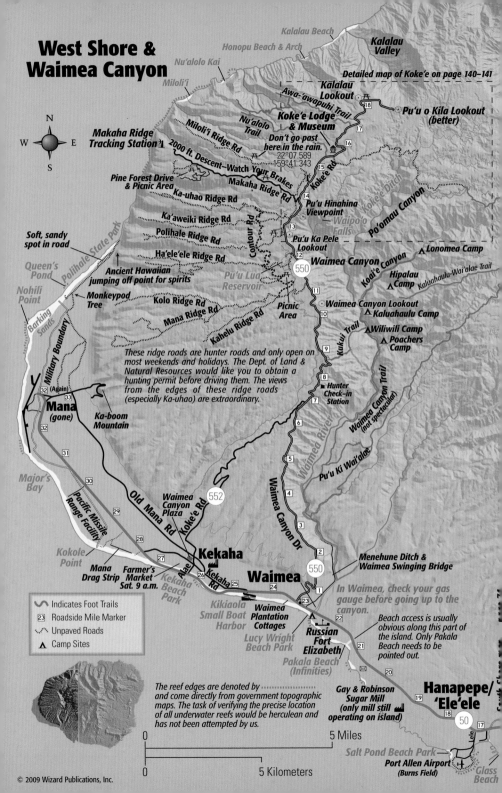

bachelors, and underground opium shops could be found there as recently as the 1930s. Hanapepe was the only non-plantation town on the island, and it gained a reputation as Kaua'i's wildest spot. In 1924 they had a riot that killed 16 Filipino workers and four police officers. This was a violent and flamboyant town that had as many bars as churches. It began to decline in the late '70s. The 1982 opening of Kukui Grove Shopping Center in Lihu'e marked the end of an era for Hanapepe's business community.

A good analogy for Hanapepe today is that of an old chair. Whereas some people look at an old stick of furniture and see a priceless antique, others see it as an old, used item to be replaced by a newer one. Depending on your outlook, you will either find downtown Hanapepe charming or a quasi-ghost town. Although we probably agree with the ghost town description, improvements *are* taking place and a certain amount of rehabilitation is occurring, so Hanapepe is sort of a moving target. If you have a couple minutes to spare, you might want to blow through downtown just to decide for yourself. There are several shops and galleries that might be worth exploring. Friday night is *art night,* and it's really starting to become a draw. Check out some of the galleries we mention on page 93. There's a swinging footbridge over the Hanapepe River. It replaced the old bridge that swung off during the 1992 hurricane.

This area is where most of our power is generated. People assume that, living on a tropical island, we must have some exotic way of making

our electricity. Sorry to burst your bubble, but we burn oil—it's just that simple—and we have the electricity bills to prove it! In a few years we hope to burn wood chips from local tree farms to help supplement that.

If you take Lele Road (Hwy 543), you come to **Salt Pond Beach Park**. This is where they continue to make salt out of seawater (see BEACHES chapter). This park usually offers very safe swimming as well as **restrooms**. (Hard to find in this area.)

Before you get to Waimea, you will see a road to **Fort Elizabeth** just past the 22 mile marker. (The sign is misspelled.) Here are the vague remains of a Russian fort built in 1816 by George Scheffer.

Scheffer was a German-born doctor working for a Russian company. A difficult, quarrelsome and conceited man, he had a habit of eventually alienating most people he met. (Know the type?) He did make a good first impression, however, and managed to sufficiently impress a Russian official, who sent Scheffer to

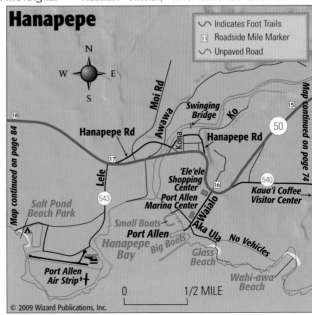

Hanapepe

N / W / E / S

Legend
⌇ Indicates Foot Trails
11 Roadside Mile Marker
⋰ Unpaved Road

Map continued on page 84

Map continued on page 74

Moi Rd
Awawa
Swinging Bridge
Kona
Ko
Hanapepe Rd
Hanapepe Rd
18
17
50
15
Lele
'Ele'ele Shopping Center
543
Salt Pond Beach Park
Port Allen Marina Center
16
540
Kaua'i Coffee Visitor Center
Awaialo
Small Boats
Port Allen
Big Boats
Aka Ula
No Vehicles
Hanapepe Bay
Glass Beach
Port Allen Air Strip
Wahi-awa Beach
0   1/2 MILE

Hawai'i to ingratiate himself with King Kamehameha and recover a lost ship's cargo. When Kamehameha eventually became suspicious of Scheffer, the German moved on to Kaua'i. There he found a receptive King Kaumuali'i who, although he had officially given his kingdom to Kamehameha, still resisted offshore rule. Kaua'i's king-in-name-only saw a chance to get the Russians involved and perhaps restore his power. The two men realized how much they could help each other and soon hatched plans to conquer the other islands using Russian ships. By this time Scheffer had become intoxicated by his status on Kaua'i and lost sight of the fact that he could not deliver on any of the promises he was making to Kaua'i's king. He even renamed Hanalei Valley, calling it Schefferthal, with the king's blessing.

As Scheffer began building the Russian Fort in honor of Elizabeth, a Russian consort, his sponsors back in Russia were beginning to get a hint of Scheffer's tactics. They sent a ship to Hawai'i to tell Scheffer that he was to pack and leave the island. Scheffer ignored the message and continued building the fort. By this time Kaua'i's king was becoming suspicious, and a group of American businessmen saw an opportunity to rid the island of Scheffer and Russia. They started the rumor that Russia and America were at war. Kaua'i's king abandoned Scheffer, who fled the island in a leaky old ship and set sail for O'ahu. Once there, Scheffer was told he would be taken prisoner. He fled to Brazil where he changed his name to Count von Frankenthal and tried to lure colonists to his estate of the same name.

Why are we telling you all this? Because the story's more interesting than the actual site—little more than a perimeter of rocks from the foundation. (By the way, there are lots of bees here.)

If you drive through Fort Elizabeth and take the dirt road, you'll come to the **mouth of the Waimea River**. This can be a beautiful area to linger and watch the interaction of the ocean with the river, especially when the river flow is low. The dark, rich sand separating the ocean from the river is saturated with water from the river. White waves some-

The dark sand at the mouth of the Waimea River beautifully contrasts the ocean foam slithering into the river.

times gently lap up and down the sand without sinking in, creating a delicate show of contrasts. You'll notice an olive green tint to the sand here. This is from a semi-precious gem called olivine, which the Waimea River tirelessly mines from its lava bed along with black flecks of lava, making the floor of the Waimea Canyon lower and lower in the process.

WAIMEA

Back on the main highway you come to the town of Waimea. This part of the island usually looks best (and greenest) in the winter. Off to your right you will see the **Captain Cook Monument**. It was in Waimea that the great explorer first set foot in Hawai'i in January 1778. (He was later killed on the Big Island in a petty dispute over a stolen rowboat.)

Travel 1⅓ mile up Menehune Road on the *mauka* side of the highway to see the **Menehune Ditch**, a smooth, lined irrigation ditch designed to bring water from the Waimea River to the taro fields. Only 50 or 60 feet are now visible. It's impressive to think that the rocks used for its construction came from a quarry more than six miles away. This is one of the few Hawaiian relics that almost certainly wasn't created by the current race of Hawaiians who came from Tahiti around 1,000 AD. *That* group didn't cut and dress stones—as is the case at Menehune Ditch—they simply stacked them. This irrigation ditch is much older and was probably built by the initial inhabitants—the original "native Hawaiians"—who came from the Marquesas Islands around 300 AD. These first settlers lived a peaceful though less structured life until the Tahitian invaders displaced them and their culture 700 years later, establishing the Hawaiian culture we know today.

Across from the ditch is the **Waimea Swinging Bridge**. Like the one in Hana-

pepe, it, too, is a replacement for the old one blown away in 1992.

The **Waimea** (meaning red water) **River** is full of sediment that dyes the water red. All the beaches in the vicinity of the river are murky due to river runoff, and the swimming is correspondingly poor. (In fact, you can see the runoff from the Space Shuttle photo on the cover.) According to legend, there was a beautiful chief's daughter named Komali'u who was sought after by many men in the village. One day a man named Mano asked her to marry him. When she refused, he killed her at a waterfall where her blood ran into the river. The chief named the village, canyon and river Waimea in memory of his daughter.

While in Waimea, **Jo-Jo's Clubhouse** (across from the 23 mile marker and not to be confused with Jo-Jo's Anuenue) serves some of the best shave ice on the island. (Yes—we've tried it everywhere else. It's our duty.) They offer a staggering 60 flavors and big portions at a cheap price. Only problem is the sometimes *slooooow* service.

KEKAHA

From Waimea, most people go up the road to the Waimea Canyon, but we will get to that later. Assuming you are continuing along the coast, you arrive in Kekaha. This is the last town on this side of the island. Past the 25 mile marker the highway hugs the beach for 2 miles. It's a nice place to stop and enjoy views of Ni'ihau past the 26 mile marker, and beach access here is accomplished by simply falling out of your car onto the sand.

Waimea Canyon Plaza is the last area with food along here. The **Menehune Food Mart** has sandwiches, hot dogs and very good bread pudding. Things aren't as hideously expensive there as you'd expect given the remoteness of the location.

While driving along the west side past Waimea, take note of the cliffs to your right. Those are former sea cliffs cut off from the sea. The land you are driving on is different than most other land in the island chain. It's not technically volcanic. When the massive Waimea Canyon (described later) was formed, the river carried the rock and soil out of the canyon where the ocean's current drove it along the shore to the northwest (as it still does today). Much of it washed up on shore, forming the large plain you see today. It's an odd cocktail of fine sediment, the remains of a gigantic, now drained fringing marshy lagoon, sand, the shells of countless sea creatures and plant remains. The result is one kickin' place to grow sugar—just ask the Robinsons, who grow 7,000 acres of it here. (Oddly, tour guides around the island—who apparently need to get out more—are constantly telling visitors that no sugar cane is grown on Kaua'i anymore.) Sugar is a money-loser here on Kaua'i, and the Robinsons are converting their sugar cane operation to make ethanol.

Many maps list a town farther north called Mana. It was once a thriving little community until the mid-1900s. This area was formerly marshy and famous for its mirages. Now the town of Mana is a mirage, nothing more than two mango trees and a mule. Some of its homes were moved and are now part of Waimea Plantation Cottages Resort. You can tell a former Mana cottage because it always had a door facing north and one facing south so passing spirits wouldn't get stuck inside.

From here on the coastline is pure sand. There's a great opportunity to have a huge stretch of sand to yourself along here. See Kokole Point on page 116.

You will pass the Pacific Missile Range Facility. About every two months they do a Star Wars missile test. Offshore, submarine hunting exercises take place almost continuously. This is a repository for some of the most sophisticated sensing equipment in the world, and they are capable of detecting a bottle bobbing up and down in the choppy water. (But for some reason, when a fishing boat is missing in the area, they seem incapable of finding it.) Fronting part of the base is Barking Sands Beach. The sand grains at this beach have a thin coating of silica and are supposed to make a barking sound if you walk on them when conditions are right (see BEACHES). Access is awkward. See BEACHES chapter for more.

A well-known surf site here is Major's Bay, so called because it's off the old commanding officer's quarters. *Hey, wait a minute. This is a navy base. Isn't major an army rank?* True, but it *used* to be an army base, and the name stuck.

POLIHALE

Looking at the map, you'll notice that the highway ends after the first 32 mile marker. Follow the map, and the first dirt road will take you to Polihale. (It's a *public access*, misleading signs notwithstanding.) On the very rare occasions that it rains heavily here, the road to Polihale can get pretty sloppy. (It also gets potholed at times and officials at State Parks like to close it once in a while as they wait to re-scrape it.) From the extreme northern end of the beach, the magnificent cliffs of Na Pali beckon you with their sheer majesty. The dunes of Polihale are up to 100 feet high. The BEACHES chapter provides more information on Polihale.

As soon as you leave Hwy 50 on your way to Polihale, look at the mountain in front of you. It's a military restricted area. They've bored caves into the mountain where they store ammunition, such as bombs and bullets. With so much explosives, you're about as welcome there as a pack of matches.

A lone boat cruises Polihale on a trip down Na Pali.

If it's summer, you might see kayaks coming (or rolling) in for a surf landing. From here you could walk to the left for 17 miles in the sand. (Maybe another day, huh?) Winds are usually calm here. There are facilities, including showers, restrooms and drinking water.

The Hawaiians believed that the cliffs at the end of Polihale Beach, called Ha'ele'ele, were the jumping off point for spirits or 'uhane leaving this world. There they would leave this life and join their ancestors forever. If there was no 'aumakua, or family of spirits, to receive them, they would wander around the area, attaching themselves to rocks and generally causing mischief. That's why it's considered unwise to take anything, such as stones, from this area. You may bring back a wayward spirit itching to get back home.

WAIMEA CANYON ✳

The Waimea Canyon is a spectacular gorge that defies description. Island legend states that when Mark Twain was here, he dubbed it "the Grand Canyon of the Pacific." (Unfortunately, when you read his biography, you find that when he visited Hawai'i, he never set foot on Kaua'i. Oops, there goes another urban legend.) Regardless, the layers evident on the sides of the canyon are reminiscent of the grander canyon in Arizona. Each layer represents a different eruption and subsequent lava flow. The canyon is 10 miles long, 1 mile wide and more than 3,600 feet deep.

To get to the canyon, take Waimea Canyon Drive from Waimea. They *want* you to go up from Koke'e Road in Kekaha because they hope you'll buy something there, but the views are better going up from Waimea. On your return from the canyon, you can take Koke'e Road (between the 6 and 7 mile markers) down for a different view of the coast.

✳ Before you go up the road, check your gas gauge. There are no stations up there (but restrooms at the major lookouts), and you've got a 40-mile round trip ahead of you with a 4,000-foot elevation rise. The temperature is 10–15 degrees cooler up there, and a sweater might be wise, depending on conditions. There are more good hiking trails in this area than anywhere in Hawai'i. For more hiking information and a detailed map of the

Splendid Waimea Canyon provides yet another facet of Kaua'i's personality.

trails in the Waimea/Koke'e area, see HIKING on page 138.

To reach the canyon, turn *mauka* onto Waimea Canyon Drive just past the 23 mile marker near a church. The road twists and turns its way up the canyon's side. On the way, keep an eye out for **Ni'ihau**. There are some great views of that private island from up here. (Even on cloudless days there's almost always a cloud over Ni'ihau. Its land mass causes them.) Past the 10 mile marker is the Waimea Canyon Lookout. This is one of several vantage points and definitely worth a stop. From here on, you will probably see lots of wild chickens about. They thrive in this environment.

NOT TO BE MISSED!

The canyon lookout is an awesome vista. At one time three rivers, fed from the island's center by the Alaka'i Swamp on Mt. Wai'ale'ale, all ran down the gently sloping shield volcano, emptying into the ocean at separate points like the spokes of a wheel. That's what created the now-dry valleys you see on your way out to Polihale. When a fault caused the collapse of part of the volcano's flank,

the three rivers were forced to combine as they ran down into the fault. This new, opportunistic river carved a place for itself in the splintered and fractured lava flows. The results are extraordinary.

As you drive upward, there are numerous areas along the road from which to view the canyon. From the **Pu'u Ka Pele Lookout**, the **Waipo'o Falls** are visible after a heavy rain, especially in the winter. The hike there (see HIKING in the ACTIVITIES chapter) is fabulous. The **Pu'u Hinahina Lookout**, located past the 13 mile marker, has a **Ni'ihau Viewpoint** in addition to its canyon lookout. If it's clear, the view of Ni'ihau is great.

Shortly after this lookout, there is a paved road on your left leading to the **Makaha Ridge Tracking Station** run by the military in conjunction with the **Pacific Missile Range Facility**. The road drops 2,000 feet over a relatively short distance and can be a real brake burner. Not far before the gate at the station you will see several dirt roads leading into a pleasant forested area with picnic tables.

Looking at the map, you'll see that there are dirt hunter-roads all along this part of the coast. The views from the edge of the ridges are mind-boggling (it's where we took the photo on page 89), but they are only open on weekends and are *supposed* to be used by hunters. The only one that's always open and available is Miloli'i Rigde Road. See ADVENTURES on page 196.

Past the 15 mile marker is the **Koke'e Museum** (335–9975). This is a good place to stretch your legs. The museum itself has several interesting displays and their three-dimensional map of the canyon really gives you a sense of what you are seeing. We've found the personnel there to be extremely knowledgeable. The **Koke'e Lodge** (335–6061) next door is the *best place in Koke'e* to get lunch. (It wins first place in a contest of one.)

As you ascend the road, note how different the vegetation is up here. Remember how dry it was down at the bottom near Waimea? Here it is always cool, and there is more rainfall than on the plain below.

Just past the lodge (on the opposite side of the road), driving Waineke Road to Mohihi Road makes a wonderful di-

version if you happen to have a 4WD vehicle. You can drive 6 miles into the interior of Koke'e, visiting beautiful sights along the way. The map of the area is on page 140.

At the 18 mile marker is the **Kalalau Lookout** where most people stop. We suggest that you drive right past it and go to the *far* superior, but less used, **Pu'u o Kila Lookout**.

A REAL GEM You are not about to see another canyon lookout. You are about to be treated to one of the greatest views in the Pacific. The **Kalalau Valley** is the largest valley on **Na Pali**. It was inhabited until 1919, and its beach is only reachable by an 11-mile hike or by kayak (see ADVENTURES chapter). For now, just revel in the view. Clouds are always moving in and out of the valley, so if it's cloudy, wait a while before you give up. It's well worth it. The earlier you go, the fewer clouds there tend to be. You can usually see clouds coming from the interior of the island. When they encounter the valley, they sink. Sinking air warms, and warmer air can hold more moisture. So if conditions are right, during normal trade

The sometimes misty forests of Koke'e demonstrate the contrasts found on the Garden Island.

winds, the clouds disappear into humidity in less than a minute right before your eyes. If the winds are coming from the ocean (not the norm), clouds back up in the valley, and it won't clear up.

According to historians, there used to be a *steep* trail into the valley from here leading down across a ridge called *kapea*, a Hawaiian word for scrotum. It was so-named because the trail was so steep that it made your…well, *you* figure it out.

Hawaiian geese, called **nenes**, tend to hang out at the lookouts. These are endemic to Hawai'i (found nowhere else) and are what you get when you take wayward Canada geese and isolate them in the tropics for a million years. They've adapted to higher altitudes, lost most of the webbing on their feet and have no fear of cars or people, so be careful driving around at the lookout. They also try to make their living begging food from visitors. Please try to resist.

This is the end of the road. As the crow flies, Ha'ena on the north shore is less than 7 miles away, but you ain't no crow. They tried to build a road from here to Ha'ena in the '50s. Anybody who has ever hiked the **Alaka'i Swamp Trail** before they installed a boardwalk could tell you that a road in these parts is next to impossible. The results of this boondoggle are monuments in the form of heavy earthmoving equipment still stuck in the swamp where the prison work crews left them. A stroll from here down part of the **Pihea Trail** can be a pleasant diversion. This is where the road to Ha'ena was supposed to start.

In 1870, Queen Emma made a famous trek through the **Alaka'i Swamp** to the Kilohana Lookout. (As an aside, Alaka'i means "to lead," because it's impossible to get around in there without a guide.) She had a hundred people accompany her and stopped at awkward times to insist on hula demonstrations. Her guide vowed never to go into Alaka'i again, and the trip became legendary throughout the islands.

The Kalalau Valley is best viewed not from the Kalalau Lookout, but from the Pu'u o Kila Lookout.

By not having a road completely encircling the island, Kaua'i has been able to escape the fate that has befallen O'ahu. As long as the dots aren't connected, there will always be parts of Kaua'i that are remote.

WEST SHORE SHOPPING

In Waimea, check out **Collectibles & Fine Junque** for Hawaiian collectables from artwork to vinyl record albums, china to jewelry and everything in between. **Hidden Dragon Imports** has jade, specialty teas and other items direct from China. **Aloha N' Paradise** has a nice selection of local artwork for sale. Pick up your fresh deli foods from **Ishihara Market** or **Big Save** across the street. Don't miss **Aunty Lilikoi** (near Big Save) for outstanding passionfruit products made on premises. They'll even share recipes. On the west end of town is **Kaua'i Granola/Sugar Cane Snax**. They are generous with free samples. If you like your coffee and cereal in the morning, they have *Espresso Granola,* which combines both. (Who'd a thought?)

Hanapepe has many galleries. Some of our favorites are: **Puahina** for original silkscreened Hawaiian warrior T-shirts and clothing items screened with native plant motifs. **Timespace Gallery** has spectacular modern artworks for those with contemporary tastes and deep pockets. Behind them is **Keiki Kovers** for adorable island-made clothes for babies and young kids. Across the street is **Talk Story Bookstore** specializing in used and rare books, as well as new works by local authors. <u>**Banana Patch Studio**</u> is where artists can be seen making a multitude of pottery items for sale. They also carry many other items such as baskets and jewelry that are worth a look. **Robert Bader/Becky Wold Gallery** creates gorgeous wood bowls and plates carved al-

The nene of Koke'e are accomplished beggars. This one flew off in a huff when we said no.

most paper-thin, and fine silk scarves in one-of-a-kind marbleized print designs. Try **Sheldon Gate Jewelry Designs** for tide-pool bracelets made of glass. Get a custom Hawaiian shirt made at **Jacqueline on Kaua'i**.

In 'Ele'ele, at Port Allen Marina be sure and look at **Malie** for beauty products made from Kaua'i-grown plants and botanicals. Across the street try the <u>Red Dirt Shirt Factory Outlet</u> for the best prices and selection on T-shirts made from Kaua'i's famous red dirt.

WEST SHORE BEST BETS

Best Sunset View—A Couple Miles up Waimea Canyon Drive

Best Treat—Shave Ice at Jo-Jo's Clubhouse in Waimea

Best Hearty Food—Chili and Cornbread at the Koke'e Lodge

Best Place for Quiet Contemplation—To the Right of the viewing Platform at Pu'u o Kila Lookout

Best Swimming—Salt Pond Beach Park or Queen's Pond at Polihale (if calm)

Best Place to Get Away From It All and Write the Great American Novel—Waimea Plantation Cottages

Best Place to Have Good Brakes—Makaha Ridge Road

Ke'e Beach and its reef lagoon offer some of the best swimming on the north shore.
This is how it looks from the Kalalau Trail.

Because Kaua'i is older than the other major Hawaiian islands, it is blessed with having more sand beaches per mile of shoreline than any other. No part of the island is without sandy beaches. Many are accessible by merely driving up and falling into the sand. Others are deliciously secluded, requiring walks of various lengths. Some are local secrets; others are unknown even to most locals. In this section we will describe virtually all of Kaua'i's beaches starting from the north shore and working our way around the island clockwise. All of these beaches are located on the maps of the various areas.

BEACH SAFETY

The beaches of Kaua'i, and Hawai'i in general, are beautiful, warm and unfortunately can be dangerous. The waves, currents and popularity of beachgoing have caused Hawai'i to become the drowning capital of the United States. If you're going to swim in the ocean, you need to bear several things in mind. We are not trying to be killjoys here, but there are several reasons why Hawai'i's beaches can be particularly dangerous. The waves are stronger here in the open ocean than in most other places. Rip currents can form, cease and form again with no warning. Large "rogue waves" can come ashore with no warning. These usually occur when two or more waves fuse at sea, becoming a larger wave. Even calm seas are no guarantee of safety. Many people have been caught unaware by large waves during ostensibly "calm seas." We have swam and snorkeled most of the beaches we describe in this book on at least two occasions (usually more than two). But beaches change. The underwater topography changes throughout the year. Storms can take a very safe beach and rearrange the sand, turning it into a dangerous beach. Just because we describe a beach as being in a certain condition does not mean it will be in that same condition when *you* visit it.

Consequently, you should consider the beach descriptions as a snapshot in calm times. If seas aren't calm, you probably shouldn't go in the water. If you observe a rip current, you probably shouldn't go in the water. If you aren't a comfortable swimmer, you should probably never go in the water, except at those beaches that have lifeguards and protected pools, such as Lydgate State Park. But during abnormally high seas, even these are potentially hazardous. Kaua'i averages nine drownings per year—58% of these are visitors. We don't want you to become part of that statistic. There is no way we can tell you that a certain beach will be swimmable on a certain day, and we claim no such prescience. There is no substitution for your own observations and judgment.

In general, the north shore beaches are calmest during the summer months (meaning April–September). The south shore is calmest during the winter months (meaning October–May). North shore high surf is stronger than south shore high surf since our location in the northern hemisphere makes us closer to northern winter storms than southern hemisphere storms.

A few of the standard safety tips apply. Never turn your back on the ocean. Never swim alone. Never swim in the mouth of a river. Never swim in murky water. Never swim when the seas are not calm. Don't walk too close to the shore break; a large wave can come and knock you over and pull you in. Observe ocean conditions carefully. Don't let small children play in the water unsupervised. (In fact, it's best to keep them at the protected ponds such as Lydgate.) Fins give you far more power and speed and are a good safety device (besides being more fun). If you are comfortable in a mask and snorkel, they provide considerable peace of mind, in addition to opening up the underwater world. Lastly, don't let Kaua'i's idyllic environment cloud your judgment. Recognize the ocean for what it is: a powerful force that needs to be respected.

When frolicking at a beach, especially a rocky one, **reef shoes** are invaluable for protecting your feet from cuts. They can turn a marginal beach into a fun beach.

People tend to get fatigued while walking in sand. The trick to making it easier is to walk with a very gentle, relaxed stride while lightly striking the sand almost flat footed.

Beach conditions are usually best in the first half of the day. And remember that weekends—like weekends everywhere—are more popular with local beachgoers, so it's best to plan your beach activities for weekdays, if possible.

One thing you should be aware of is that in Hawai'i, all beaches are public beaches. This means that you can park yourself on any stretch of sand you like. The trick, sometimes, can be access. To get to a public beach, you might have to cross private land. The county and state have procured easements to many of the beaches. On our various maps, we have marked these public access routes in yellow. This, along with descriptions and directions, will assist you in finding the beach of your choice. But public access is an involved and often murky subject. We did our best to get it right, but there *may* be some that are marked where *somebody* may object. (E.g., "This *used* to be public access, but the county easement wasn't filed properly when the moon was full, and my attorney talked to their attorney, and together they drafted this 85-page document describing the protocols necessary when accessing every fourth Tuesday...") You get the idea. Use your best judgment.

The beaches that are *supposed* to have **lifeguards** daily are Ha'ena Beach Park, Hanalei Beach Park, Kealia, Lydgate, Po'ipu, Salt Pond and Kekaha. Lifeguards *may be* present on weekends and holidays at Anahola Beach Park and Wailua.

When we mention that a beach has **facilities**, it usually includes restrooms, showers, picnic tables and drinking water. Facilities are sometimes less than pristine.

A WORD ABOUT SHELLS

Hawai'i's creatures produce only a tiny fraction of the shells you'll find in other parts of the world, so it's illegal to take any from the beach. Once we were snorkeling at Larsen's when a visitor asked us, "How come I don't see any such and such type of shells anymore? We were here five years ago and saw lots of them. I have a whole bag of 'em back home in my garage." We told him, "Maybe we don't have much anymore because they're all in that bag of yours in the garage."

NORTH SHORE BEACHES

❖ Ke'e Beach

This is as far as you can go *by car* on the north shore. The beach here is called Ke'e (also called Ha'ena *State* Park), and

A REAL GEM

it's a swimming, snorkeling and sunbathing favorite that can get crowded. The sand volume here varies tremendously. Some summers the sand fills the lagoon, creating a knee-deep sand swimming pool. During these times *on calm days* the snorkeling just *outside* the reef is unreal. Tons of fish, clear water and so many turtles you'll lose count as you cruise out the reef opening on the left side and head right. Maybe it's our imagination, but the snorkeling seems to get a little better every year. But calm seas are the *only* time you should consider *leaving* the lagoon. During winter months and at other times, large waves may wash over the reef, creating an excess of lagoon water. Since Ke'e has the only reef opening, this water has only one place to go to equalize the volume—out the reef opening on the left side. That's why it's important to observe ocean conditions carefully. Big waves mean big currents in the reef openings and big problems for you unless you stay away from the reef opening.

The park is equipped with facilities. If the showers are full, the stream you crossed ³⁄₁₀ mile back makes an ideal place to rinse off the saltwater, but be careful—the rocks can be slippery.

The highway's end is also where the Kalalau Trail begins. It leads to **Hanakapi'ai Beach** and **Kalalau Beach**, which are described in the ADVENTURES chapter.

❖ Ha'ena Beach Park

This very pretty beach has complete facilities and lifeguard. It is located across from the **Dry Cave**. Plenty of parking near the beach. Sand is very coarse (and therefore, comes off very easily). Although you might see people swimming here, the shore is totally exposed,

A beachgoer wonders if it's too late to return his snorkel gear.

lacking any reef protection. The smallest of waves has a surprising amount of force. A popular surf spot off to the left of the beach is called **Cannons**. Since the beach is very steep, a small wave could knock you over and the backwash could pull you in; therefore, swimming is hazardous except during very calm seas. Camping with county permit.

❖ Tunnels (Makua) Beach

A REAL GEM

One of Kaua'i's snorkeling nirvanas. This superb beach has a wide-fringing reef that is so large it can be seen from space. (Don't believe me? Locate it on the map, then look at the cover of this book. The reef is very prominent in this shot taken from the space shuttle.) There is often a lateral rip current, but it's *normally* quite weak, making Tunnels a good snorkeling spot most of the time. The beach is quite popular, and you will often see SCUBA divers here, as well as surfers and windsurfers. All this makes it sound crowded, but a lack of street parking keeps the numbers relatively low. The kaleidoscope of underwater life is usually profuse and definitely worth your time to explore. See section on SNORKELING on page 177 for some useful tips. See also the SCUBA section; both are in the chapter called ACTIVITIES. Public access is by either of two short dirt roads past the 8 mile marker on Hwy 560. The first (and best if you're snorkeling) one is $^4/_{10}$ mile past the 8 mile marker. The second one is almost $^6/_{10}$ mile past the 8 mile marker and, although it has shorter access to the sand, you may have to scramble down some tree roots, which might be difficult for some. Get there early to assure a parking spot. If they're full, park at Ha'ena Beach Park and walk to the right. You could also take Alealea Street before the 8 mile marker, park near the sand, and walk to the left along the beach. (It's a half-mile walk in sand that way, but it's pretty.) You should know that if you park on the highway itself, they *do* give tickets.

❖ Kepuhi Beach

The snorkeling is good here but not nearly as good as Tunnels. You'll rarely find many people on this beach, so if you're in the area and want easy access but no crowds, this is the beach for you. This long strip of sand is fronted by an even longer coral reef. The makeup of this reef causes a slightly stronger current. Check out conditions before you snorkel. Because most of it is not located directly off the main highway, it tends to be forgotten, even by locals. It is, however, still used on occasion by throw-net fishermen. Access is at the eastern end of Alamoo Road. See map on page 48.

❖ Wainiha Beach Park

Hazardous surf and its location at the mouth of the Wainiha River make it murky and unsuitable for anything other than shoreline fishing and beachcombing. And squatters at press time created an unwelcome feeling.

❖ Lumaha'i Beach

This is the long, wide, golden, glorious beach you see just after you've passed Hanalei Bay. Pictured on countless postcards and posters, this beach was made famous as a location for the movie *South Pacific*. This is where Mitzi Gaynor spent considerable time washing that man right out of her hair. If you're looking for a huge, picture-perfect stretch of sand on the north shore, Lumaha'i shouldn't be missed. If you're looking for safe swimming, Lumaha'i shouldn't be touched. This beach and Hanakapi'ai on the Na Pali Coast are the two most dangerous beaches on Kaua'i. Exposed to open ocean, the waves here, even small ones, are frighteningly powerful. We've come to this beach after seeing it absolutely flat at Ha'ena Beach Park, a few miles away, only to be utterly assaulted by Lumaha'i's waves. Put simply, most of Lumaha'i is almost never safe to swim. The waves, currents and backwash are not to be underestimated. Lumaha'i Stream on the left side is sometimes crossable during calm seas and low stream flow. It serves as an estuary for 'o'opu during the summer when the shifting sands tend to cut off the river from the ocean. During this time, the closed river mouth is sometimes safe to swim. But absent these conditions, swimming in Lumaha'i Stream has caused numerous individuals to be swept out to sea. Surfers and boogie boarders often use the left side of the beach near the rocks, but unless you're an expert on Hawaiian surf, this should not be attempted.

Separated by lava rock to the right (east) of Lumaha'i is **Kahalahala Beach** (technically part of Lumaha'i, but who's quibbling?). Swimming here is a different story. You access it from a marvelous 3–4 minute walk down through lush jungle to the beach 100 feet below. During calm summer days the water here can be like a crystal-clear swimming pool. There's a tide-pool for keiki to splash about, a fair amount of shade and a tall rock that some people love jumping off. (Our general rule is, never jump off anything you haven't checked out first.) When seas are calm here, this area is utter paradise. Big surf, however, which is not uncommon in the winter, makes this part of the beach nearly as dangerous as the rest of Lumaha'i.

Access to these beaches can be obtained either via a trail from the top of the lookout at the eastern edge of the beach *before* the 5 mile marker on Hwy 560 (this gets you to the eastern part, which is the best part), or from the parking area just before you get to the Lumaha'i River. See map on page 48.

❖ Hanalei Bay

The four beaches described below are all part of Hanalei Bay. With its single long

The Hawaiian Monk Seal

The endangered Hawaiian monk seal occasionally comes ashore after a heavy meal or to avoid a predator. Many people assume the seals are sick or injured and attempt to coax them back into the water. If you are lucky enough to encounter one, please leave it alone. Beaching is perfectly normal. The fines for disturbing one can range as high as $25,000. The seals dive as deep as 400 feet to feed and are considered the most primitive seals in the world with ancient social behavior. Unlike other seals, they don't come ashore in large numbers.

A monk seal snoozes at a Kapaʻa beach, oblivious to the kite surfers just offshore. Then again, this photographer watched the same kite surfers for over 5 minutes, oblivious to the monk seal 10 feet away.

If you can negotiate the steps and path on the right side coming down to the sand, Hideaways delivers the right ingredients that make a great beach. And in the summer it's twice as long as this.

crescent of sand, the bay is beautiful to look at but not great to swim in. Pounding shore break, backwash and rip currents, especially during the winter months, make Hanalei Bay less than ideal as a swimming beach. But that doesn't make it any less pretty. Large surfing waves make Hanalei Bay very popular with surfers, who come from other islands to experience the extremely long-lasting waves.

❖ Waikoko Beach

Easy access and good reef protection at this one portion of Hanalei Bay make this a popular beach during moderate surf periods, but the water is shallow, which makes for marginal swimming conditions. The snorkeling is better than the swimming if stream flow isn't high. Located between the 4 and 5 mile markers as the road begins to ascend. There is a 20-foot-long path near the 15 MPH sign. See map on page 49.

❖ Wai'oli Beach Park

Located at the end of either He'e or 'Ama'ama Roads in Hanalei and often referred to as **Pine Trees**, the underwater topography focuses more of the ocean's force here, making the swimming hazardous except during very calm seas. Access is from Weke Road in Hanalei. A reader recently pointed out (and we verified) that this beach has particularly good sand for building **sand castles**. The stuff sticks together like cement.

❖ Hanalei Pavilion Beach Park

Also located on Weke Road in Hanalei, it includes facilities and a lifeguard. Popular with boogie boarders and surfers, the shore break and backwash make for less-than-ideal swimming conditions most of the time.

❖ Black Pot

Located near the mouth of the Hanalei River, swimming conditions are marginal. During calm summer surf, boogie boarding is possible near the pier area. Black Pot refers to a large black cooking pot residents used to keep at the beach. This is the area where kayakers put in to paddle up the Hanalei River. The picturesque pier here makes a good sunset photo. Facilities available at beach. Camping with county permit.

❖ Pu'u Poa Beach

Located next to the St. Regis in Princeville, the beach has a fringing reef and offers good snorkeling possibilities during calm seas. During the winter, the waters off the outer edge of the reef offer some of the best and most challenging surfing in the state (for experts only). Access is through a cement path starting just to the left of the gate house at the St. Regis. Getting to the beach necessitates negotiating 191 steps. (Yes, we counted…it was a slow day.) From here you can walk all the way to the mouth of the Hanalei River. The other access is to come from Black Pot Beach and wade across the usually shallow water at the mouth of the Hanalei River.

❖ Pali Ke Kua (Hideaways)

A REAL GEM

Fifty feet before the St. Regis in Princeville gate house is a corridor off to the right (next to the Pu'u Poa tennis courts). This path leads *down* (120 feet below) to Pali Ke Kua Beach, also called Hideaways. The first half of the descent consists of stairs and a railing. The remainder is trail. All told, it takes 5–10 minutes to get there. There are actually two beaches here, with the second one off to the right separated by a rocky point. Both offer excellent snorkeling during calm seas. The salient underwater features are good relief and a diverse fish community punctuated by the occasional turtle. With

marvelous coarse sand, large false kamani trees for shade and good snorkeling when calm, this beach is a wonderful place to spend the day. You won't usually find too many people here since it's still poorly marked and parking near the trailhead corridor is limited.

While the beach can be a nice place to bring the kids, some may have trouble negotiating their way down the path. (In fact, *you* might have trouble, too, if it has been raining and the path below the steps is muddy. Ropes might be there to help, if that's the case.) When seas aren't calm, rip currents can form. Check ocean conditions carefully. Unusually high surf has been known to generate waves that can sweep across the entire beach. The *other* part of Pali Ke Kua beach can be reached by swimming to the right from Hideaways or by walking a paved trail leading down from the Pali Ke Kua condominiums. That *other* path is a private trail available only to guests at Pali Ke Kua.

❖ Queen's Bath

A REAL GEM

When we revealed it in our first edition, Queen's Bath was an unknown gem accessible via a vague trail through the jungle and exclusive to our readers. I guess we're a victim of our own success. It's now so popular that they installed a parking lot and signs. Queen's Bath is actually a large pool the size of several swimming pools carved by nature into a lava shelf with an inlet from the ocean for fresh seawater to flow. (Shown on page 24.) If the surf is too high, you would never recognize this place as anything special. But at other times, Queen's Bath is a marvelous pool to swim in. Fish get in through the inlet, making it all the more charming. (Bring your mask; no fins needed.) It's a great place to take your underwater camera. During the summer,

The 2-mile long fringing reef at 'Anini usually gives this beach the calmest water on the north shore.

if the ocean is *too* calm, the water is not refreshed as much as it should be. During high surf, it's dangerous as the water flows in and out of the pond. But the rest of the time, Queen's Bath is one of those places you will return to each time you visit Kaua'i. To get there, follow the trail off Kapiolani Road near Punahele Road in Princeville. See map on page 49. During winter months (generally October–April), high surf often assault the area. Even when the ocean appears calm, it's aways possible for a rogue wave to snap at this part of the shoreline, knocking people around, maybe even dragging them back into the open ocean. That's why winter surf typically makes Queen's Bath unusable. The trail (slippery when wet) passes a marvelous seasonal waterfall on your right after a few minutes. (Good for rinsing off the salt when you're done.) After dropping 120 feet, the trail encounters the ocean at the lava shoreline where a small waterfall drops directly into the ocean. Go to the *left* along the lava for 260 yards. (It'll seem like more.) Queen's Bath is recessed in the rock and

is part of a horseshoe-shaped lava cut. Use the photo on page 44 or the inside cover to identify it. If you can't find it, the ocean probably isn't cooperating.

❖ SeaLodge Beach

A REAL GEM

This wonderful pocket of sand is set in an indentation in the cliff. With plenty of shade courtesy of false kamani trees and heavenly coarse sand (the kind that won't stick to you with the tenacity of a barnacle), SeaLodge Beach is a real find. This beach is sometimes empty of people because most don't know it's there. During the summer in particular, it's an ideal secluded beach. Access is from a trail at *Building A* at the SeaLodge Resort which is at the end of Kamehameha Road in Princeville. See map on page 49. Where the trail encounters the ocean, it veers to the left. Look for turtles in the water here. The snorkeling can be outstanding during very calm seas, but entry and currents need to be respected. Depending on the weather, the trail can be slippery and a bit tricky in areas. During periods of unusually high surf, waves have been known to travel all the way to the base of the cliff. Don't come here if this is the case. The entire picturesque hike should take between 10 and 15 minutes and is well worth it.

❖ 'Anini Beach Park

Protected by a *long* fringing reef, 'Anini Beach has become a popular place for the rich and famous to build homes. The water can be very shallow, and the snorkeling is usually good in many areas when visibility cooperates. The swimming is among the safest you'll find on the north shore. The channel at the western end of the beach is where the water flows out, so stay away from this part. (See the left side of the map on page 46.) There are numerous areas along this stretch of sand to swim, snorkel or just frolic. There is a polo field across from the beach; check it out if you're there during summer. 'Anini Beach is a good place to learn windsurfing. Camping with county permit, facilities at the pavilion.

The name used to be *Wanini Beach,* but the "W" was blasted away with a shotgun by an irate resident who felt it had been misspelled. Other residents assumed the gun-toting spell-checker must have corrected a mistake and the "new" name stuck. (*That's* typical Hawai'i.) Take the northern Kalihiwai Road (between the 25 and 26 mile markers) and stay to the left on 'Anini Road.

The far (west) end of the beach, on the other side of the channel, is known as **Wyllie Beach**. Residents of Princeville access it by taking a ¼ mile-long trail from the end of Wyllie Road, which drops 20 stories. The easier way is to park near the channel on 'Anini Road and wade across the stream. Wyllie Beach is a thin ribbon of sand with lots of shade from false kamani trees (whose fallen leaves turn yellow, red, orange and brown). It makes a very nice stroll as the ocean gently laps at your feet (though the sand can disappear during high tide and surf). There is a touch more sand in nearshore waters (though still plenty of rocks) than at other parts of 'Anini.

Local children often play in the shallow stream at Kalihiwai Bay.

❖ Kalihiwai Beach

Located at the mouth of Kalihiwai Stream, you drive down from either Kalihiwai Road. (It used to be a loop, but the bridge was knocked out by a tsunami in 1957, and they haven't rebuilt it.) At the bottom of the road, you encounter a picturesque bay with a wide sand beach lined with ironwood trees to park under. There are houses on the other side of the road. The beach is popular with boogie boarders in the summer and is a good place to see local keiki learning to ride waves. It's also a good place to just enjoy the water during the summer. During the winter, surfers ride the large waves under the cliff area. The eastern (first) Kalihiwai Road is the best road to take to the beach. The only ding is that local dogs occasionally roam free, leaving—well, *you* know what they leave behind.

❖ Secret Beach

A REAL GEM

Also known as Kauapea Beach and known to most locals by the more enticing name of Secret Beach, this is a stunningly beautiful beach only accessible via a 10–15 minute hike. This fact, along with its former anonymity, caused it to become Kaua'i's premier nude beach. For the record, public nudity is illegal in Hawai'i, and police issue tickets there, so it's not as prevalent as it once was. This long, golden sand beach is not swimmable during the winter, but on calm summer days it can be a delight for swimming and offers good snorkeling. It's worth the trip year-round just to see its exceptional scenic beauty. There is usually a small waterfall to rinse off your gear and a few places where water squirts from the side of the cliff. The island off to your right is Moku'ae'ae Island, a bird sanctuary. To get to Secret Beach, turn right off the first (eastern) Kalihiwai Road, then right on the first dirt road you encounter. (See map on page 46.) Take the trail to the bottom. (It's real slippery when it's raining.) Make a mental note of where it encounters the beach for your return. If you go to the *left* at the bottom of the trail, the shoreline leads to the **Secret Lava Pools** described on page 151.

❖ Kahili Quarry Beach

Where Kilauea Stream encounters the ocean is a beach sometimes called Rock Quarry Beach. There is good swimming on the left (western) side and good snorkeling on the right side during calm seas. Since this is a river mouth, the water can get murky at times. (Sharks, which like murky water, have been sighted here during periods of heavy stream flow.) This is a popular boogie boarding and surfing site. The river mouth can cause rip currents. Easiest access is from a dirt road off N. Wailapa Road. See map on page 46. A good hike near here is described under HIKING on page 148.

❖ Waiakalua Beach

A marvelous and undiscovered north shore beach. Although from your car it requires a steep, 5–10 minute walk to the beach 160 feet below, Waiakalua is an undisturbed, serene place to spend the afternoon. Medium coarse sand, a long, fringing reef, numerous pockets of shade and a freshwater spring at the far end add to the charm. Observe the reef from up on the bluff. Calm summer snorkeling can be interesting but shallow; watch out for rip currents. During other times, swimming can be hazardous. At the far end of the beach is a rocky point separating the two halves of the beach. The snorkeling around this point is exciting, featuring clear water teeming with big life. However, the rips, surges and surf make this

Larsen's Beach has an excellent reef, but stay away from the channel near the top left of the photo.

area tricky—only advanced snorkelers need apply. Otherwise, just enjoy the beach. The cool spring at the far end offers sweet, fresh water. Bring an empty container and some water treatment pills—all fresh water obtained anywhere in nature should be treated to prevent bacterial disease. (It barely trickles during dry months.) To get to Waiakalua, turn onto North Waiakalua Road and take the dirt road on the left side just before the end of the road. Park when you can't drive any more, and take the trail off to the left. The beach on your left at the bottom is Waiakalua Beach. The beach boulders off to your right lead to **Pila'a Beach**. It can take 10–30 minutes to reach **Pila'a Beach**, depending on your boulder-hopping prowess. Otherwise, just stay at Waiakalua Beach. You'll probably have either one all to yourself. See map on page 47.

❖ Larsen's Beach

This has crystal-clear water, lots of beachcombing and seclusion. The beach is named after a former manager at Kilauea

A REAL GEM

Plantation named L. David Larsen (the rascal who introduced the hated blackberries to Koke'e). This beach is splendidly isolated but can be accessed by walking down a gently sloping trail. Off to the right are a bunch of lava rocks that make for good snorkeling if conditions are right. To the left is a long crescent of sand broken by occasional outcroppings of rock and reef. Underwater topography creates good conditions for beachcombing. Pakala Point is on the left side where the first beach ends and lava rock protrudes out into the ocean. Just before these rocks is **Pakala Channel**. (Shown near the top of the photo and on the inside back cover.) Most of the water you see breaking over the reef drains through this channel; therefore, *don't swim in or near the channel*. The water leading just up to the channel moves so swiftly at times that it seems more like rapids than a rip current. If the ocean is calm and you stay away from the channel, if the tide is right and you have some experience snorkeling, this place can be a

The south side of Moloa'a Bay on a calm, sunny day is paradise found.

snorkeler's paradise. Lots of coral and fish in shallow, crystal-clear water greet the eye. Relatively few beachgoers use this beach during the week. This beach is *not* a swimming beach, just for snorkeling, due to the sharp reefs and shallow water.

One thing that can be *very cool*—if you're careful—is to get in the water at the southeast end (where the trailhead is) and let the current take you toward (but not into!) the Pakala Channel. Then get out and walk back.

The end of summer is when water at reef-fringed beaches like Larsen's has the poorest visibility because it has usually been many months since it has had a good flushing by the high surf.

During periods of high surf, waves *tower* above the reef, breaking on the edge, which can be quite a spectacle.

On the opposite side of Pakala Point are two pockets of sand that are even more secluded and offer good snorkeling

and a chance of spotting a monk seal. Larsen's is about 20 minutes north of Kapa'a; take the *north* end of Ko'olau Road (the second Ko'olau if you're coming from Kapa'a) just before the 20 mile marker. $1^2/_{10}$ miles from the north end of Ko'olau Road, take the left Beach Access road all the way until it ends. (See map on page 47.) Go through the cattle guard and follow the trail to the bottom (which is 140 feet below you). The beach is a 5–10 minute walk down the hill. Note where the trail hits the beach for your return. We've noticed that the beach sometimes attracts nudists.

❖ Moloa'a Beach

A REAL GEM

A wonderful beach on calm days. The right (southeast) side is much nicer than the northwest side. Very pretty beach, but not a great swimming beach when seas aren't calm. It's off the main highway and not as well known as other beaches. Take the first (southeastern) Ko'olau Road (before the 17 mile marker) to Moloa'a Road. The public access is near the end of Moloa'a Road. Parking is *very* limited. There are a few stalls toward the end of the road, otherwise park where there are *no* NO PARKING signs to dissuade you. You might have to walk a ways to the beach, but it's worth it. To get to the southeast side, you'll have to walk 100 yards along the beach. There you'll find the wading, swimming and boogie boarding the best, and shade is plentiful. See map on page 47. Some residents lost access to their nearby houses when the tiny bridge to their neighborhood collapsed in the late '90s. Rather than make them wait years while county agencies squabbled over jurisdiction, the military base on the west side sent a dozen Navy Seabees to build them a new one in one day using donated materials.

❖ Papa'a Bay

Very picturesque. The beach access involves a 5-minute trail through the brush down to some rocks below. After that you'll have to boulder-hop about a hundred yards. You need to use the access to North 'Aliomanu Beach (see map on page 47) and look for a beach access when the road turns to the right. In addition, it is one of the few beaches on Kaua'i where you may detect a fishy smell. When the producer of the movie *Six Days/Seven Nights* was here to film the plane crash scene, he apparently liked the location so much, he purchased all *171 acres* around the bay and has built quite a compound, which he calls **Tara**. At press time it was for sale for over *$46 million*. Although Captain Hollywood owns the land and house around the bay, the *beach* is public.

❖ 'Aliomanu Beach

This is really two beaches with different access points. The long, fringing reef offshore of the south beach is used heavily by locals for throw-net fishing, octopus hunting, pole fishing, torch fishing and limu harvesting. This beach, along with Pila'a and Larsen's, attracts families who have been limu (an edible seaweed) harvesting on the outer parts of the reef for generations. They pick the top part of the plant, leaving the roots to regenerate.

The northern (and better) beach is accessed from a parking lot 80 feet above the beach, requiring a 5-minute walk. (See map on page 47.) Although the nearshore waters are rocky, the beach is sandy and very pretty.

❖ Anahola Beach Park

The area around Anahola is designated Hawaiian Homelands, and most of the beach users are Hawaiian. Visitors aren't common but are certainly welcome. Swimming is safest where it is protected on the right (eastern) side of the bay to just before Kahala Point. Watch for rip currents near the pier. Also nice is the northern end, which is lightly used and can be accessed from the first Aliomanu Road.

EAST SHORE BEACHES

❖ Donkey Beach

A REAL GEM

So named by drifters in the '60s who observed burros and mules being used by the sugar company to haul seed cane to the fields nearby. Donkey Beach has been a popular nudist beach on Kaua'i due to its location, but the land's current owners are doing much to end this practice. (After purchasing the land from a defunct sugar company and selling house lots for $2 million plus, they're not too thrilled with the idea of naked beachgoers.) This long stretch of sand is also popular with surfers. Interestingly, surfing in ancient times was usually done nude. (I wonder if that's where the term *hang loose* came from…)

Access is ½ mile north of the 11 mile marker, north of Kapa'a. Look for a hiking sign guiding you to the parking lot with facilities. The uncrowded beach is very attractive, with a convenient tree in the middle for shade. The foreshore at the beach is steep, creating a pounding shore break and strong backwash. Swimming is sometimes hazardous. It's about a 10-minute (550 yard) walk on the paved path to the beach. As you near the shoreline, veer to the right for the beach. To the left (north) past the stream and over the small hill is a secluded cove (cleverly labeled "secluded cove" on our map) where the snorkeling can be very good at times. You will probably have that cove all to yourself. During rainy times, there might be a small waterfall and swimming hole behind the cove.

❖ Kealia Beach

Drive north of Kapa'a and you will often see lots of boogie boarders and surfers in the water here. (See map on page 59.) The powerful waves are fantastic but can be treacherous. The currents and backwash are sometimes ferocious. The northern end of the beach is more protected by a breakwater and can be good for wading and occasionally snorkeling on a calm day. If you have never ridden waves, be very careful here or you might get drilled into the ground. If the surf is high, definitely leave it for the big boys. Lifeguard and facilities.

❖ Kapa'a Beach Park

Located in the heart of Kapa'a, this is heavily used by locals. Like any beach located close to a population center, Kapa'a Beach Park is not as pristine as other beaches you will find. That said, the northern section (the part just before the lookout as you leave Kapa'a going north) offers interesting but shallow snorkeling.

Check for currents. The rest of the park is not as memorable. It is, however, a good place for a beach stroll or to watch the sunrise. There are a few large sand pockets along the beach that are swimmable when the surf isn't high. Regular facilities here plus a swimming pool. The best thing about Kapa'a Beach Park is watching the kite surfers on a windy day.

❖ Waipouli Beach

Pretty, but not a good swimming beach. There are a few small pockets along the southern portion of the beach that are relatively safe for swimming during calm periods, but be cautious. The area seaward of the beachrock fronting the beach is subject to strong currents year-round. This is normally considered a dangerous beach. There is a paved shoreline trail along much of this beach, which is perfect for jogging or a leisurely stroll.

Just north of Waipouli Beach is **Waipouli Beach Park**, also called **Fuji Beach** and sometimes **Baby Beach**. Conditions there are different. This can be a nice place to let keiki splash around in the ocean. Part of it (on Moanakai Street between Pahihi and Makana) is often protected by a long, natural sandstone breakwater. Only when the tide or surf are high does water flow over the sandstone and form a slight current to the left. Otherwise, it's usually flat calm. The sand is coarse, so you'll sink a bit more into it. Check to make sure the ocean isn't making a liar out of us and that it's clean enough. Since it's located in the middle of town, it sometimes gets a little dirty.

❖ Wailua Beach

Across from the Coco Palms Resort, from the mouth of the Wailua River to a rocky point to the north, this is an easily accessible beach. Just drive right up. It is popular with surfers and boogie boarders who appreciate the unprotected waves. Winter swells sometimes keep even these users out of the water. Swimmers should be aware of rip currents in several areas along the beach and pounding shore break during high seas. The river itself, which is crossable only during periods of *low flow*, can cause tricky water conditions, so caution is advised. The ocean and the river are constantly battling for supremacy, and the struggle can be dramatic. The ocean builds up a sand bar, and the river attempts to erode it. Sometimes the river is completely stopped up. When it finally breaks through the sand bar, it can be fascinating. The sand bar can erode in a matter of an hour or two, taking large amounts of sand with it. For a short time thereafter, ancient Hawaiian petroglyphs are exposed on rocks in the river mouth.

❖ Lydgate Beach Park

A REAL GEM

Located just south of the Wailua River, Lydgate is composed of a picnic area, a large patch of grass, restrooms, two nice playgrounds, showers, lifeguard and two marvelous boulder-enclosed ponds. These ponds are nearly always safe to swim, with the smaller one meant for the keiki (kids). These ponds were created to allow fresh seawater and fish into the pond, while protecting you from the ocean's force. And they work quite well. Lydgate is the most popular fish feeding place on the island. Mornings are the best times. Some chips, bread or rabbit food sparingly squeezed through a hole in a plastic baggie will usually win you lots of new underwater friends. If you are having trouble attracting a crowd, keep swimming slowly while staying reasonably close to the rocks. Fish like the rocks since they offer protection from predators. Once a few start eating, continue to swim slowly to attract the maximum crowd. For more tips on feeding the fish, see page 180. Please be careful to take the plastic baggie out with you. There are plenty of turtles in the area that can choke on the plastic. Access is just off Leho Drive in Wailua. (See map on page 59.) Note that if Portuguese man-o-wars happen to be present, it's usually near the rocks at far right end.

❖ Nukoli'i Beach Park

From Lydgate to the far end of the Hilton Kaua'i is a long sand beach called Nukoli'i Beach. This beach includes the area fronting the Wailua Golf Course. This entire stretch of sand, more than 2 miles long, is never crowded, often deserted. This is surprising given its proximity to Kapa'a, but good for you. There is a road fronting much of the golf course, until it erodes at the very end. If you just want to easily claim a large spot of beach for yourself, this is as good a place as any. The swimming conditions vary along the beach but are usually marginal. Currents and surf are the usual villains. The area in front of the golf course is the only part worth considering for swimming purposes. The snorkeling can be good when it's calm, and it's fun to hunt for golf balls in the water. You might even find a club hurled by someone having an off day. Access? Just drive right up from the dirt road between the golf course and the Hilton Kaua'i entrance (not far from the 4 mile marker). Or take the Hilton entrance to access the southern portion of the beach. Facilities near the Hilton. One caveat: Natural currents often bring to this beach flotsam, such as netting and ropes from passing ships.

❖ Hanama'ulu Beach Park

Water is usually murky due to the Hanama'ulu Stream. Sharks are often seen in the area. The waters around Ahukini Pier can offer interesting snorkeling when it's very calm. In general, a mediocre beach with fairly good park facilities, such as BBQ grills next to the picnic tables, a nice pavilion and playground.

❖ Ninini Beach/Running Waters

Located below the Marriott, there's good snorkeling off to the left in front of the rocks on a calm day. However, even then it can be surgy and a bit tricky. Access via a walk along a golf course fairway, then a right turn at the shore and down a steep trail to the beach; see map on page 65. Take a drive over to the Ninini Lighthouse. If someone is working there at the time, ask if you can go to the top. The view from there is outstanding.

❖ Kalapaki Beach

With a gently sloping sand bottom and partial protection from the open ocean, Kalapaki is popular with visitors and locals alike. Swimming, bodysurfing, windsurfing (no kite surfing because of the nearby airport), beginner surfing and boogie boarding conditions are usually good except during periods of high surf. Adjacent Nawiliwili Park behind the Anchor Cove Shopping Center is a popular picnic spot. Canoes and twin-hulled sailing catamarans often come ashore here. Facilities near Anchor Cove Shopping Center. Access is by a road behind the shopping center or through the Marriott. See map on page 65. This is a good place to be when a cruise ship goes by. Because it's at Nawiliwili Bay (where the Hule'ia and Nawiliwili streams empty), the water won't be as clear as other water around the island. When calm (which is most of the time), it's a good place to teach your little one how to ride a boogie board.

❖ Niumalu Beach Park

Good place to launch kayaks for trips up the Hule'ia Stream (where the opening scenes from *Raiders of the Lost Ark* were filmed). Camping by county permit. Other water activities are lousy due to its location so far up the river.

SOUTH SHORE BEACHES

❖ Maha'ulepu Beaches

A REAL GEM

This marvelous coastline is wild and undeveloped, actually consisting of three separate areas known as Gillin's Beach, Kawailoa Bay and Ha'ula Beach.

The whole of Maha'ulepu makes for fantastic exploring and beach walking, hence the gem. The swimming can be hazardous, and seas here are often choppy. Winter is best. Ocean entry is difficult in many places. There is an abandoned guard shack on the road to the beaches, and they close off access between sunset and sunrise. Please take everything out that you bring in. The land company can close this access down any time they wish, so locals are bending over backward not to give 'em a reason.

Maha'ulepu is located past the Hyatt on Po'ipu Road after the road becomes dirt. Turn right at the dead end and follow the telephone poles. See map on page 75.

To get to **Gillin's Beach**, drive past the old shack and park at the lot where the road otherwise continues to the left. A short trail takes you to the beach. (See map.) This beach is named after the late Elbert Gillin whose rebuilt house (now a pricey vacation rental) is on the beach just off to your right. If you walk past it, you'll see a stream that may or may not reach the ocean. Take the trail that follows the stream on its far (southern) side. After about two minutes you'll see a small, triangle-shaped opening off to your left. This is an ancient, open-roofed sandstone sinkhole with some cool features. The local community college has been doing some archeology studies here and sometimes has it gated off. This area is identified as a cave on the map rather than as an amphitheater because we didn't want the casual map reader to think that rock concerts were held there.

To get to **Kawailoa Bay**, continue on the dirt road until it is directly next to the beach. Windsurfing is popular from here to **Gillin's Beach**. They ride the waves faster than the wind, and it is a real treat to watch.

The trail to **Ha'ula Beach** (see map on page 75) requires a walk along an elevated field of lithified sand. (The trail starts where a fence ends near the cliff's edge.) The constant assault from sea spray has caused the sandstone to erode into short but fantastically sharp and strangely shaped pinnacles. This is a great place to observe the power of the ocean as it smashes into the cliff. Local fishermen drop their lines into the water from here since they can see their prey before they cast. When you reach **Ha'ula Beach** (about a 10–15 minute walk), you will almost certainly have it all to yourself. The beach is backed by high sand dunes. Behind one you will find an old picnic table and BBQ. The beach is rarely visited except by occasional horseback tours from CJM Stables. The swimming isn't very good; in fact, it can be quite hazardous depending on conditions. But the beach is a beautiful place to enjoy your solitude. Over the ridge to the northeast is **Kipu Kai Beach**. Totally isolated, the only way to get to it is by sea or over that ridge. And the horse trails over the ridge are generously sprinkled with evil, spiked stickers. Bring your Kevlar pants.

The area between **Ha'ula Beach** and **Kawailoa Bay** contains other lithified sand dunes as well. Fishing from the top (labeled Cliff Cracks on the map) is incredible, but be careful—the dunes can be brittle, so don't fall in. The beach area just north of these lithified dunes often provides lots of goodies for the beach comber. Check out the dry, sometimes gasping blowhole near the shoreline at the eastern edge of Kawailoa Bay.

Maha'ulepu was the scene of a terrific slaughter in the spring of 1796. When King Kamehameha launched the first of two invasion attempts, he and his fleet of 1,200 canoes carrying 10,000 soldiers left O'ahu at midnight, hoping to reach Wailua on Kaua'i by daybreak. They were in the middle of the treacherous Kaua'i Channel when the wind and seas picked up. Many of his canoes were swamped. Reluctantly, he ordered a retreat but too late to stop some of his advance canoes. When they landed at Maha'ulepu, they were exhausted. They awoke to the sound of enemy troops who proceeded to kill all but a few escapees. The last thing these escapees wanted to do was go back to O'ahu and tell their boss what happened. So they bolted all the way to the Big Island and kept their mouths shut.

❖ Shipwreck Beach

This beach was named for an old, unidentified wooden shipwreck now long gone. Also called **Keoniloa Beach**, it fronts the Hyatt. The public access road is between the Hyatt and the Po'ipu Bay Resort Golf Course. The beach is used mostly by surfers, boogie boarders, body surfers and windsurfers who stay toward the eastern end. High surf can create very unfavorable conditions. Even during calm seas, swimming is sometimes difficult. The Hyatt erects

The water is nice, but entry can be a bit awkward from this spot. Shipwreck Beach can be a good place to sit and watch frustrated fishermen cast off (literally).

colored flags to signal ocean conditions—green meaning safe. (Though we've *never* seen a green flag. Their lawyer probably confiscated it.) The cliff off to your left is called Makawehi Point and is a popular place for pole fishermen. You will often see foolhardy young men jumping off the cliff into the waters below. (As did Harrison Ford and Anne Heche—or at least their stunt doubles—in the movie *Six Days/Seven Nights*.) The cliffs are a fascinating place to hike and are described in HIKING on page 158. The Hyatt has some outdoor showers near the beach area to rinse off, but they are technically only for the guests.

❖ Brennecke Beach

This beach was badly mauled by a hurricane back in 1992, but community volunteers brought it back to life by hauling in sand and removing an ill-conceived seawall. Great boogie boarding and lots of turtles. Since it is so small, surfboards are not allowed near the shore. The waves are usually great and tend to break both far away and close to shore—perfect for both beginners and advanced. You can rent boogie boards across the street at Nukumoi Surf Co. Observe conditions carefully before you go in. Since this beach is more susceptible to change than most island beaches, you'll have to evaluate its boogie viability.

❖ Po'ipu Beach Park

A REAL GEM This is the major center of beach activity on the south shore. The swimming is nearly always safe just to the left of the offshore sandy islet. Snorkeling around the right side of the islet can be fantastic. Park facilities and lifeguard are present. To the left is an area semi-protected by a breakwater. It's very popular with children. This park is a nice place to enjoy the ocean. The far right side isn't as protected but features excellent snorkeling and swimming if the surf isn't high.

❖ Kiahuna Beach/Sheraton Beach/ Po'ipu Beach

A REAL GEM

Take your pick with regard to the name. This beach fronts the Sheraton Hotel and Kiahuna Resort. It is post-card pretty and often safe to swim thanks to an offshore reef. Surfers ride waves outside the reef, but you should stay inside unless you really know your stuff. Boogie boarding and snorkeling help make this one of the most user-friendly beaches around. Access from the end of Hoonani Road. See map on page 75.

❖ Koloa Landing

An old boat launch used as a SCUBA spot. See SCUBA in the ACTIVITIES chapter.

❖ Baby Beach

This stretch of sand is partially protected from surf by a natural breakwater of lava boulders forming a quasi-protected pool. The sand only extends a little way into the water, giving way to a lining of lava stones, so you'll be grateful for those cheap reef shoes you brought with you. These same shallow stones also capture some of the sun's heat, making the water a little warmer here. A REAL GEM for people terrified of the ocean, as well as little crumb-crunchers, hence the name. Check conditions first. On Hoona (loop) Road off Lawa'i Road. See map on page 74.

If high surf is rockin' at other beaches, Baby Beach near Po'ipu usually provides a calm respite.

❖ PK's

Named after the Prince Kuhio monument across the street on Lawa'i Road. Almost no sand and entry can be awkward, but snorkeling is good at times. Also used for SNUBA and SCUBA.

❖ Lawa'i Beach/Beach House

This tiny pocket of sand next to the Beach House Restaurant nearly disappears at high tide. The snorkeling in front of the restaurant is great, but the water is subject to currents during periods of high surf and needs to be respected. At other times it can be calm and a good place for the less-experienced snorkeler. SNUBA (not SCUBA) is also done here. Just stay near the shore around the restaurant.

❖ Keiki Cove

A minuscule pocket of sand just past Lawa'i Beach where the road almost clips the ocean. (A break in the wall hides stairs.) It's usually protected and an excellent place to let rug-rats experience the ocean, but check it yourself first.

❖ Lawa'i Bay

Access is the problem here. There's no way to get here by land without crossing private property. But you can kayak here from Kukui'ula Harbor only a mile to the east. The beach is in a particularly lovely setting, backed by the National Tropical Botanical Garden. If you visit the beach, you're not allowed to venture into the private garden.

❖ Palama Beach

The only way to get to this beach is to take Kaua'i Coffee's dirt road past the 4 mile marker on Po'ipu Road. From there, take one of the feeder roads to the beach. (The feeder road is on the map, but the gate's probably locked.) All this requires permission from Kaua'i Coffee, which they probably won't give. If you're still with me, the beach is quiet and nearly always deserted.

WEST SHORE BEACHES

There aren't a lot of listings under West Shore Beaches. That's because it's almost *all beach*.

❖ Glass Beach

If someone told you that you gotta check out the beach near an old dump, would you believe them? Then if they said the reason to check it out was because stuff from the dump washes ashore, would you go? Well... you should. Glass Beach makes a rotten first impression. It's in the industrial part of 'Ele'ele backed by huge, ugly tanks full of gasoline. Add to that millions of pieces of broken glass, washed in from broken bottles and auto glass. The result? A colorful tapestry of sand and multicolored glass. (Come to think of it, doesn't glass *come* from sand?) This isn't a beach to frolic at or swim in. It's a good strolling beach, especially if you want to tie in a visit here with a hike along the Swiss cheese-type of lava farther east. That hike is described on page 158. The amount of glass varies with tides and surf—sometimes there's almost none here or ultra-fine; sometimes it's everywhere. Please don't take any of the glass litter. (Now *there's* a bizarre statement if taken out of context.) To get to Glass Beach, drive toward Hanapepe, turn left on Waialo Road going toward Port Allen. Before the ocean, go left on Aka Ula until it's dirt. Then take a right in the dirt and park at the beach. A 20 minute or so walk further east leads to **Wahi-awa Beach**, a dark sand beach where tour boats sometimes moor for lunch and kayaks visit in the winter. See map on page 85.

Two lovers live their sunset dream at a west side beach.

❖ Salt Pond Beach Park

This area is distinguished in that it has the only natural salt ponds in Hawai'i still used to make salt. Seawater is pumped into containers and allowed to evaporate. More water is added, and then it is transferred to shallower pans. The process is repeated until the water is loaded with salt. This is allowed to evaporate completely, leaving crystallized salt behind. (Excellent in kalua pig.) During the summer you'll likely see people practicing this process. The nearby park and its facilities are a popular place for locals to bring their families. The beach is separated by two rocky points. A natural ridge of rock runs between the two points, creating an area of relative calm inside. Swimming is usually safe, and children play in the semi-protected ocean water. The exception is during periods of high surf, which can make it unsafe. In Hanapepe past the 17 mile marker off Lele Road. Usually windy, especially in the afternoon. Camping with county permit, full facilities and lots of wild cats.

❖ Pakala Beach

Those cars you might see parked on the side of the road shortly after the 21 mile marker belong to surfers carrying their boards to a very famous surfing site also known as **Infinities**, so named because the ride seems to last forever. The water is murky and only used for expert surfing.

❖ Lucy Wright Beach Park

Lucy Wright was a prominent member of the Waimea community when she died in 1931. It is a testament to how the townsfolk felt about her that the beach was named in her honor, especially in light of the more historic event that happened here. For it was at this spot that Captain James Cook first set foot in the Hawaiian Islands in January 1778. The beach itself is not a particularly good beach. The Waimea River mouth is nearby, and the silty water is less enticing than clear waters elsewhere. Some guidebooks label this a black sand beach, like the black sand beaches on the Big Island or Maui. That's not quite accurate. Though there *is* lots of black sand here—flecks of lava along with a green stone called olivine chipped from the river bed by the Waimea River—much of the "black sand" is simply fine sediment carried by the same river. Camping by county permit, though we noticed lots of illegal long-term campers at press time. Across the river are the remains of the

Part of the longest beach on the island, Polihale is the ultimate beach stroll.

Russian Fort called Fort Elizabeth State Historic Park. For more information on the fort, see page 85. The best part of the beach is watching the interplay of the ocean and river mouth, described on page 86. Full facilities.

❖ Polihale

A REAL GEM

This area consists of more than 15 *miles* of uninterrupted sand beach. There are three regions, called **Kekaha Beach Park**, **Pacific Missile Range Facility** and **Polihale State Park**. Except for a few small areas, the entire stretch is unprotected, which means it is exposed to the ocean's force. During periods of high surf, waves can travel up the beach and pull you in, so be wary. When the seas are calm, you might enjoy the water. The sand can get pretty hot out on this side—hot enough to fry your feet, so watch it. Take water with you. It's available only at Kekaha Beach Park and at the other end at Polihale State Park.

Kekaha Beach Park is the first region you encounter. High surf generates a particularly powerful rip current and waves can be unbelievably strong; stay out or ask the lifeguard unless the water is real calm.

Past Kekaha is one of the least appreciated (and used) stretches of beach on the island. **Kokole Point** marks the beginning of PMRF (below). The dirt road ⅔ past the 27 mile marker leads to the shoreline. 4WD drivers should read the part about driving on sand under the Polihale description below if you want to drive on the beach. At the beach here you can often walk for a mile (especially to the west) and not find a soul. Ni'ihau seems so close from here. There's no shade, and the same swimming warnings apply as Kekaha Beach Park. But it's a great place to enjoy a wide, sandy beach and an awesome place for a late afternoon BBQ.

Pacific Missile Range Facility (PMRF) is operated by the U.S. Navy. It is here that they train for ASW or Anti Submarine Warfare. They also conduct "Star Wars" missile tests here. Since the Sept. 11th attacks, the access situation has changed. You need to apply for a background check and pass, which takes 3 weeks. The beach on the northern part (adjacent to Polihale State Park) is **Barking Sands Beach**. If conditions are right, the sand dune (which has numerous kiawe trees) is supposed to make a barking sound with your every step. The likely cause is a combination of uniform grain size coupled with a thin coating of silica that sticks when dry. Don't feel bad if it doesn't happen. We've jumped up and down like idiots on that sand until we're blue in the face, and we haven't even gotten it to whine. The sand needs to be *real* dry. Local legend has it that the barking sound comes from nine dogs buried in the sand. They belonged to their master, a fisherman, in the days when dogs didn't bark. (Sometimes I wish those were *still* the days.) One day, they started acting antsy as the master tied them up before he went fishing. While he was out, a storm broke and forced him off course. A god gave the dogs the power to bark so they could guide their master home. Unfortunately, the dogs were so fearful waiting for their master that they ran around the stakes they were tied to. Around and around and around they ran until they buried themselves in the sand. The fisherman was depressed when he returned and couldn't find his dogs. He would go down to the shore every day looking for them, but he never found them. The dogs remain there to this day, barking for their master, hoping he will find them. (My neighbor's dog seems to bark for the same reason.)

Polihale State Park is the end of the line. You can't go any farther north on this part of the island without a boat. This is where the Na Pali Coast starts. Rain is rare in these parts. On the few occasions that it does rain hard, the road can get pretty sloppy. Other times potholes might slow you down, but regular cars can almost always make it. The sand can get *real* hot in the summer. The four facility areas here tend to be poorly maintained but include showers, restrooms, picnic tables and drinking water (which you'll need).

The dunes of Polihale are famous throughout the islands. The beach averages 300 feet wide, and the dunes can get up to 100 feet high. Walking down a dune like that can be fun; walking up is a monster. Better to walk around unless you are training for the *Ironman Triathlon*. Locals drive their 4WD vehicles right onto the beach. If you try it, be aware that you are a *long* way from Lihu'e. The first thing a tow truck driver will probably ask you is, "Do you own your own home?" It's probably cheaper to buy a new car. And AAA won't tow a *stuck* car, only one that won't start, so yank an important-looking wire before you call them. Remember the 4WD drive trick to driving on sand is to have low air pressure in your tires (15 psi is what we use), be gentle on the gas and *don't stop* in soft sand; let your momentum carry you. A cheap air pump from Wal-Mart that plugs into the cigarette lighter can refill the air. Even with all that, it's still possible to get stuck. Consider taking the carpet out of the trunk and driving on it if you're stuck.

To get there, take Hwy 50 till it ends, veering right at the fork. (See map on page 84.) The first dirt road leads $3^{2}/_{10}$ miles to a large monkeypod tree. To the left is **Queen's Pond**. This is the one part of Polihale that often offers safe swimming. It is partially protected by a small fringing reef, and the swimming inside the reef is good except during periods of high surf.

If you go to the right at the monkeypod tree, there's a soft sandy spot in the road $4^{1}/_{2}$ miles from where you left the pavement. If you drive past it *(don't stop in the sand),* look for the large parking lot on your left with three small pavilions and restrooms. You'll be able to fall out of your car onto the sand.

Beaches along **Na Pali** are not reachable unless you're up for an adventure. That's why they are described in the ADVENTURES chapter.

Wet, warm and happy. Life is good...

If you want more from your Kaua'i vacation than a suntan, Kaua'i offers a multitude of activities that will keep you happy and busy. Among the more popular activities are helicopter tours, ocean tours of Na Pali, golfing, hiking, SCUBA diving and kayaking. You will find lots more to do here as well.

We've listed the activities here in alphabetical order. Beware of false claims on brochures. We've seen many fake scenes in some brochure racks. Computers have allowed photo manipulation to imply realities that don't exist (which *we* don't do).

Activities can be booked directly with the companies themselves. Ask them if they have any coupons floating around in the free publications or if there is a discount for booking direct. You can also book through **activity brokers** and **booths**, which are numerous and usually have signs such as FREE MAPS or ISLAND INFORMATION. Allow me to translate: The word FREE usually means I WANT TO SELL YOU SOMETHING.

What we're about to tell you has gotten this book pulled from some shops and badmouthed in some circles, but the truth's the truth. Their objective, as is the case with many concierges, is to sell you activities for a commission. *Occasionally,* you can get better deals through activity booths or your concierge, but not often, because 25–30 percent of what you're paying is their commission (which they call a "deposit") for making the phone call. That's why calling direct can sometimes save money. Companies are so happy they don't have to give away ¼ to ⅓ of their fee to activity booths, they'll sometimes give you a discount.

Many of the activity booths strewn about the island are actually forums for selling timeshares. We are not taking a shot at timeshares. It's just that you need to know the real purpose of some of these booths. They can be very aggressive, especially with so many timeshares on the market. (To use a wilderness analogy— they are the hunters; you are the hunted. Don't let them see the fear in your eyes.)

Selling activities has become a *big* business on Kaua'i, and it's important to know *why* they're pitching a certain company. If an activity booth or desk steers you to XYZ helicopter company and assures you that it's the best, that's fine, but consider the source. That's usually the company that the booth gets the *biggest commission* from. We check up on these booths frequently. Some are reputable and honest, and some are outrageous liars. Few activity sellers have ever done any of the activities unless they got it *free* and the company *knew* who they were. On the other hand, we *pay* for everything we do and review activities *anonymously*. We have no stake in *any* activity company we recommend, and we receive *no* commission. We just want to steer you in the best direction we can. If you know who you want to go with (because you read our reviews and decided for yourself), call them direct first.

A Warning: Many of the companies listed have a 24-hour cancellation policy. Even if the weather causes you (not them) to cancel the morning of your activity, *you will be charged*. Some credit card companies will back you in a dispute if the 24-hour policy is posted, some won't. Fair? Maybe not. But that's the way it is.

Lastly, consider booking by e-mail before you come. Good companies can fill up in advance, and the Web can pave the way for your activities. Our site at **www.wizardpub.com** has links to *every* company listed here that has a site, even the ones we recommend *against*.

ATVs (also called quads) can be a fun way of seeing the back country. They are like Tonka Toys on steroids with knobby tires. The two companies here offer *very* different experiences.

Kipu Ranch Adventures (246–9288) is our favorite. The scenery is much nicer than Kaua'i ATV (below) and their guides are better and will stop often to narrate. Their tour is of Kipu Ranch, a *very* beautiful ranch. In the 3-hour tour ($125), you're treated to the lump-in-your-throat backdrop of Ha'upu Range along the pastures. They'll descend into woodsier areas, along a stream and usually end up at a viewpoint almost no one on Kaua'i *ever* gets to see—the hidden valley and beach of Kipu Kai from the road that drapes across the mountain. (Because it's private and closed, we *never* thought we'd get to see this sight.) The 4-hour tour ($150) omits that grand view of Kipu Kai but visits two small waterfalls. They use big bikes and run their tours well. You won't be allowed to totally cut loose on your bike, if that's what you're aiming for, and their average moving speed is slower. It's a tour, and you *will* get dusty or muddy. But it's a fun way to see exceptional scenery.

On the other hand, **Kaua'i ATV** (742–2734) in Koloa is the exact opposite in almost every way. They lack the good views of Kipu Ranch and instead concentrate on the thrill of riding an ATV. The average moving speed is 15 MPH and you may reach 25 MPH at times; it depends on the guide. Some guides might give you more freedom to cut loose; others might be stern taskmasters who keep you on a short leash and get on your nerves with their nastiness. If you get one of them, you'll hate the whole experience. Get the right guide and it can be a hoot for those who like busting loose. If it's been raining, you're encouraged to crash through every puddle. During dry times, it's pretty dusty. Either way you'll get dirty. They almost never cancel due to weather. Groups are bigger (up to 20), and lunch is simple sandwiches. Service is scant if not downright surly at the baseyard. If it's pouring rain and you ask for a jacket, you're likely to be indifferently told you "should have bought a poncho back at the store." And the helmets are disgusting, with no obvi-

ous effort that we saw to clean them from the previous riders. (Bring a bandanna or buy one from their shop.) Their playground is mostly old sugar cane roads plus two stops at small waterfalls and a cool trip through a ½ mile-long tunnel. Two- and four-person mud buggys (which are a blast) are also available in addition to the ATVs which set the pace. Narrations are minimal, which is good, because when they *do* talk, the information is often inaccurate. The waterfall tour is $155. It's $125 for the shorter tour.

BIKING

Bike lanes or shoulders of some kind line the main highway from Princeville all the way around to Mana on the west

Beachside biking along the east shore.

side (though some are narrow in spots, and some bridges force you into the traffic). Past Princeville, forget it.

For mountain biking, the dirt roads in **Po'ipu**, especially near **Maha'ulepu,** can be fun, though a bit dusty. Another good place is the cane road between **Kealia Beach** and **Anahola.** (Start at Kealia Beach and pedal north.) The **Kuilau** and **Moalepe Trails** can be exciting. (Described under HIKING on page 153.) The roads past the end of **Kuamo'o Road** in Kapa'a leading toward Wai'ale'ale and the **Jungle Hike** described on page 153 are excellent for mountain bikes.

If you don't mind a long drive, the roads of Koke'e offer good choices. See the Koke'e map on page 140 and the west side map on page 84. Pay attention to **Mohihi-Camp 10 Road** on the Koke'e map, and the roads on the west (ocean) side of Waimea Canyon Drive starting from near the 11 and 13 mile markers on the west side map. The latter offer marvelous opportunities. The **contour road** is always fun. You can even travel down the spine of some of the ridges, such as Ka-uhao and Ka'awe-iki, if you have the stones to pedal back up. The ADVENTURES chapter has a bike/hike combo.

If you're interested in renting a mountain bike, call any of these companies: **Kaua'i Cycle** (821–2115) in Kapa'a, the friendliest bike shop on the island; **Outfitters Kaua'i** (742–9667) in Po'ipu and **Pedal 'n Paddle** (826–9069), beach cruisers and hybrids only, in Hanalei. You'll pay $12–$45 per day. Bikes with shocks are better but more expensive.

If you just want to go downhill, road trips down Waimea Canyon Drive are available. They're fun but pretty short. With **Bicycle Downhill/Outfitters Kaua'i** (742–9667) you meet at 6 a.m. or 2:30

p.m. in Po'ipu, then drive up to the canyon in their van. Near the 12 mile marker you get out and coast downhill almost the entire way on 550 and 552, ending up in Kekaha before noon. $98. (Interestingly, one of their ads says "100% downhill" but shows a woman riding *uphill!!)*

Kaua'i is in the process of spending 50 million federal dollars to construct a shoreline walking/biking path from Nawiliwili to Anahola, scheduled to be completed when Paris Hilton draws her first social security check. Currently the only completed section is the 5-mile section from Kapa'a to just north of Donkey Beach. The northern section is the prettiest, and the smooth concrete path is easy to ride on beach cruisers. Two shops in Kapa'a rent them. **Coconut Coasters** (822–7368) is near the north end of town and has the newest bikes. **Hele On Kaua'i** (822–4628) is a stand next to Roxy Square with a smaller selection. It's $10–$45 for the day, and both have tandems available.

Boogie boarding (riders are derisively referred to as *spongers* by surfers) is where you ride a wave on what is essentially a sawed-off surfboard. It can be a real blast. You need short, stubby fins to catch bigger waves (which break in deeper water), but you can snare small waves by simply standing in shallow water and lurching forward as the wave is breaking. If you've never done it before, stay away from big waves; they can drill you. Smooth-bottom (hard shell) boards work best. If you're not going to boogie board with boogie fins (which some consider difficult to learn), you should do it with reef shoes or some other kind of water footwear. This allows you to scramble around in the water without fear of tearing your feet up on a rock or urchin. Shirts are *very* important, especially for men. (Women already have this aspect covered.) Sand and the board itself can rub you so raw your *da kines* will glow in the dark.

Your hotel activity desk may have boards. It should cost you $5–$8 per day, $15–$30 per week. Other places include:

North Shore—Hanalei Surf Co. (826–9000), **Kayak Kaua'i** (826–9844) or **Pedal 'n Paddle** (826–9069).

East Shore—Kayak Kaua'i (826–9844) and **Boss Frog** (822–4334).

South Shore—Seasport Divers (742–9303) in Po'ipu, **Progressive Expressions** (742–6041) in Koloa or **Nukumoi Beach & Surf Shop** (742–8019) across from Po'ipu Beach.

Below are some beaches worth considering. Also check the BEACHES chapter.

- **Kealia Beach** in Kapa'a is excellent, but the waves are powerful.
- **Kalapaki Beach** in Lihu'e is a smart choice for beginners and the timid.
- **Brennecke Beach** has returned to its former glory. (For a decade it was poor after being chewed up by a hurricane.)

Keiki shreddin 'em.

CAMPING

The ultimate in low-price lodging is offered by Mother Nature herself. Kaua'i is a great place to camp with 13 different areas—six state camping areas and seven county campsites. See map on next page. To camp at a state-controlled site, you need to contact the **Hawai'i DLNR, State Parks** at 3060 Eiwa St., #306, Lihu'e, HI 96766, (808) 274–3444. (Our Web site has a link to a page where permit applications are downloadable.) You are *strongly* advised to get your permit before you arrive because the sites can fill up, especially during peak season (May–December). The state requires that you send a copy of the driver's license or passport of *every* adult who will be camping, as well as the names of any minors, along with your dates of travel. The permits are $5 per group per night (except Na Pali, which is $10 *per person*) and should be acquired as far in advance as you can. They recommend at least six months in advance during the busy months. *More* for Na Pali.

The state enforces permits with uncommon zeal, so when officers swoop in to check your permits, stand at attention and wipe that smile off your face.

For more on beach campsites see BEACHES chapter.

County sites require a county permit. They will send you an application or you can do it online. The cost is $3 per adult per night. Call:

County of Kaua'i Parks & Recreation
4444 Rice St. #150
Lihu'e, HI 96766
(808) 241–4463

Camping Sites—County Sites in Black, State Sites in Purple.

Haena Beach Park
Hanakapi'ai
Hanakoa
Kalalau State Park
Miloli'i State Park
Koke'e State Park
Polihale State Park
Hanalei (Black Pot Beach)
'Anini Beach Park
Anahola Beach Park
Hanama'ulu Beach Park
Lucy Wright Park
Salt Pond Beach Park

The county also has regional neighborhood offices for permits. Call for the nearest location.

Car camping from 4WDs at Koke'e State Park is lovely—especially Sugi Grove—and is convenient if you plan to hike much there.

If you need to rent camping or hiking gear, your best sources will be **Pedal 'n Paddle** (826–9069) in Hanalei or **Kayak Kaua'i** (826–9844) also in Hanalei.

Propane can be found at **Kmart** or **Wal-Mart** in Lihu'e. For white gas or butane call **Gaspro** (245–6766) in Lihu'e, **Waipouli Variety** and **Da Life**.

Good places to buy gear include: **Da Life** (742–2734) in Koloa, **Pedal 'n Paddle** (826–9069) in Hanalei, **Waipouli Variety** (822–1014) in Kapa'a and **Discount Variety** (742–9393) in Koloa. Others are **Wal-Mart**, **Kmart** and **Costco** in Lihu'e and **Cost-U-Less** in Kapa'a for food.

Kaua'i's waters contain abundant fish. Of course, it's one thing to have 'em and another thing to catch 'em. Whether you want to go deep sea fishing, sit by a lake or cast off a cliff, you will be pleased to know that all are available on Kaua'i.

Deep Sea Fishing

If deep sea fishing's your game, there are several charter companies around. They all provide the necessary gear. Tuna, wahoo (ono) and marlin, among others, are all caught in these waters. The seas around the islands can be rough if you're not used to it, and it's fairly common for someone ·on board (maybe you) to spend the trip feeding the fish. We advise that you take Dramamine or Bonine *before you leave.* Scopolamine patches work well but have side effects that can temporarily affect vision. (It can make close-up vision poor for a week.) Other alternatives may be available. See your doctor. (I've always wanted to say that.) Some people feel that greasy foods or citrus before or during your trip is a no-no; *many* swear by ginger tablets. Some seriously suggest putting a cherry seed in your bellybutton. (And hope the fish don't laugh at you.)

Most boats troll nonstop since the lure darting out of the water simulates a panicky bait fish—the favored meal for large game fish. On some boats, each person is assigned a certain reel. Experienced anglers usually vie for corner poles on the assumption that strikes coming from the sides are more likely to hit corners first.

You should know in advance that in Hawai'i, the fish belongs to the boat. What happens to the fish is entirely up to the captain, and he'll usually keep it. You may catch a 1,000-pound marlin and be told that you can't have as much as a steak from it. If this bothers you, you're out of luck. If the ono or another *relatively* small fish are striking a lot and there is a glut of them, you might be allowed to keep it—or half of it. You *may* be able to make arrangements in advance to the contrary.

Before deciding *who* to go with, decide if conditions warrant going at all. It might be calm on one side of the island and rough on another. Current ocean conditions can be obtained by calling the **National Weather Service** (245–6001) for weather, for **Hawaiian Waters Forecast** (245–3564).

Reputable charter companies are:

West Shore Charters

Na Pali Sportfishing (635–9424) has a 35-foot power cat and is based out of Kikiaola Harbor near Waimea. They are slightly cheaper than other charters, but they like to set sail at 6 a.m., which can be hard to do if you're staying in Princeville. $130 for a half day. They'll also fish off Ni'ihau for a 10-hour private charter.

Na Pali Explorer (338–9999) has half-day shared charters for $145 on a 41-foot Concorde.

We've had astonishingly bad experiences with **Deep Sea Fishing Kaua'i** (634–8589).

East Shore Charters

Hawaiian Style Fishing (635–7335) has 25-foot boat that goes out of Kapa'a. Unlike most boats there's no deckhand, so it'll be a bit more hands-on (literally). If the trolling's not working, they'll bottom feed. A good, flexible outfit. $125 for a half day.

Leaving from Nawiliwili Harbor, **Lahela Sportfishing** (635–4020) uses a 34-foot Radon. They do mostly private charters with 14 people max and allow you to take all of the catch if you like. *Shared* charters are expensive at $219 because they only take 4 anglers.

Kai Bear (652–4556) has a 38-foot and a 42-foot Bertram. Their new motto is, "We do sportfishing for the discriminating big game fisherman." Sounds a little snooty for cheap beer and fish guts. Half day is $159; deluxe is $239. Half day private is $795.

Freshwater Fishing

There are dozens of lakes (actually manmade reservoirs) strewn throughout the island. Largemouth bass are plentiful. You'll also find smallmouth bass and a tough-fighting South American import called tucunare or peacock bass. Avoid fishing when the water is real muddy after a heavy rain; fish won't bite.

The **Pu'u Lua Reservoir** in Koke'e (on the west side, see map on page 84), as well as several feeding streams, are stocked yearly with rainbow trout finger-lings. Lake waters are too warm for trout to spawn. Trout season in Koke'e is restricted to the first Saturday in August, then 16 consecutive days, then weekends and holidays until the end of September. (Subtract from this the square root of *pi*, and the result is your birthday.)

Division of Aquatic Resources, Department of Land and Natural Resources (274–3344) can fill in any additional blanks you may have.

Companies that do guided freshwater fishing trips: **Cast & Catch** (332–9707).

Places to obtain licenses are: **Lihu'e Fishing Supply** (245–4930) in Lihu'e and **Waipouli Variety** (822–1014) in Kapa'a. Squid and shrimp can be obtained from most supermarkets.

GOLFING

With its bountiful nightly rainfall and warm, sunny days, Kaua'i is a perfect environment for golf. Its nine golf courses are diverse, ranging from a wealthy sugar magnate's private course donated to the island, to a world-class resort course rated #1 in the all the islands by *Golf Digest*. If golf is your game, Kaua'i is sure to please.

The prices described under Fees in the table (below) reflect the highest category of fees. Check the specific course descriptions below for more information and possible discounts. Many have additional twilight specials.

If you're an avid golfer, Princeville, Kaua'i Lagoons and Po'ipu Bay have teamed up to offer the **Kaua'i Challenge**

Course	Par	Yards	Rating	Fees
Kaua'i Lagoons Golf Course 72		6707	72.2	$175*
Kiahuna 70		6234	70.3	$95*
Kukuiolono (9 hole x 2) 72		6154	70.0	$9
Po'ipu Bay Resort 72		6127	69.5	$220*
Princeville Resort Kaua'i:				
Makai Course 72		6306	70.5	$175*
Prince Course 72		6521	72.1	$200*
Puakea Course 72		6471	71.0	$99*
Wailua Municipal Course 72		6585	71.3	$60–$70

* Indicates power cart included in fee.

for $390. When you buy your first round at any one, ask for it by name and you'll get vouchers to play the other two, saving almost $200.

Princeville Resort Kaua'i:
The Makai Course (826–3581)

Designed by Robert Trent Jones, Jr. and first opened in 1972, the **Makai Course** consists of 3 sets of 9 holes called the **Ocean,** the **Lakes** and the **Woods.** For 18 holes you get your choice of two, with **Ocean/Lakes** being the most popular. The **Woods** course has a windy reputation. The **Lakes** offers an impressive 9, with holes 3–7 commanding outstanding views. Hole 9 requires a buttery touch as it shoots over the water onto a small green located just behind it. The **Ocean** is the most challenging and interesting of the three, as well as the longest. The 6th and 7th holes offer dramatic views of the north shore coastline from the edge of a steep cliff. In fact, hole 7 shoots across a menacing gorge.

Located off Highway 56 inside Princeville; see map on page 49. Fees are $175 for standard, $140 if you're staying at the St. Regis Resort. Kama-'aina rate is $55. Carts are included. Walking is allowed, but you pay for a cart anyway. Note: The proper golf attire rule is more rigidly enforced at Princeville courses.

Princeville Resort Kaua'i:
The Prince Course (826–5070)

Now you've reached golfing nirvana. This course is often rated #1 in all the islands by *Golf Digest*, and for good reason. With 390 gorgeous acres to work with, Robert Trent Jones, Jr. took full advantage of the cliffs, gorges and natural rolling scenery. When it opened

in 1990, the Prince Course was hailed by *Golf Digest* as the best new resort course in the country. Since then, it has become known throughout Hawai'i as one of the most challenging and rewarding courses one can play, usually rated as the best in the state. The design stresses unobstructed expansiveness, with the rolling topography and deep gorges serving as the main hazards and obstacles. There are 9 miles of cart paths, and the layout allows for considerable room between holes. Hole 6 offers a delightful march toward the ocean cliffs. At hole 7, you must shoot over a gorge onto a narrow finger of land containing the green and little else. The 13th green is accompanied by a charming waterfall coming out of a hole in the mountain. You won't find a lot of flat areas on this course, but you will find tough, challenging, world-class golfing. In fact, if you're *really* into self-flagellation (*hey,* getting pretty personal, aren't we?), the black tees measure a whopping 7,309 yards with a rating of 75.2. If it's your first time here, the $5 course guide is handy to have. The clubhouse is spectacular (except for the restaurant). If you've never played golf before, this probably isn't the course on which to learn. But if you have a little experience and don't mind being humbled a bit, this course can't be beat. One thing to note: The overabundance of rain here is actually *bad* for the grass. Don't expect manicured fairways. They tend to keep grasses long and since it can be muddy, they are quick to inforce the 90° rule and might even prevent you from driving some fairways, which makes for a long game. Come for the scenery and layout, not for the grass.

Located just before Princeville off Hwy 56; see map on page 46. Fees are

$200 for standard, $155 if you are staying in Princeville, $140 if you're staying at the St. Regis Resort and $70 for kama'ainas.

Wailua Municipal Course (241–6666)

At one time this course was rated the best *municipal* course in Hawai'i and one of the best in the United States. Although it certainly has fallen from its once vaulted position, today Wailua still rates as a pretty good municipal course with a great location.

As it parallels the beach on Kaua'i's Coconut Coast, Wailua constantly reminds you that you are near the ocean. The smell of sea air, the constant crosswind and the roar of the surf are all comforting companions, making this course extremely popular with locals. (The $15–$20 kama'aina rates might also be a factor). Weekends are very busy; Tuesday and Thursday are slowest. While the course is long, there are relatively few hazards, making it a leisurely course. Wind is always a consideration here. Hole 17 requires restraint, lest you drive it into the sand (the *real* sand and its accompanying surf). The locker room and other facilities are no-frills. Singles are paired up. Rates are $60 on weekdays, $70 on weekends (plus $18 for the optional cart, $6 for a push cart). A five-round pass is $275. Club rentals start at $32. (Credit cards for club rental only.)

Kaua'i Lagoons
(241–6000 or 800–634–6400)

This is a moving target. Formerly two separate 18-hole courses called the Mokihana and the Kiele, Jack Nicklaus and the resort owners were tearing out holes, building new ones and overall making things difficult for us poor guidebook writers. Things are in flux until sometime in 2010, when this will emerge as three separate groups of nine. In the mean-

For those who venture off the fairway here at Po'ipu, we have some advice: Take the stroke.

time, you can still play 18 holes; we're just not sure which ones.

Located at Kaua'i Lagoons, take the Rice Street entrance and proceed past the hotel. Fees are $175 with discounts if you are staying at one of several resorts. (For example, Marriott customers pay $115.) Kama'aina rates are $60. Carts are included in the price and are mandatory. Price drops to $125 at noon.

Puakea Golf Course (245–8756)

This is the island's newest course, and it's in great shape. Fairways are spaced fairly far apart, but the course tends to be pretty windy. You don't have many ocean views, but nearby Ha'upu Mountain makes a very pretty backdrop. Hole 3 requires some restraint. Go for the green and you'll simply get wet. Use your 3 wood and come up short of the water, and you'll live to shoot another day. And stay to the left at hole 8, or you'll be presented with a posse of bunkers lined up with their mouths open to arrest you.

In all, Puakea is a fun and moderately difficult course. Located behind Kukui Grove Shopping Center; see map on page 65. Fees are $99 for the general public, and the kama'aina rate is $50. Carts included in price and mandatory. Collared shirts required. Club rental available for $40, and they have surprisingly nice clubs for rentals.

Po'ipu Bay Resort–Hyatt (742–8711)

With its location on the "sunny south shore," **Po'ipu Bay Resort** is a sprawling 210 acres of wide-open golfing. In fact, if it has a flaw, it's that it is *too* wide open. Even course personnel privately mumble about a dearth of hazards. But this nitpicking aside, **Po'ipu Bay Resort** offers spectacular scenery, impeccable grooming and attention to detail. (They like to brag that they imported their bunker sand from Australia and Idaho.) Designed by (here he is again) Robert Trent Jones, Jr., our only real complaint is that the grass in the rough is allowed to get too soft and shaggy. If you roll just slightly off the fairway, even when you see where it went, it's easy to lose your ball unless you step on it. (Go ahead...say it: *If I shot better, I wouldn't* be *in the rough*. Ooo, that hurts.) The links style course is nicely designed with particularly smashing views from holes 15–17. Look for turtles in the water when you're near the heiau (an ancient Hawaiian structure) on hole 16. During winter months you might even see whales off the coast. The course is not as challenging as Princeville's Prince Course (but it can be windier), and players less comfortable with the game will enjoy it as much as the more advanced. Collared golf shirts are requested. They have GPS distance locators in the golf carts—which is cool—but we're uncertain as to their accuracy. We found we could drive carts to within 15 yards of a hole, yet the locator would indicate 40 or 50 yards to go.

Located off Po'ipu Road (520); see map on page 75. Fees are $220 for the general public, $150 for Hyatt guests and a kama'aina rate of $68. Carts are included in the price and are mandatory. At noon price drops to $135. By the way, so you don't go blind looking for it, there *is* no such place as Po'ipu Bay.

Kiahuna Golf Club (742–9595)

Another Robert Trent Jones, Jr. design, this course has been renovated by its new owners and is in the best shape we've seen it. The greens are fast and the fairways manicured. Holes 3 and 7 share a water hazard and a green, so be sure to shoot for the correct pin. The back nine has five left doglegs, the biggest being at 15. At 495 yards from the blues, you have to play short to set up the second shot. Drive too far and you'll have to contend with a Saharan-sized trap to the right of the green. Rock walls and rock gardens dot the course and will devour your balls.

Homes are being constructed all around the course, detracting from the natural beauty and ocean views are scarce. (The mauka views are better.) But the nice range conditions and price (half that at Po'ipu Bay) make it tempting. Behind the Poipu Shopping Village along Kiahuna Plantation Drive. Standard fees are $95. Carts are included and have GPS that is fairly accurate. Kama'aina rate is $45. Club rentals are $50 for Pings.

Kukuiolono Golf Course (332–9151)

In 1919, sugar magnate Walter Mc-Bryde donated his personal 9-hole golf course and some surrounding land to the people of Kaua'i. This land, complete with a trust, has been cherished by Kaua'i residents ever since. To get into the park, you pass through a magnificent metal gate with lava stone pillars. Once inside, the personal nature of the course is apparent. The links are not as lavish as others on the island; its location in Kalaheo does not afford it much rainfall, and the maintenance budget is not in the same league as the big boys. And it was not designed by Robert Trent Jones, Jr.; in fact, they don't know *who* designed it. But this course might leave you with a smile. They even sell bird seed to feed the ubiquitous tame chickens. The price can't be

touched. $9 *per day* with power carts costing $9 and pull carts $3 per nine holes. Club rental for $9 are available, but check in advance. Course personnel can be snotty and unprofessional, but don't let it get to you. It's the course that's the star here. If you're playing 18 holes, play from the blue tees for the back nine—6,154 yards of pleasant, easy-going golf. Especially good for beginners since there aren't many hazards. If you want to personally thank Mr. McBryde, you'll find him buried near the 8th tee in the middle of his lovely and cherished Japanese garden. This charming garden is worth a look, and local weddings occur here almost every weekend.

Open to everyone, this course is located $^8/_{10}$ of a mile from Hwy 50 on Papalina Road (the only stoplight in Kalaheo). From Papalina look for a gate on your right. No advance tee times.

First, I need to get something out of the way. Flying a powered hang glider (known as a trike) is different than any other type of aircraft. When I was growing up, I used to have a recurring dream that I could flap my arms and fly like a bird. My father flew little Cessnas, which, though fun, felt more to me like a car in the air than flying like a bird. I had forgotten my flying dreams until **Birds in Paradise** (822–5309) began giving lessons in these odd-looking aircraft. I was skeptical at first. Is this for real? Is it safe? Are you *really* allowed

Flying along in a powered hang glider is as close as you'll ever get to feeling like a bird.

to do this? After checking into it a bit, I discovered that these newest generation crafts are *far* safer than they were two decades ago. As soon as my instructor and I took off, I realized that a person *really could* fly like a bird. *This* was what the flying bug felt like! I was so smitten with the craft that I eventually paid the owner to teach me, and now I fly trikes myself in addition to fixed wing airplanes. So, although I have *no* personal interest in any company teaching trikes in Hawai'i, my perspective isn't as remote as it is for most activities. After all, it's not possible to *anonymously* review Birds in Paradise because I now know the pilots. (We're all members of the small microlight community.)

With that explanation, powered hang gliding is an activity I love and recommend. Don't confuse this with hang gliding. This craft has an engine, it's bigger and more stable, and it even has a powered parachute attached to the craft…just in case (a safety feature rare on

traditional airplanes). Trikes take off and land on regular runways, and the ease and grace of the craft is glorious. (Rent the movie *Fly Away Home* if you want to see what they're like.)

Trikes have become quite a love of mine and are, in my opinion, the safest form of ultralight flight available. (I'm not a daredevil and wouldn't fly them myself if I felt unsafe in them, though any time you're in the air you're potentially at risk— even on the airlines.) I grin like a fool *every* time I fly and have never reviewed an activity that generates more enthusiastic responses from other participants. It seems that whenever I see people coming off a trike (I sometimes use the same airport that Birds in Paradise does), passengers are *frothing* at the mouth with excitement, proclaiming that it's the best thing they've ever done on vacation. (Unless they're on their honeymoon, of course; then it's the *second* best thing.)

Birds in Paradise has a camera mounted on the wing to take photos of you during the lesson at $85 extra for a DVD—just in case no one back home believes you. They often have two trikes running so couples can fly together in formation. There's a 270-pound weight limit. The cost of a half hour in-air lesson is $135. It's $215 for an hour *plus* a fuel surcharge. Expensive? Perhaps. But it's so unspeakably cool that the memories will stay with you for a lifetime.

HELICOPTERS

If ever there was a place made for helicopter exploration, it's Kauaʻi. Much of the island can be seen only by air, and helicopters, with their giant windows and their ability to hover, are by far the preferred method for most. Going to Kauaʻi without taking a helicopter flight is like going to see the Sistine Chapel and not looking up. You will see the ruggedly beautiful Na Pali Coast and marvel at the sheerness of some of its cliffs. This is an area where razor-thin, almost two-dimensional mountains rise parallel to each other, leaving impossibly tall and narrow valleys between them. You will see vertical spires and shake your head in disbelief at the sight of a goat perched on top. The awe-inspiring Waimea Canyon unfolds beneath you. A good pilot will come up over a ridge, suddenly exposing the glorious canyon, often timed to coincide with a crescendo in the music you hear in your headphones. You will see the incredible Olokele Valley with its jagged twists and turns and stair-step waterfalls. It is impossible to keep track of all the waterfalls you will see on your flight. You will get a different view of Kauaʻi's fabulous north shore beaches and reefs. You might see whales, depending on the time of year. And best of all, you will be treated to the almost spiritual splendor of

Na Pali by air is like no other place in the world.

Wai'ale'ale Crater. You have never seen anything like the crater—a three-sided wall of waterfalls 3,000 feet high, greens of every imaginable shade and a lushness that is beyond comprehension. Many people find themselves weeping when they enter the crater. Others find that they stop breathing—it happened to me the first time. If it has been dry lately, it's simply great; if it's been "pumping," it is spectacular.

When you are finished with the flight, you will either be speechless or babble like a fool—it happens to everyone.

Bear in mind that we're not rabidly pro-helicopter statewide. In our Maui book, *Maui Revealed*, we were lukewarm on flights there (fearing a bang-for-your-buck deficit). O'ahu, too, doesn't lend itself well to air tours. But on Kaua'i it's absolutely worth it.

One concern you may have is safety, and that's a valid point. As far as the industry safety record is concerned, there have been crashes and "incidents," when a craft has had to make an unscheduled landing. You can ask the companies directly about safety, but you should be aware that over the years when we've tried it, we were often misled or directly lied to. Not every time, but many times.

When we checked with the FAA, we discovered that, like many things, safety evaluation isn't that simple. A company might be cited for maintenance violations—*that* sounds ominous. Then you find out that the maintenance was carried out properly, but a log was dated incorrectly, or the company didn't fill out a particular form. Should we steer you away from them for this reason?

In the end it comes down to a matter of judgment. Below is a list of companies that we feel are qualified. Not all have spotless safety records. Things happen—a warning light comes on, and they have to land immediately. Even if it was a false alarm, it is still considered an "incident." These companies struck us as honest and forthright in their concerns about safety.

One issue that all the companies have to deal with is weather. As a pilot myself, I appreciate a company that will *cancel* due to marginal weather. Setting aside the safety factor, if it's too cloudy to see much and it's dumping rain, how much will you get to see? When we don't like the weather, we call the companies to see which ones are canceling. The companies that most often fly when we wish they *wouldn't* are Air Kaua'i, Will Squyres and Inter-Island.

As far as seating is concerned, the front seat is the best. To console you, some companies might tell you otherwise when they direct you to a back seat. From the front, the island rushes at you with incredible drama. The problem is

Company	Phone #	Status	Helicopter Type	2-Way *	Departs
Blue Hawaiian	245–5800	Recommended	Eco-Star	Yes	Lihu'e
Jack Harter	245–3774	Recommended	A-Star, Hughes	Yes	Lihu'e
Inter-Island	335–5009	Qualified	Hughes	Yes	Hanapepe
Safari	246–0136	Qualified	A-Star	Yes	Lihu'e
Will Squyres	245–8881	Qualified	A-Star, Eco-Star	No	Lihu'e
Island	245–8588	Qualified	A-Star	Yes	Lihu'e
Ni'ihau	335–3500	Specialized	Agusta	No	Hanapepe

* Indicates whether craft contains a microphone for you to talk to the pilot.

that seating arrangements are made on the basis of weight. Lighter people are generally seated up front. If you are seated in the back, the **right seat** is the best since much of the action will be on the right side. (By common agreement, companies fly clockwise around the island, making Na Pali and other areas best from the right side.) Although companies won't guarantee you the *front* seat, ask them if they'll at least keep you on the *right side* of the craft and let them know you'll consider them weasels if they don't comply. Most will accommodate. If they don't, consider going elsewhere.

There are different types of helicopters. **A-Stars** seat two passengers up front and four in the back, leaving two people in the middle. Helicopter companies like these crafts since they can fly six passengers at a time. There are usually no windows to open, so glare may be a factor with your pictures. **Eco-Stars** are a roomier and more luxurious version of A-Stars. They have lots of window space, are quieter and cost more, so tours are sometimes more expensive. **Blue Hawaiian** and **Will Squyres/Sunshine** use Eco-Stars. At press time nobody was using **Bell Jet Rangers**, but it's a popular tour helicopter nationwide and one we try to avoid due to poor seating. **Hughes 500** aircraft seat two passengers in the front and two in the back, a great arrangement. The Hughes has the pilot sit on the left side, out of the way. (*Some* A-Stars like Jack Harter's do, as well.) Hughes have large, removable windows. While the back is a bit cramped and doesn't allow the forward view that other back seats do, their side views are better. Currently, only **Inter-Island** and **Jack Harter** have these because the Hughes cost more per person to operate than A-Stars. Both companies fly with

the doors off. Windy and cold in back but an awesome experience.

All helicopters on Kaua'i are allowed to fly 500 feet over most scenic areas. (Companies that claim *only* they can fly that low...are full of beans.)

This is a hard section to write. You're going to spend a lot of money, and we *really* want to point you in the right direction. Most of the companies do a pretty good job, but they're very different. (Of course, like another activity that comes to mind—*wink, wink*—even when a helicopter ride over Kaua'i is bad...it's still good.) The difference between helicopter companies is the difference between a very pleasant flight and really experiencing the island. It's the difference between coming off the craft with a pleasant smile and coming off with a stupid grin on your face that won't leave you all day—between having a tale to tell and experiencing something so moving that it will stay with you for a lifetime. All this said and done, our favorites are **Blue Hawaiian** and **Jack Harter**.

Prices

We hesitate to print the prices for helicopters these days because, with wildly fluctuating fuel prices and cutthroat competition, it's too variable. At press time it was *around* $200 per person for hour-long flights before fuel surcharges and so-called discounts. This means they like it when you book direct and avoid the commission-driven "activity booths" and some might give you a 25% discount, maybe even more if you book on the Internet. Many companies have coupons available in ads or give discounts for booking directly or online. (Just ask them.) Charter rates for the whole bird are between $1,000 and $1,900 per hour.

If you ever saw Jurassic Park, you'll remember this waterfall (real name Manawaiopuna Falls). The only other way to see it is by helicopter (unless your last name happens to be Robinson).

Recommended Companies

Blue Hawaiian (245–5800)—This is the company to go to if you want the cushiest flight. Their Eco-Stars are the most comfortable choppers on the island and the roomiest. Giant windows (with gobs of glare, too, if you're into photos) provide a great viewing area. Price *might* be a bit higher than similar A-Star tours. They make DVDs of the trip from their four on-board cameras.

Jack Harter (245–3774)—This was the guy who started it all on Kaua'i in the early '60s, and his company's tours are still in demand, so book in advance. Their A-Star layout keeps the pilot on the left side, which is good for the front seat passengers. Harter has 60–65 minute flights and an excellent comprehensive 90–95 minute flight for about $110 more. They're the only one with such a flight and the experience is relaxed and unhurried. Their narration has been super accurate in the past, but they've been a little sloppy with the facts lately. If you want a sportier trip (we think it's more fun), they also have a 4-passenger Hughes with the doors off similar to Inter-Island's without the waterfall landing. *Very* cool and great for photographers. Unlike their cheaper A-Star flights, the Hughes has no background music.

Other Qualified Companies

Inter-Island (335–5009)—The most unusual helicopter trip on the island. When you get into the Hughes helicopter from Hanapepe's Port Allen Airport (a good take-off point), the first thing you notice is that the doors are off. Now *that's* a view! During the flight they do something no one else was doing at press time—they *land* at one of several inaccessible waterfalls. (You may get a good one or you may get a boring falls.) After 45 minutes or so of frolicking in the pool and deli lunch, it's back in the chopper to finish the trip. Their route is a bit different than other operators with some impressive locations. It gets pretty cold and sometimes wet in the back, and the wind in your eyes and hair might be an annoyance (so pony-tail those long locks), but the 60+ minutes in the air and 45 on the ground provide a flight that you can't get elsewhere. While not as comfortable or cushy as the other flights, it's a fun, if pricey, adventure for about $100 more than similar flights without the landing. One thing: Your pilot might be friendly and helpful or stoic and

a bit negative, which can put a damper on the atmosphere.

Safari (246–0136)—We're not a big fan of their tours. One interesting difference, however, is that they record your entire trip from multiple on-board cameras. (It's $40 extra.) The quality may be pretty bad (we get hypnotized by watching the dirt on the camera lens moving back and forth), and frankly, we think you'd be *much* happier with a professionally made DVD, rather than one taken on the fly (so to speak). But at least you'll get to hear your voice if you asked the pilot questions. Readers have told us that they are the most accommodating to larger passengers. They also have a trip that lands at a remote canyon where you get out and listen to a lecture about the Robinson Family history and their plans. Insanely overpriced at $329.

Will Squyres (245–8881)—Owned and operated by Sunshine Helicopters, they use A-Stars and Eco-Stars (which they call Whisper-Stars). Although helicopter companies always claim that weight distribution decides who sits up front, if you pay an extra $50 (on top of the $279 for the Whisper-Star), they'll distribute your butt up front. (They call them "first class seats.")

Island Helicopters (245–8588) has standard 50–60 minute tours in their A-Stars. For $266 (check for discounts) they'll land at Manawaiopuna Falls and let you get out for photos and some area info. No swimming and people over 250 pounds may have to purchase an additional ticket.

Be wary of some of the information imparted during some of these flights, especially from bigger companies that may have pilots from the mainland with little knowledge of Kaua'i. They mean well, but often their "facts" are way off.

Helicopter Tips

- Never take a flight of less than an hour; you will only get your appetite whetted. It's too rushed.
- With a still camera, zoom lenses work best since the size of the field changes rapidly.
- Use a fast ISO speed of 200 or 400.
- Beware of the glare from the inside of the windows, and don't let your camera touch a vibrating window while shooting. Circular polarizers (which you'll have to adjust constantly) are *vital* for reducing glare. Wearing dark clothing helps, too. Polarized sunglasses help in the glare department.
- Don't get so caught up taking pictures that you lose the moment. It's hard to soak up the magic of your flight through a camera viewfinder.
- If you're in a craft that has two-way communication, don't be afraid to ask the pilot to turn so you can take a shot of something. Most will.
- If you're prone to motion sickness, take something *before* you fly.
- Remove any earrings before putting on the headphones.
- If you can't hear the pilot over the music, ask him to adjust the sound.
- If there are four or more of you, consider chartering a helicopter. It might actually be cheaper and will allow you to call many of the shots during the flight. "Pilot, please hover here for a few minutes, and turn a little more to the right." If only your group is on the flight, you are effectively chartering the flight whether you realize it or not, so take advantage of it.
- Morning is usually the best time for flights (though Na Pali looks best in the afternoon). Rainy weather brings more waterfalls.
- If you take a helicopter trip, do it early in your stay. It'll help orient you to the island.
- When you see people getting off a helicopter after their tour, try not to be downwind from them. They are often foaming at the mouth from their experience and might drool on you.

For an off-island helicopter experience, **Ni'ihau Helicopters** (335–3500), owned by the powerful Robinson family, flies groups to their privately owned island of Ni'ihau. For $385 you get a 1-hour flight, circumnavigating Ni'ihau and landing at one of its beaches for snorkeling and a picnic. The problem you encounter with them is that they require at least 5 people on a flight and don't usually have enough customers to ensure a flight for you. Even if they do, their twin-engine Agusta is often being chartered for commercial work (such as the military, which uses it for electronic warfare exercises). If you are determined to take the flight, contact them as much in advance as possible to maximize the chance that they can organize a flight, but don't be surprised if it doesn't work out.

Airplane Tours

If you don't like helicopters and still want to see Kaua'i by air, **Air Ventures Hawai'i** (651–0679) does tours in their 6-seat airplane for $145 for the hour. It's nowhere *near* as thrilling as a helicopter tour, and if your objective is to see the sights, go with helicopters. But if you just want a plane ride over Kaua'i, here's your chance.

Tropical Biplane (246–9123) also provides tours, but in a biplane (two wings). At $366 per couple for an hour-long flight ($188 for 30 minutes), it's not much cheaper than helicopters, but they only take 2 passengers at a

We defy you to find a finer setting for lunch than this one along the Po'omau Canyon Ditch Trail.

time, so tours are more personalized. Biplanes have fairly rotten views. The wings dominate everything you see.

HIKING

Of all the Hawaiian Islands, none offers more trails or better hiking than Kaua'i. You could spend an entire month on Kaua'i, hiking *every* day and not see half the trails that the island has to offer. And those are just the officially *maintained* trails.

We have *lots* of hikes in this book. We've also made some close-up maps to assist on specific hikes. Additionally, there are several *excellent* hikes listed in the ADVENTURES chapter since they're a bit...different.

If you plan to do a lot of hiking, contact the agencies below for information packets on their trails:

Hawai'i DLNR Division of State Parks
3060 Eiwa St., #306
Lihu'e, HI 96766
(808) 274–3444

County of Kaua'i Parks & Recreation
4444 Rice St., #150
Lihu'e, HI 96766
(808) 241–4463

If you need to **rent** camping or hiking gear, your best sources will be **Kayak Kaua'i** (826–9844) in Kapa'a and Hanalei or **Pedal 'n Paddle** (826–9069) in Hanalei. For walking in streams or anything slippery, nothing beats **tabis**. Like felt-covered mittens for your feet, they provide impressive traction on mossy rocks. (No ankle support, though.) **Waipouli Variety** (822–1014) and **Kmart** in Lihu'e are your best bets.

Good places to buy other gear include: **Village Variety** (826–6077) in Hanalei,

Waipouli Variety (822–1014) in Kapa'a and **Discount Variety** (742–9393) in Koloa. Also in Koloa is **Da Life** (742–2925), which has lots of outdoor clothing, shoes and camping gear. Don't forget **Wal-Mart** and **Kmart** in Lihu'e.

Lastly, a **hiking stick** can be helpful on some trails. We sometimes even use two on long hikes and find that they greatly ease climbing and descending and give better balance, in addition to their usefulness in probing mud puddles. It's also handy during the months when tiny **crab spiders** are active. Their minor bites aren't dangerous, just annoying, especially if you get one in the face. Just wave a stick in front of you if you notice any on the trail. In a flash of brilliance, they were brought to the islands on purpose to attack a farming pest. Didn't work—smooth move, guys! (Next, they'll probably want to bring in *tarantulas* to get rid of the mosquitoes.)

KOKE'E/WAIMEA CANYON AREA

In Koke'e State Park you'll find exceptional hiking, with the additional benefit of higher altitude and its accompanying cooler temperatures. The map on page 140 shows the layout of the trails and dirt roads. The dirt roads, even when graded well, become *very* slick when wet. As a result, you may have to walk to some of the trailheads, lest you find yourself stranded. It's a good idea to check in at the **Koke'e Museum** (335–9975, open 10 a.m. to 4 p.m.) before you hike to get up-to-date information.

By the way, some of the trails in Koke'e require a 4WD vehicle (or a *long* walk) to get to them. As an alternative to a 4WD, consider renting a mountain bike and bringing it up to the canyon in your car. Then ride it out and hide it in the forest near the trailhead, and you will find that your hiking options greatly increase. One such hike is listed in ADVENTURES on page 198.

Po'omau Canyon Ditch Trail

Formerly called the Ditch Trail, this is an outstanding hike and one of our favorites in the park. This trail was closed for over a decade after 1982's Hurricane 'Iwa and a series of landslides scuffed it up, but it was reopened in the 1990s. It sports incredible views, lush and exotic surroundings and a dizzying finger of land that sticks out into the canyon and overlooks two glorious waterfalls at one shot. It also has a smashing grassy overlook with a canyon view custom made for a picnic lunch. This is a truly beautiful trail. Originally cut in 1926 to assist Koke'e Ditch workers, it's unofficially kept up by volunteers. There are two segments. The first is moderately strenuous, if that, and the second is more strenuous and less maintained. Long pants can be useful if the blackberry bushes (and their evil thorns) are sticking out into the trail. The footing is occasionally obnoxious, especially on the second half, and there are opportunities for the genetically clumsy or the vertiginous to take a long roll.

To get there, take Waineke Road (across from the Koke'e Museum) to Mohihi-Camp 10 Road and drive on the main dirt road. Either park at the intersection of Mohihi and Kumuwela Road and walk a mile on Mohihi Road to the trailhead, or drive farther, until you're 1⁶⁄₁₀ miles from Hwy 550. From here, it's a ¾ mile walk to the trailhead. (4WDs won't have a problem with the last ¾ mile, but cars may unless it's *real* dry and you're *real* confident it will stay that way.) The unmarked trailhead is *on your right* angling back toward the road exactly 2¼ miles from Hwy 550. (If you come to a bridge with metal slats, you've gone 600 feet too far. The trailhead is *just before* a road turnout and might be marked with a metal sign post (missing a sign). Look for it on your right when the 30-foot-high, road-cut wall of rock and dirt on your left is about to end. See map. If you have to cross a concrete walkway at the beginning of the trail, *you're on the wrong trail!*

Almost as soon as you start the trail, you will come to a small valley with a running stream. This is your canary in a coal mine. If the vegetation is too thick to walk through, it means you are unlucky enough to be here toward the end of this trail's volunteer-run maintenance cycle, and that the rest of the trail is overgrown, as well. Might want to do a different hike.

The trail winds its way through primordial-looking jungle with ferns, birds and often the sound of running water to keep you company. Toward the end of the first half, there is a narrow ridge of land on your left; look for it. This is only for the intrepid, as the drop on either side is rather conclusive. At the end is a vista from a poet's dream. On the far wall is a thunderous cascade pounding its way down. Next to it is a multi-step waterfall plunging into a deep pool with the awesome canyon all around you. You will probably interrupt other visitors—bleating goats are almost always perched up here.

After the ridge, continue on the trail until it encounters a spur to Kumuwela Road. Either circle around on the road, or continue on the second half of the trail. It's hairier in spots but worth it. The worst part involves traversing a landslide over 200 feet across. It requires a sturdy gait and some focus. Look for the trail on the other side before you choose a path to cross on and don't try to go across the top. Half a mile from the end, you cross a stream. If you take the short trail to the left first, you will be rewarded with a perfect place to have your lunch. It's the grassy bank of an old waterfall (before the ditch cut it off), which overlooks the valley in a setting that is right out of a movie. Sit under the sugi tree for a while, and you won't *ever* want to leave.

At the end of the trail, you can walk 2 miles on Kumuwela Road (or take Kumuwela and Waininiua Trails) back to Mohihi-Camp 10 Road and your awaiting car. Now *there's* a hike to savor!

Pihea Trail to Alaka'i Swamp

This trail starts at the end of Waimea Canyon Drive at the Pu'u o Kila Lookout. It combines awesome views of Kalalau Valley and takes you through the highest swamp in the world. The terrain in the swamp is like nothing you've ever seen, and we've been told many times that it was the highlight of many people's hiking experience on Kaua'i. You're insulated from the mud *most* of the time by a wooden boardwalk.

The Pihea Trail skirts the edge of Kalalau Valley, passing through native 'ohi'a and fern forest. (See map on previous page.) About a mile into it, a very short but *steep* spur trail leads to the Pihea Vista. Nice, but tricky to walk up to—it's optional. (Long legs help.) Just past this junction, the trail is covered in most spots by a boardwalk to keep you from wallowing in the mud. (The part of the trail before the boardwalk is sometimes pretty muddy, so be forewarned.) When the trail intersects the Alaka'i Swamp Trail, go left (east); it's about 2 miles to the end. The Alaka'i Swamp Trail leads to the edge of a cliff where the

Koke'e Trails

The nature of the terrain at Koke'e makes it difficult to convey the type of hiking each trail provides. This accurate, computer-generated, shaded relief map is drawn from an angled perspective to give you a feel for the lay of the land. Since this is a perspective map, the mileage scale should be a little smaller at the top of the map (since it's "farther away" from your eyes) and a little bigger at the bottom of the map.

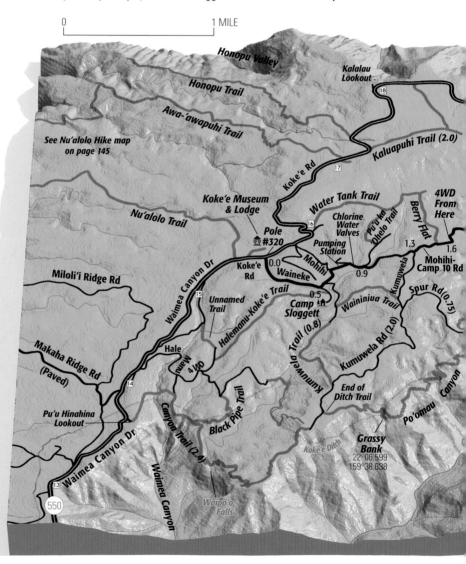

0   1 MILE

Honopu Valley

Kalalau Lookout

Honopu Trail

18

Awa-'awapuhi Trail

Kaluapuhi Trail (2.0)

See Nu'alolo Hike map on page 145

Koke'e Rd

17

Water Tank Trail

4WD From Here

Koke'e Museum & Lodge

Chlorine Water Valves

Pu'u ka Ohelo Trail

Berry Flat

Nu'alolo Trail

16

Pole #320

Pumping Station

1.3

1.6

Mohihi

0.9

Mohihi-Camp 10 Rd

Koke'e Rd

0.0

Waineke

Kumuwela

Miloli'i Ridge Rd

Waimea Canyon Dr

15

Unnamed Trail

Halemanu-Koke'e Trail

0.5

Camp Sloggett

Waininiua Trail

Spur Rd (0.75)

Makaha Ridge Rd (Paved)

Hale

Manu 4WD

14

Kumuwela Trail (0.8)

Kumuwela Rd (2.0)

Po'omau Canyon

Pu'u Hinahina Lookout

Canyon Trail (2.4)

Black Pipe Trail

End of Ditch Trail

Grassy Bank
22°06.599
159°38.638

Koke'e Ditch

Waimea Canyon Dr

13

550

Waimea Canyon

Waipo'o Falls

Note: Distances given for trails are one way. Distances listed along Mohihi-Camp 10 Road are from the intersection of Waineke Road and Kokee Road near telephone pole 320. Don't be fooled by a sign at that intersection saying Kumuwela.

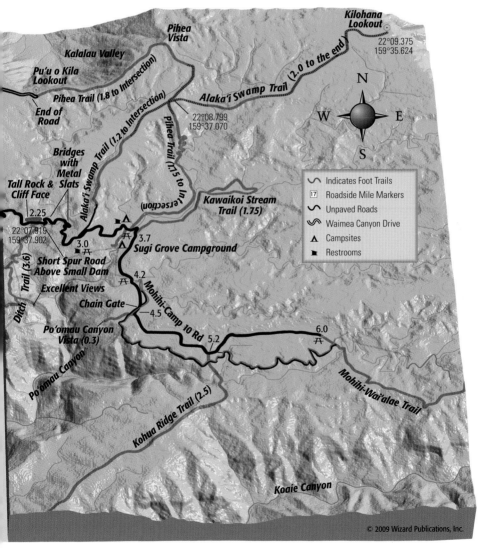

Kilohana Lookout
22°09.375
159°35.624

Pihea Vista

Kalalau Valley

Pu'u o Kila Lookout

Pihea Trail (1.8 to Intersection)

End of Road

Alaka'i Swamp Trail (2.0 to the end)

22°08.799
159°37.070

Alaka'i Swamp Trail (1.2 to Intersection)

Pihea Trail (1.1.5 to Intersection)

Bridges with Metal Slats

Tall Rock & Cliff Face

2.25

22°07.919
159°37.902

3.0

3.7

Kawaikoi Stream Trail (1.75)

Sugi Grove Campground

Ditch Trail (3.6)

Short Spur Road Above Small Dam

Excellent Views

Chain Gate

4.2

4.5

Mohihi-Camp 10 Rd

5.2

6.0

Po'omau Canyon Vista (0.3)

Po'omau Canyon

Mohihi-Wai'alae Trail

Kohua Ridge Trail (2.5)

Koaie Canyon

N W E S

Indicates Foot Trails
17 Roadside Mile Markers
Unpaved Roads
Waimea Canyon Drive
▲ Campsites
■ Restrooms

© 2009 Wizard Publications, Inc.

Kilohana Look-out affords a majestic view of Ha'ena on the north shore, clouds permitting. Imagine hiking to this point before the boardwalk was installed. Then imagine that the hard part was *still to come*. That's because the ancient Hawaiians used this trail to get to the north shore when the surf precluded going by sea. Once at Kilohana, they went over and down the 3,400-foot cliff to the valley floor and along the sloping valley to the ocean. All this for westsiders to visit family on the north shore in the winter. (Remember this the next time you think you're too busy to drive across town to see Mom.) Along the trail you'll see old telephone poles. They were erected by the military after the attack on Pearl Harbor and stretched across the swamp, down the cliffs of Kilohana and into Hanalei. They served as a backup communications line in case the Japanese captured Lihu'e.

Even without the view at the end, it's probably the most unusual hike on the is-land. Full grown trees on the flats rarely exceed 5 feet tall. Submerged grasses, vines and moss-covered trees sheltering endemic birds (found nowhere else) make this a memorable hike. Fog rolls in and out constantly, adding to the mystery of the scenery. You've *never* seen wilderness like this. While you're on this boardwalk, you'll have the same thought as everyone else—"My *God*, this must have been a wretched hike before they installed this." Darned straight! It's about 8 miles round trip from your car, but you can just go as far as your desire takes you. The boardwalk system was created in the late '90s and was quite a task. Even with it, expect to get a little muddy from patches where the boardwalk was left out. If you want to avoid the some-times sloppy stretch of the Pihea Trail, you can just do the Alaka'i Swamp Trail from its beginning off Mohihi-Camp 10 Road. (See map.) You'll probably need a 4WD or mountain bike to get to the Alaka'i Trailhead off Mohihi. Pihea's car

The Alaka'i Swamp Trail's boardwalk meanders to a spectacular end at a sheer cliff overlooking the island's north shore 4,000 feet below the lookout.

access from the end of Waimea Canyon Drive makes it the better route.

Canyon Trail to Waipo'o Falls

Another favorite, this one is also moderately strenuous and will probably take you 2–3 hours, depending on how long you linger. Along the way you will get unparalleled views of the canyon from the other side, visit two waterfalls and find a cold pool to swim in, if you like.

You park your car at the Puæu Hinahina Lookout between the 13 and 14 mile markers, walk to the back of the parking lot, through a clearing and to the trail to your left. If there's no parking, you can park at the top of Hale Manu Valley Road between the 14 and 15 mile markers on Waimea Canyon Drive and walk 8/10 mile down the road (with a 240-foot loss in elevation) to another trailhead, unless you have a 4WD. (See map.)

About ½ mile into the trail from Pu'u Hinahina you have the option of going to the lookout off to your right. You might want to save that for the end, since other views will be better.

You'll end up between these two falls when you do the Waipo'o Falls hike.

After you are exposed to the great canyon views, you will come to the top of a ridge. Keep an eye out for goats on the opposite walls. Look south for a provocative-looking rock arch, out where it's impossible for man to have created it. (You will see it closer from the larger waterfall ahead.) The light in this part of the canyon is usually best in the late afternoon (around 3 p.m.).

Just past and below the ridge, you'll come to an intersection, with a small falls to your left and a bigger one to your right. The first one is tiny, but the pool is cool and refreshing. The bigger falls takes a two-step plunge down 800 feet. You're at the top. These falls sometimes flow a bit low, especially in the summer, so don't be disappointed. Just enjoy the delicious scenery, complete with wild

Nu'alolo Valley looks radically different from every angle.

ginger everywhere, before making your way back.

Nu'alolo Trail/Nu'alolo Cliffs/ Awa-'awapuhi Grand Loop

This is a great hike! It takes most of a day and is strenuous, but you're treated to views that will stay frozen in your mind for a lifetime. If you're up for a long day hike on Kaua'i, this is the one. And you may be surprised at how few people you see along the way.

First, the gory details. It's either 9⁸⁄₁₀ or 11³⁄₁₀ miles (the latter if you have to walk Waimea Canyon Drive back down to your car) and involves about 2,000 feet of altitude change, 1,500 of which is climbing the last leg. But *oh,* the sights you will see. The vertiginous may object to a place or two, but they won't want to miss it.

There are three trails. Nu'alolo Trail starts near the Koke'e Lodge and heads toward the ocean, Awa-'awapuhi brings you back up, and Nu'alolo Cliffs links the two. When you finish at the Awa-'awapuhi trailhead, you're 1½ miles up the road from your car. So either leave a car there, or you'll have to walk back down narrow Waimea Canyon Drive to your car.

This hike is downhill for the first third, mostly flat for the second and a somewhat gentle but constant incline for the last third.

Start at the Nu'alolo Trailhead just south of Koke'e Lodge. (This is better than doing it from Awa-'awapuhi first.) *Coming from the lodge,* the 3⁸⁄₁₀ mile-long trail is on your right. After a short climb you'll descend through a landscape that will change from bird-filled koa forest to patches of wild flowers to dryland forest to exposed ridge. All are a tribute to the rain's infatuation with increasingly higher altitudes. The trail will split in a few places but quickly rejoins. By the way, part of this trail is open to hunting during some parts of the year. It's highly unlikely that you'll encounter a hunter, but it's probably best to avoid practicing those new pig calls you just learned.

About 3 miles into the hike is the turnoff for a hunter trail. Bypass it and stay to the right. At 3⁴⁄10 mile is the intersection of Cliff Trail. Don't take Cliff Trail just yet; instead continue another ⅓ mile to Lolo Vista Point. Swallow hard. You're on the upper edge of an Eden-like valley. The view will take your breath away—and then some. Nu'alolo Valley is unimaginably beautiful, and the Na Pali Coast looks endless beneath you. This is the bluff where Harrison Ford had his tree-choking tantrum in *Six Days/Seven Nights.* (Though *he* got here by helicopter.) Surely it can't get better than this. Think again. As you go back and start the 2¹⁄10 mile-long Nu'alolo Cliffs Trail, you are almost immediately presented with an even more dramatic view—if that's possible. So here *you* are, at the back of the valley looking toward the ocean, half a mile below and a mile in front of you. *This* has got to be the best view on Kaua'i, right? So you'd think. A liability sign tells you to proceed at your own risk. We're assuming you do. It refers to a washed out section ahead that can be unnerving, but it's short.

After a rest at the picnic shelter a little farther, the trail turns into deeper forest. This stretch is one of the loveliest in the park, where birds abound and the scenery is delicious. There are a few false trails that lead to nowhere. Stay on the main trail. After playing in your own personal waterfall (yep, it's got one of those, too, though it's sometimes dry), you hit the Awa-'awapuhi Trail. The highway is to your right, but you head left ⅓ mile.

Nothing can prepare you for what you are about to see. Just when you thought it couldn't get any better, the Awa-'awapuhi Lookout steals your heart with cliffs so sheer and green they can't possibly be real. Can *this* be the same Nu'alolo Valley you saw before? High altitude-flying, white-tailed tropic birds laugh and soar *beneath* you. Knife-edge ridges you didn't even know were there stand against the cliff. This is a side of God's handiwork that you never knew existed. Revel, savor, remember.

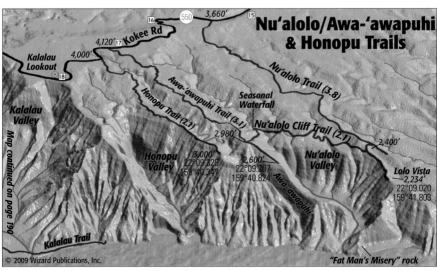

Map continued on page 190

© 2009 Wizard Publications, Inc.

Take a break along the Nu'alolo Cliffs Trail.

The view from past the guard-rail is even better, but you're unprotected. If you fall, the first step is a fairly jarring 2,000 feet. To the right is the almost vertical Awa-'awapuhi Valley. Check out the spires at the valley mouth.

Rested? Good. It's time to pay the piper. You're at 2,600 feet, and the road is 3¹⁄₁₀ miles away at 4,120 feet. Fortunately, it's fairly gentle most of way.

Some Warnings: You should start this hike no later than 10 a.m. (earlier if possible). Hiking boots are a good idea. This is not a good trail if it's been raining a lot in Koke'e. Avoid when muddy, or bring your bobsled. Hiking *up*

Nu'alolo when it's muddy is awful—another reason we come back up via Awa-'awapuhi. As for water, bring at least twice as much as you think you'll need. After all, the first ²⁄₃ is downhill or fairly flat, so lugging the water that far is relatively painless. Drink up before you start your ascent, and dump any water you don't want to carry. That's infinitely better than walking up Awa-'awapuhi dry (as *we* did the first time). There's a brochure at the museum that identifies marked plants on the Awa-'awapuhi Trail. It's great if you took the trail *down* (which we advise *against* since you're better off taking Nu'alolo down), but you're probably too pooped to care coming up. Besides, many of the markers have been removed.

Kuku'i Trail

While gazing into Waimea Canyon, you may wonder if there's a trail down into it. Yup. And lucky for you, it's down the road at a lower elevation near the 9 mile marker, so you *only* have to descend (and, of course, *ascend)* 2,300 steep, unrelenting feet. Ah, but what views you'll see on your way down as the canyon changes in appearance. It's 2½ miles to the river below. (Not much distance to lose almost half a mile in elevation, so the grade is steep.) At the bottom is Wiliwili Camp (pretty trashed at press time). Make *sure* you bring enough water for the trek back up. Too many people underestimate the climb, and they're fantasizing about water on the way up. The climb back up is pretty grueling, and you'll be sore for a few days.

If you don't want to go all the way down, there's a good viewpoint ⅓ mile into the trail and a *spectacular* viewpoint 1 mile into (and 750 feet below) the trailhead. Past this, the trail goes through forest.

Mohihi-Wai-'alae Trail

First things first. If you don't have a 4WD vehicle, you probably won't be doing this trail unless it's *real* dry and you have *lots* of confidence it won't rain. That's because it starts at the end of Mohihi-Camp 10 Road, 6 miles from Waimea Canyon Drive (Hwy 550). See map on page 141 and the description of the road in the Po'omau Canyon Ditch Trail hike.

If you are blessed with a 4WD vehicle, you'll be treated to one of our favorite trails on the island. Not for any sweeping views—you only get one or two of those. This trail shines because it passes through one of the finest forests you'll ever see.

After parking at the end of Mohihi Road near picnic tables, you'll take the trail down a few minutes, across a footbridge, and walk toward and to the right of more picnic tables. A sign there saying FOREST RESERVE marks the continuing faint trail to the right of the sign.

Down through a forest of sugi trees, you'll have to cross a stream that you can usually boulder-hop. A few dozen feet after the stream there's a shack. Don't pass it! The trail angles back to the right.

From here it's not so confusing. The trail gains 250 feet, levels out and climbs a bit more until you come to a broken bench. From here there's a grand view of Koai'e Canyon, part of Waimea Canyon.

For another 1½ miles the trail undulates then brings a plateau with a rain gauge. Until now the trail has been fairly wide. From here it's narrower, with passages through ferns, and there are a few areas that require care as they're on the side of a hill.

If you're game, the next mile is well worth it. It will drop to a luxuriant fern forest, then keeps getting better and better. When you're about 2½ miles from

In all Kaua'i it's unlikely you'll ever find a more pristine forest than along the Mohihi–Wai-'alae Trail.

Ti plants grace the end of the 'Okolehao Trail. Turn around and you'll see more of the island from up here than perhaps any other trail on the island.

your car, the trail completely levels out. The forest has gotten more and more exotic looking. Gone are the introduced plants of Koke'e. This is an old growth, native forest that looks utterly primeval. It's as if someone had a bucket of life and splashed it all over the ground. Be careful not to walk on the mosses themselves.

The ground is soft and gentle, like walking on a thickly padded carpet, and the area feels ancient and undisturbed. The 87 inches of rain this area gets per year are absorbed by the forest floor. Walk slowly and observe how life bursts from every nook and cranny. Native birds, though not numerous, show little or no fear of humans. We've been lucky enough to be here on a sunny day, but even rain won't obscure the healthiest, happiest and most prosperous forest you may ever walk through.

Although the trail keeps going for many, many miles, 3–3½ miles is a good

turning-around point. (There are mile markers.) Though this last portion is *reasonably* marked, keep track of where you've been for your return. Try to start early—by 9 a.m., if possible, so you can take your time on this trail. Camping at Sugi Grove can be handy for this.

NORTH SHORE HIKES
Hanalei 'Okolehao Trail

So you've been especially gluttonous since you've been here, and the guilt is keeping you awake at night. Here's your chance to work off that lu'au you attended. This trail is a puffer. It gains 1,250 feet in less than 2 miles. That means the grade is steep, tiring and unrelenting. It will seem much longer than it is.

Most of the first ⅔ mile is on the dull remains of a steep old dirt road. By the time the road ends and the *real* trail starts (at a huge power pole whose lines swoop into the valley below), you'll probably hate the trail and hate us for mentioning it. Look to the left, and the trail continues through forest. It's prettier, as it quickly starts climbing the ridge, but just as strenuous. Climb, climb, climb, climb. Then climb some more. There are breaks in the vegetation affording grand views, but you couldn't care less because you're puffing so hard. After about 30 miles (really 1⁸⁄₁₀, but you'll swear we're lying) you are richly rewarded. A lovely plateau dotted with ti plants offers impossibly sweeping views. (Just before the trail ends at the plateau, a different spur trail to the right leads to a separate ridge. Nasty, scary, hard core and death-defying make that a *must-miss* alternative.)

From the trail's end at the plateau you can see ⅕ of the entire island, weather cooperating, from Anahola all the way around to the end of the road at Ke'e. Behind you, you'll see Wai-'ale'ale and the Hanalei River chiseling its way out of the mysterious center of the island, the Kilauea Lighthouse, Hanalei Bay...nowhere is there a more expansive view.

Was it worth it? Only you can say, but we think so. Is the hard part done? 'Fraid not. Coming down is also hard because the constant downhill is hard on the knees...and 'okole if it's wet and you slip.

To get to the trailhead, drive past Princeville and turn left just after you cross the Hanalei Bridge at the bottom. (See map on page 49.) At ⁷⁄₁₀ mile from Hwy 560 is a parking lot on your left. The trailhead's on the opposite side at a small foot bridge. After 500 feet you'll encounter a chain gate with an old road rising steeply to your left. Climb till the end or until you run out of sweat.

Incidentally, the word 'okolehao refers to liquor made from ti roots. In the old days, bootleggers planted ti up here to supply them with raw materials.

Pools of Mokolea

For those looking for a beautiful, wild shoreline hike but who don't want something too long and strenuous, this

The Pools of Mokolea top off a short but sweet shoreline hike.

may be the ticket. It only travels ¼ mile each way from your 4WD car (or ½ mile from a regular car) but has some tasty rewards.

From the 4WD trailhead (directions below), you either go up and down next to a wire fence, or around—either way ending on the lava bench. You'll soon see tide-pools. Fish and crabs scatter at your approach. Lots of ancient metal equipment and parts are scattered along the shore. For 100 years the sugar company dumped worn-out gear here. What was once junk has been transformed by a century of melting rust into an intriguing part of the landscape.

More tide-pools and more lava. It's slow going because you're mostly boulder-hopping on lava rocks, so take your time. Only 800 feet from the end of the road is a large, Jacuzzi-sized hole in the lava where the ocean surges in and out. It's great to watch, but beware of large sets of waves that can surprise you. (This goes for much of the walk along here. Monster surf needs to be evaluated.)

At ¼ mile is Mokolea Point. What a spectacular place! Waves often pummel the area, creating rivulets of water flowing across the lava bench. During low surf a wonderful lava pool graces the area. Several small pools behind the large rock make nice soaking pools if the surf isn't too high. Moderate waves sometimes wash over the bench, replenishing the pools. Overhead, white-tailed tropic birds and shearwaters often soar on the thermals. Kilauea Lighthouse and Crater Hill are 1⅓ mile across the water.

Just past the pools is the end of your hike. The ocean has cut a trench in the lava all the way to the cliff. When there's surf, the ocean comes roaring into the trench, which gets narrower and narrower, eventually undercutting the cliff in a small pocket. The result is a violent ricochet as the water and compressed air ex-

Surprises, such as this freshwater cave at the shoreline, await those who hike to Kalalau Beach.

plode out of the trap that the lava has set for it. It's like a dragon, breathing water instead of fire. Some waves even hiss as they are expelled. Sometimes rogue waves pound with such ferocity you think the ground will split beneath your feet. Some explosions of water may shower you, so be careful.

You can get to the marginally defined trailhead from one of two ways. A road off Kilauea Road in Kilauea is ¼ mile from Keneke and the Kong Lung Center. (See map on page 46.) This 1⁷⁄₁₀ mile road terminates on the Mokolea peninsula. (The first ⁴⁄₁₀ mile is paved; after that it's 4WD.) Though an unattributed road sign may imply it's private or closed, county documents show it as a *public* access. An alternative way for *any* car is to take Wailapa Road between the 21 & 22 mile markers off Hwy 56 near Kilauea. Then take the smooth dirt road to Kilauea Bay. Park and find the best place to wade across the stream (unless it's raging) and head toward the right.

Kalalau Trail

The ultimate hike is also the most famous hike in all Hawai'i. Eleven miles of switchbacks, hills and beautiful scenery. This hike can be a real adventure. Because of this, we discuss it in detail in ADVENTURES on page 190.

Secret Lava Pools

People often assume that when you live on an island with several editions of a guidebook already out, there must not be anything left to discover. Well, maybe on some islands, but they don't know Kaua'i. This place is constantly revealing new wonders to us, and the potential discoveries are seemingly endless. Take this location. We'd hiked around this area many times and flown

over this point at least a hundred times by ultralight. Yet it wasn't until a flight during the last edition that we saw this area for what it is.

Near Kilauea, it's about a 10-minute walk down the path to Secret Beach 200 feet below. (See directions to Secret Beach on page 104.) Once at the bottom, nearly everyone is attracted to the large, beautiful beach section to the right. Too bad. The most unusual part is to the left. Walk along the sand until it ends. Some lava rock may make further progress awkward, depending on the surf and tide. Beware of getting slapped by a rogue wave here. You shouldn't consider this hike if the ocean is angry.

After about 500 yards, a large channel/tide-pool filled with small fish much of the time makes a fascinating diversion.

About 600 yards to the left of where you first encountered Secret Beach at the bottom of the path (it'll seem like more because of some awkward footing), you'll come to one of the most perfect bathing pools on the island. Over 6 feet deep in one place, cut off from the ocean's waves during low to moderate surf, the calm, clear and beautiful water beckons. Oh, yeah. Life is good.

If the surf is not up and you want more action, another pool closer to the ocean gets jostled at bit by waves. Only consider this other pool when the ocean is calm. Big surf or a rogue wave can turn that second pool into a washing machine and turn you into a limp rag. Enjoy the natural black bottom pool, which is a bit warmer than the ocean.

Yeah, but what about the salt from the ocean? I don't want to drive back all salty. Oh, aren't *we* getting spoiled? OK, if you insist. Past the pools around the rock cliff, look for a place to scramble up the short lava wall, continue a

A family enjoys the Secret Lava Pools—what's not to love?

few minutes to the right, and you'll come to your very own waterfall to rinse off. The rocks below the falls (which you access by walking *way* past the top of the falls, then doing a U-turn) are *exceptionally* slippery, so either bring tabis (page 137) or rinse in the shallow pool above the falls.

We want to stress that this whole hike isn't doable when the surf's up. The ocean can clobber this coastline, especially in the winter, and could kick the living daylights out of you if it wanted to. Even calm seas could surprise you. Stay observant and don't push it just because you're itching to visit. This hike, like so much outdoor activity in Hawai'i, depends on nature being in a good mood.

An easier, if less dramatic route, is to take the first Kalihiwai Road for ⁷⁄₁₀ miles and park at a pullout on the right near a skinny, yellow fire hydrant. A possibly hard-to-spot trail here leads 10 minutes down to the top of the falls. There may be two metal rungs in the cliffside to the

right of the falls to help you down. The trail can be slippery, but it's shorter.

EAST SHORE HIKES
Sleeping Giant (Nounou Mountain)

This is a moderately difficult trail. Actually, it's three different trails. The vertical elevation you will gain from the East Trail is 1,000 feet. A thousand feet sounds like a big rise (OK, it *is* a big rise), but this is a hike worth experiencing. Nearly the entire hike is through forests with pretty views. This is a real trail, not an abandoned road like some hiking trails. Of the three trails, the East is the prettiest, longest (at around 2 miles each way) and the least steep, though it involves the most elevation gain. If you take the eastern route, at the third switchback after the ½ mile stake, the trail seems to split into two paths. *Do not take the left fork, which is on the side of the mountain!* This is probably a pig trail and not part of the main trail. You won't like it. In fact, other trails that deviate from the main trail are usually bad. Take the time to savor some of the luscious views of the entire east shore from spots. When you get to the main fork in the trail (diligently guarded by hala trees with their A-frame, cage-like roots), take the fork to the left for 3 or 4 minutes to the picnic table. From here you can see the entire Wailua Valley from Anahola to Lihu'e. The view is not to be missed and well worth the climbing effort expended. Anyone who becomes dizzy from heights should be aware that there are areas along the east side trail where the beautiful sweeping view off to one side is quite steep.

Up at the picnic table, there is a short trail dipping south across the giant's neck up to his forehead and nose. Or is it his chin? Hard to say. The view from up there is, literally, a once-in-a-lifetime experience. The vista is without rival. Think *real hard* before you take this part. It is steep, and the spine is almost vertical on both sides. A wrong step, or a slip anywhere near the nose, would almost certainly cost you your life. Just before the summit there is a short trail to your left leading to the hole in the giant's chin, seen from the bottom of Kuamo'o Road. This part of the Nounou Trail is what they call a real 'okole squeezer. Stop at the picnic table unless you are very brave, very foolish and very well insured.

If you take the West Trail or the Kuamo'o-Nounou Trail, you'll find the climbing steeper. It's a good workout; we like to climb it daily if we've enjoyed a few too many restaurant reviews lately. Kuamo'o-Nounou Trail and West Trail combine at a magnificent strand of Cook Island pines (a very tall and straight pine tree thought, during the Age of Discovery, to make good ships' masts).

Of the three trails to the top, we recommend either the East Trail or the Kuamo'o-Nounou Trail. (The latter has a stretch where mosquitoes might mug you. Use a repellent.) The map on page 59 makes it easy to find the three trailheads.

Kuilau Ridge Trail

This trail begins 1¾ miles past the Kaua'i Research and Extension Center. The trailhead marker is on the right side as you are driving west on Kuamo'o Road and there are a few parking stalls. Otherwise, park at the nearby Keahua Arboretum.

This is a very nice hike. The first part is a gentle but constant incline that takes you past a myriad of birds. Watch and listen for them. At the end of the incline (about 30 minutes), you will come to a small picnic area overlooking a lovely valley. If it's clear, you will get a stunning view of Mount Wai'ale'ale. This is a nice place to have lunch or just enjoy a long sip of water. *Make sure you go past the picnic tables.* The payoff is 5 minutes later. You will be rewarded with a wonderful razorback, winding, rolling, trek into paradise. *Gorgeous!* There are lush hillsides filled with ferns of every size and shape. Off in the distance you can see the ocean at Kapa'a and all the way to Lihu'e at another point. Very nice. Turn around where the Kuilau Trail ends and the Moalepe Trail begins (see map on page 58) at a quaint wooden bridge. (Or continue onto Moalepe Trail, if you like, though Moalepe isn't in as good condition due to horses stomping the snot out of the trail base.) The entire hike should take you 2½ to 3 hours if you hike at a semi-steady pace. Bring water. Hiking boots recommended, but tennis shoes OK.

Jungle Hike

If you want a *taste* of the steamy jungle and forest (but without the need for a ma-

This jungle hike is fairly easy and rewards you with a nice place for a picnic.

chete and a gallon of insect repellent), this might be what you're looking for. It leads to a government stream gauging station and passes through some magnificent scenery. Your reward at the end is a small, picturesque stair-step little falls where two streams come together adjacent to a water diversion ditch. (The word ditch has ugly connotations, but often these small dams can make a nice place for a picnic.)

To get there, take Kuamo'o Road (580) all the way until it becomes dirt. (A sign at the Keahua Arboretum says 4WD ONLY, but the road's not *that* bad...usually.) The pavement stops, but you won't. You'll cross *under* a couple streams and stay on the dirt road for over 2½ miles. When you come to a Y take the left fork and reset your odemeter. Then at almost 1 mile is another Y, then a gate; take the left fork. (If the gate's locked, you have to walk an extra ³⁄₁₀ mile.) At 1³⁄₁₀ miles is the second gate. The map on page 199 shows all of this. (This road can get a bit junky between scheduled maintenance. Regular cars are *usually* OK, but there's a chance you may have to stop sooner without a 4WD.) Park here and walk

down the dirt road. The gate is on state land and was erected to prevent vehicles from going any farther, but it's perfectly legal to go through the gate and continue on foot. Near this gate is where they filmed the ENTRANCE GATE scenes in *Jurassic Park*. It probably won't stop a T-Rex, but it'll keep your car out. The views into Wai'ale'ale Crater from this dirt road can be exceptional, especially in the morning.

After walking 10–15 minutes from the gate (½ mile), you'll come upon an ascent. There will be an old turnout on the left side. Listen for gurgling water here. The trail leading off to the left from this turnout immediately parallels for a short time a water ditch and passes through extremely lush territory. The ferns, birds and trees are abundant along this easy-to-follow but sometimes slippery trail. A pleasant 10–20 minute trek up and over a 150-foot high ridge will bring you to a nice, freshwater pool, formed by the small dam. The area around the dam is covered with plant life and can be slippery. A wonderful, secluded spot to eat lunch.

If you don't want to walk *over* the hill to get to the falls, you can walk *through* it. Where the ditch becomes a tunnel (at a circular cement opening), you can access the tunnel that goes under the mountain. Most people will have to duck the entire 800 foot length and, of course, if the water flow rate should change while you're in there, you'd have a big problem to deal with. Hmm, maybe that over-the-hill trail isn't so bad after all. Anyway, it's an adventurous option that we've done (when the flow wasn't too high and we had a flashlight), and it's a hoot.

The falls are actually formed by two streams. If you swim across the pool and climb the rocks, then take the right fork for only a few (slippery) minutes, you'll come to a small, hidden falls. At the base is something we call the **Jacuzzi**. During low to moderate stream flow the falling water creates bubbles and jets of air that feels remarkably similar to a spa (albeit a cold one). It's *wonderful* to soak in. Just stay out if the flow is too heavy, and read page 33 for precautions on swimming in streams. Use your own good judgment.

Powerline Trail

The Powerline Trail is a dirt road cut through mostly untouched wilderness. It was carved by the electric company to facilitate the installation of (surprise!) powerlines in the early 1900s. It was recut in 1996 and goes from northeastern Kapaʻa to southern Princeville over a span of 10^4/$_{10}$ miles. If you ever wondered why some local trucks have 2-foot lift kits, this road is one reason. It has giant ruts that can swallow stock trucks.

This trail is best taken as a shuttle, starting from Kapaʻa side (the prettier part of the trail) past the end of Kuamoʻo Road, just past the Keahua Arboretum.

(See maps on pages 58 and 46 for the two trailheads.) You could leave your car there and take The Kauaʻi Bus back from the north shore, but you'd have to take a cab up Kuamoʻo Road to your car. Otherwise, just take the trail until you get tired, then come back.

There aren't any long climbs, just lots of small ones on the hilly first half of the hike. The second half is mostly a gentle descent into the north shore. The area is lush and undisturbed for most of the way—except for the road and those pesky poles. (I guess we shouldn't whine too much about the poles. If they weren't there, the trail wouldn't be either.) The area is so lush that the absence of plants on the trail is easily visible from space. Look at the front cover—the Powerline Trail is unmistakable. Watch for waterfalls along the way, though none are close enough to visit. At about halfway you will be able to see the ocean on the north shore. What a lovely sight! You can see great distances at many places along the trail. This hike, though tiring, is a fine way to see Kauaʻi's wild side.

Along the trail there are numerous short spur roads leading to individual poles. Some offer great views. Since the road stays fairly near the poles all the time, and since the main road is easy to stay on, you shouldn't get lost. It ends at Kapaka Road. (Kapaka Road is between the 27 and 28 mile markers on Hwy 56.)

Hoʻopiʻi Falls Hike

Waterfalls have an amazing ability to bring piece of mind. Although Kauaʻi is studded with many waterfalls, most of them are inaccessible for one reason or another—but not this one. There are two falls on the Kapaʻa Stream—and one of them is named Ho'opi'i. Some locals call the first one Ho'opi'i—government maps give that name to the second falls.

Look at the map on this page. There are additional trails in this area, but the one shown is on state land. The top of the map on page 59 shows you where Kapahi Road is. An old *public* dirt road (now used as a trail) is on your left as you come down Kapahi Road. Please be respectful of the neighborhood here. One resident even posted an irate review of our book on *Amazon.com* because he was upset that we told you how to get to these falls.

Walk down the dirt road, and it leads to a trail. Go downstream and eventually there's a side path leading down to the first falls. Wow, what a place! A flat lava bench offers a magnificent place to sit and breathe in the falls. The only way to get under those falls is either to go downstream and wade back upstream or jump into the pool as some of the daring locals do. (At your own risk; check out the water first to make sure there's nothing dangerous submerged.)

Back on the trail, the path eventually parallels the stream. Once there, you need to stay within 10 feet of the stream (except in one area) to stay on state land.

This area is lush and the sound of the stream hypnotic. Just before the second falls the trail crosses the stream, terminating at the top of the falls. (There's no easy way to the bottom.)

If you don't bring mosquito repellent, bring an extra pint of blood for the walk through the woods. Tennis shoes are OK unless you cross the stream for the second falls. Bring water and your camera!

Hiking to the Top of Wai'ale'ale

A question we're often asked is *How can I hike to the summit of Wai'ale'ale?* The answer is…you can't. In ancient times Hawaiians used to hike up a ridge on the northeast side of the crater (the ridge that's over the Tunnel Hike on page 198). Near the summit they had rope ladders for the final portion. A landslide and lack of use in the 1800s shut off that route. In the 1970s a person tried, with a helicopter overhead to give radio guidance, and he failed. In 2006 another person tried and had to be rescued by helicopter.

The other route used to be through the Alaka'i Swamp, and some government maps still show that trail. It's been gone for years, and even people born and raised here aren't able to make it through the swamp anymore. A few adventurers have made it, but we don't recommend it. The rain gauge at the top is now read by helicopter.

We generally shy away from describing places that the reader won't be able to see. After all, what's the point? Our books are meant to be *used*, and the things *we* see are things that *you* can see.

But over the years we've been asked *so* many times what the summit of Wai'ale'ale is like, we feel obliged to describe it. We were able to fulfill a long-

Ho'opi'i Falls

N / W–E / S

Kapa'a Stream

Kealia Stream

Falls

Old Dirt Road

Falls

Kapahi Rd

Trails approximate

Kawaihau Rd

See map on page 59 to get here.

© 2009 Wizard Publications, Inc.

time dream when we arranged a trip up here by helicopter once. It requires jumping through a lot of bureaucratic hoops—and it requires dependably clear weather at the summit—a rare event. (You need a high pressure system parked over the island retarding cloud growth.)

The summit of Wai'ale'ale is an otherworldly place. Other than a few clumps of sickly-looking 6- to 10-foot trees, there is nothing over a foot tall for more than a mile in any direction. Not even the ubiquitous ferns are genetically programmed to deal with so much rain and cloud cover. So the dominant features carpeting the ground are moss, lichen and short grasses. The 3,000-foot cliffs plunging into the crater define the eastern portion, which is so shear, you can literally walk up to it and look nearly straight down to the crater over a half mile beneath your feet.

Walking around is a bit awkward. The sponge-like ground is constantly threatening to steal your shoes. It takes about 2 hours just to go from one end of the summit to the other. Unfortunately, pigs and goats have taken up residence in this hostile terrain, so the state has fenced off a large portion to keep those pests out. No mosquitoes live up here, but huge drag-

Some call this Ho'opi'i Falls. Others use that name for the next falls down the river. These keiki couldn't care less. They're just enjoying the sound.

onflies are everywhere. Only a handful of birds can be heard, some of them endemic—found nowhere else in the world except on this watery mountaintop.

SOUTH SHORE HIKES
Po'ipu Shoreline Sandstone Hikes

The lithified cliffs of **Makawehi** next to Shipwreck Beach, as well as the **Maha'ulepu** area, offer excellent shoreline hiking. The Makawehi cliffs are easily accessed by taking the trail from the parking lot between the Hyatt and the Po'ipu Bay Resort golf course (or simply

From the summit of Wai'ale'ale, the Wailua River is a half-mile below your feet.

walking to the east end of the beach). It's over half a mile long, formed from cemented sand dunes deposited here during the last ice age. The wind and salt have clawed and thrashed at these cliffs with impressive results. Take your time and wander about. Look for (but don't remove) fossils in the sandstone, and enjoy the views.

Maha'ulepu is described in detail in BEACHES on page 110. Another good hike is to start from the end of Gillin's Beach (see map on page 75). It's beyond the stream and past the last pocket of sand. It's wonderful to walk along here when the surf is raging. At one place there's a hole in the floor of the cliff, allowing you to see the ocean exploding beneath your feet on the lithified bench below. This area looks like an alien landscape. Weekends bring fishermen who tend to leave reminders of their hobby here.

You could walk all the way to the Hyatt, if you wanted. The wind, pounding surf and beautiful cliffs create an amazingly relaxing walk, even if the ground is a bit lumpy. About ⅔ of the way to the Hyatt, the cliff gives way to a sandy pocket affording a luscious view of the cliffs.

Melted Metal & Keyhole Cave at Swiss Cheese Shoreline

Here's an area that's alluring despite numerous reminders of the sometimes untidy nature of man. It starts near the industrial part of Hanapepe (technically 'Ele'ele) and leads to an isolated beach. Along the way the Swiss cheese-type of lava shoreline provides ample opportunity to explore how the ocean carves up the land, while an old dump site makes for some surprisingly interesting discoveries.

Start by driving to Glass Beach (see directions on page 114). After the beach the road continues, terminating at an old cemetery. Here you may see trash or junk cars. That's because this area used to be (and to an extent still is) a place locals use to dump equipment. Go to the lava bench below and head to the right. You'll see that the sides of the cliff are embedded with old junk, mostly metal and glass. (That's where Glass Beach got its glass.) On the lava is an amazing assortment of ancient engine blocks and car frames. I know it sounds ugly, but you have to see what the ocean has done with them. Many of the hulks have completely melted from the rust, often interwoven with the lava itself. Nature has had almost a hundred years to reclaim the metal, and the results of this long-time environmental abuse are oddly fascinating. Even old porcelain and ceramics have been rounded so that you'd swear they're stones.

After exploring the junk area, backtrack by heading left along the shoreline. You'll see areas where the ocean has chiseled its way inland. Continue along the shore (east), and you soon come to a **lava arch**. Water floods under the arch, filling and draining the swimming pool-sized opening in seconds, creating a chaotic, washing machine effect. (Look, but don't swim.)

Tides and surf can alter the shoreline here. There are several blowholes that spout when the wave direction is just right. Always be alert to the potential of large waves.

Past the arch is a 20-plus-foot-long cave we call **Keyhole Cave**. It's got a small opening on the bottom where the ocean surges in and out. At the back is a keyhole-shaped opening. It's fascinating to watch the interplay of the cave and the ocean here.

There are other holes, then a tall column of lava looking down toward the frothing ocean. Although you've left the old dump site behind, local fishermen use this coastal area on weekends and don't always clean up their mess. Try not to let it bother you.

You can either continue along the shoreline or occasionally use the old road paralleling the coast. (Most likely you'll use both.) The landowner doesn't want you driving on the road but has traditionally let people walk along here. The coffee trees behind the shoreline, however, are off limits.

After 20–40 minutes (depending on how often you stop and explore—hopefully a lot) you come to Wahi-awa Beach. It's a lovely looking bay, though the water visibility is usually poor due to river runoff.

Keyhole Cave is just one cool reason to check out the Hanapepe shoreline.

During the week, if the tour boats aren't there for lunch, it's often empty.

GUIDED HIKES

If you want the comfort and security of a local, **Native Hawaiian Conservation** (652-0478) is run by a native Hawaiian couple that takes very small groups on personalized tours to various places. They know the island and its flora well and in addition to the hike, they'll expose you to cultural aspects you won't find elsewhere.

If you're a geology buff, **Kaua'i Nature Tours** (742-8305) is run by the authors of a geology book on Kaua'i. They do a good job of putting complicated concepts into simple terms.

HORSEBACK RIDING

If you want to let someone else do the walking while you tour the island, try horseback riding.

Silver Falls Ranch (828-6718) inland (mauka) of Kilauea is hands down our favorite. Their 300-acre ranch looks more like an palm arboretum, and the guides seem thrilled to see you and show you around their little piece of paradise. The horses are well-groomed and the trails well-kept. This is how rides should be done if you're looking to be pampered in a stunning location (although it's nose-to-tail). $95 for the 1½-hour ride. For $115 it includes another hour and a trip to their small waterfall and large pool. Swim and lunch there. The only downside is that their location is rainier than some of the others, so you take your chances with the weather. Their weight limit is fairly high but also based on your height.

CJM Country Stables (742-6096) has three rides available. The afternoon picnic ride is 2 hours of riding, 1 hour for lunch. The ride is mostly along or near the coast to a "secret" beach (it's Ha'ula). $125 per person. Then there's a 9:30 a.m. and 2 p.m. Scenic Valley Beach Ride—2 hours of riding on mountains and along the coast. Beverages included. $98 per person. No riding experience necessary. 250-pound weight limit. Don't expect much narration, just a nose-to-tail ride for up to 24 people (in three groups) along a beautiful coastline in an area that gets less rain than the others. The leader may spend the entire trip on his cell phone (which has happened to us). But fantastic scenery makes up for most of the shortcomings the company may have and creates an easy second choice for us. The experience is pretty relaxed, and the horses are cooperative. They take lots of riders and feel a bit like a rider processing machine, but the rigid structure will make beginners feel pretty comfortable. Experienced riders may be chomping at the bit (wow, I *finally* got to use that horse phrase in the proper context!) for some more spark.

Esprit de Corps (822-4688) is mostly for experienced riders. They have numerous rides. (The 5-hour is the best.) This includes up to an hour of training/refreshing. Unlike most companies, they'll let you trot and canter—a lot if you like. They ride a dirt road (Moalepe) with pleasant views of the mountains. They *strongly* stress proper riding habits—drilling you on posting (rising trot)—and it's more of a riding adventure instead of an animal tram ride like CJM. Their depth of knowledge is admirable and freely shared. Ask about the tasty rose myrtles along the way. Prices are $130 for the 3-hour intro, $250 for the 6-hour meditation ride and $390 for the all-day (includes lunch and swimming) trip. 220-pound weight limit.

Keapana Horsemanship (823–9303) is a no frills, bare bones one-woman operation that doesn't look like much on the surface and the horses aren't impressive. You don't go for the views or the polish of a fancy ranch. The lure here is the total flexibility. She'll pretty much do what you want, the way you want it, and they'll take kids younger than most along an old, abandoned sugar cane field. Every ride is a custom-made, private ride, and you can walk, run or canter, if you like. $90 for an hour, $150 for two. You'll get a glimpse of Wailua Falls.

Princeville Ranch Stables (826–6777) is our last choice and has rides that feel more like a lesson than a beauty ride, and their horses seem over-trained and overindulged to us. They call it "natural horsemanship," and it means the horses react skittishly to your moves. Don't lean too much; it signals the horse a certain way. Can't carry your camera; it might spook the little darling. No cell phones; *the horses* don't like it. You get the picture. The scenery is nice and they visit a waterfall on one of the rides, but it's hard to relax when you're worried about sending your horse into therapy if you do the wrong thing. They go to a 4-hour ride to a "secret" waterfall (Kalihiwai Falls—it's the falls seen from the bridge right after the 25 mile marker on the north shore.) $135 per person; includes 1 hour for swimming and lunch. There's a 230-pound weight limit. Bring your camera and something to swim in. There's also a 90-minute bluff ride for $80 and a 3-hour ride for $125.

JET SKIING

Jet ski rentals are outlawed on Kaua'i, so if this is what you came to the island to do, you're out of luck.

A kayak can be a marvelous way to see Kaua'i. The quiet, peaceful nature of kayak travel appeals to many. There are four rivers on Kaua'i you can kayak and, of course, there is the open ocean.

River Kayak Trips

We've kayaked all the rivers in several kinds of craft. We prefer the rigid two-person, self-bailing kayaks for beginners, single person self-bailers for those who have kayaked before. Some use canoes, but we're not as fond of them since they can fill with water if tipped. (Inflatables are terrible since they are easily deflected by wind—called weathercocking, in case you're taking notes.)

Of the four rivers, the **Wailua** is by far the most popular. (See map on page 59.) It's very scenic, and there's a waterfall called **Secret Falls** on the north fork you can hike to if you like. (Some brochures call it the most spectacular waterfall on the island. That's bunk, but it's a nice one just the same.) It's 5 miles round trip and takes most people about 3 hours plus stopping or hiking time. Since large boats take passengers to the Fern Grotto, kayakers should always stay on the north side of the river. If you want to visit the Fern Grotto, consider pulling ashore *before* or *after* the docks. To be honest, the grotto is not the same as it used to be and is barely worth

If the ocean surf's up, how about a day on the river instead?

there's nothing under the water first. The African village scene from *Outbreak* was filmed on a secluded plain here on your right; look for it. The wind will probably be in your face coming back, so hug the north bank tightly to minimize the wind. The earlier you leave (we start at 7 a.m. and strongly suggest you do, too), the less wind coming back, and you'll avoid crowds on the river and at the waterfall. To kayak this river *on your own* there are special logistical considerations—see RENTING A KAYAK FOR THE RIVER below. No kayak renting on Sundays.

The **Hanalei River** is the longest and goes mostly through plains. (Beautiful plains, but plains.) There are no powerboats past the mouth where you put in, so it'll be quieter. It takes about 3 hours (6¾ miles) round trip for most people to kayak this peaceful river. After a heavy rain, waterfalls etched in the distant valley walls can enhance the trip. The wind usually helps you a little coming back.

The **Hule'ia River** in Lihu'e is 5 miles round trip (2 hours or more). It starts from Nawiliwili Harbor, and the water flow is not great, so expect ickier water here. There are majestic mountains on your left as you go out, and you will pass the Menehune Fishpond and an area where they filmed the swing-on-a-vine-to-the-waiting-airplane scene from *Raiders of the Lost Ark*. (Keep an eye out for the opening to the fishpond.) The last navigable part is our favorite part of this river. This river goes through a wildlife refuge, but you'll see and hear more birds on the Hanalei River. The

the effort to get there. The best part about kayaking this river is the scenery and hiking to the waterfall. Just enjoy the Wailua for its lushness, and watch out for the large boat tours. Past the Fern Grotto, you *might* see a rope swing at a well-known swimming hole. (The state has an ongoing war with pesky rope swing builders. State workers, with marching orders from their lawyers, relentlessly cut 'em down almost as fast as people put up new ones.) People line up to jump off the cliff into the water there, despite a state sign warning them not to. If you do, too, make *sure* wind will probably be in your face coming back. If you're doing this on your own, you'll run into large guided groups at times.

The **Kalihiwai** is short but *very* sweet. You can kayak it in an hour if you decide not to do the additional hike to Kalihiwai Falls. Put in at Kalihiwai Beach. You might see the waterfall from where you stop kayaking. The scenery is the best of the four, and you might want to do it if you have any juice left after a Hanalei River trip. Expect to be hassled if you visit the falls in any way that doesn't bring money to the horseback company that leases the land where the falls are.

Renting a Kayak for the River

You can rent a kayak and paddle any river you like, *except* the Wailua River. The state has rules making it much harder to rent a kayak *on your own* to kayak the Wailua (which is the best one). They want you to go on a *guided* tour. (It's not a safety issue; it's a political one—long story.) So although we recommend doing river trips *on your own*, this may be hard to do on the Wailua. Of the companies mentioned below, only **Kayak Kaua'i**, **Wailua Kayak & Canoe** and **Wailua Kayak Adventure** have them for rent for the Wailua River. (The last one has the best rates.) Call weeks in advance to maximize your chances of getting one. An alternative is **Kamokila Hawaiian Village** (823–0559), which rents kayaks for $35 from a location so far up the Wailua River, that your paddle to Secret Falls is probably less than 10 minutes. They also *claim* they'll rent them on Sunday. (Nobody else is allowed.)

All the other rivers on the island you can kayak on your own without a guide.

On the Wailua River, first you kayak, then you hike...then you frolic!

Prices change a lot in this competitive business, and prices for rentals on the Wailua cost more. For single-person kayaks (which are getting harder to find) consider Peddle 'n Paddle or Wailua Kayak Adventures—rent for $20–$25 per day. Two-person kayaks are $40–$75 per day. Sometimes they are cheaper if you are willing to arm wrestle timeshare salesmen. Most cars will hold 2 or 3 kayaks on the roof.

Guided River Trips

For guided tours of the Wailua River, see list of companies below. Most companies charge around $85. Although the Wailua is our favorite *unguided* kayak trip, the best *guided* river trip we've seen is a 7-hour Hule'ia River kayak/hike trip from **Outfitters Kaua'i** called the Kipu Falls Safari. About 2 miles of kayaking then a half mile of hiking to a small falls. Then you're on a tractor-pulled wagon to lunch at a second waterfall. After eating, you head to Kipu Falls (see page 70) and its zipline. You'll finally hike back to the river where an outrigger canoe awaits to bring you back to your car. We recommend the morning trip. The hiking and paddling are not overly tough, though you'll get wet and muddy. The guides do an excellent job, they handle the food well, they're great with kids (who *love* the part where they feed some pigs and peacocks), and they don't rush you during the trip. It's not cheap at $178 per person, 20 people max. They have a less desirable trip that omits Kipu Falls and lunch for $98.

Ocean Kayak Trips

Ocean kayaking can be an experience of a lifetime. The crown jewel is a summer Na Pali Coast trip. *National Geographic* named it the second best adventure in the United States. (Rafting the Colorado was #1 and dog sledding in Alaska was #3.) Na Pali can be an *incredible* trip for those who can do it, either guided or unguided. We try to do it *every* summer and camp along the way. Because paddling Na Pali is so involved, we have a complete description in ADVENTURES on page 186.

In addition to Na Pali, **Kayak Kaua'i** and **Outfitters Kaua'i** have Po'ipu to Port Allen trips in the winter for around $145. The wind usually helps on this 7-mile, 4–5 hour paddle. Certainly not the most interesting shoreline on the island, but the Lawa'i Bay stop is nice.

What if I want to rent a kayak and paddle the ocean on my own? Well, unlike all the other Hawaiian islands, Kaua'i is a very difficult place to rent a kayak *for the ocean*. Whether it's because companies want to make more money guiding you or because Kaua'i's ocean waters are not as calm (probably a little of both), most will turn you down cold if you tell them you're taking a kayak into the ocean. Of course, if it's the sit-on-top variety (which most here are) as opposed to canoe-types, that's what we use on the ocean anyway. If you have some experience and good judgment, there's no one to stop you from taking it to the ocean.

Kayak Companies

The companies described below provide a variety of services.

Kayak Kaua'i (800-437-3507 or 826-9844) in Hanalei. From May through September they have one-day guided Na Pali tours for $205 per person. Lunch included at either Miloli'i or Nu'alolo Kai. They also have ocean trips to Lawa'i Bay on the south shore for $145. The more involved the trip, the better it is to call them in advance, *especially* for Na Pali. For the Wailua River they have doubles for $75. They have the best location if you're going to kayak the Hanalei River. Guided Wailua trips with lunch for $85.

Outfitters Kaua'i (742–9667) in Po'ipu has summer Na Pali trips for $225. Guided Wailua River kayak tours with lunch are available for $98, as well as the awesome trip described under GUIDED RIVER TRIPS.

Pedal 'n Paddle (826–9069) in Hanalei specializes in one-stop shopping. They rent kayaks for the Hanalei, camping supplies, beach cruiser bikes and snorkel gear.

Aloha Canoes & Kayaks (246–6804) does guided Hule'ia River trips (without Kipu Falls). Not so compelling.

Wailua Kayak & Canoe (821–1188) operates near the Wailua River, and you'll probably be able to walk your kayak down to the boat launch on a kayak dolly. Their gear (seats and such) are not as good as others, and customer service is scant. Doubles rent for $75. Guided Wailua trip is $90, snacks only.

Wailua Kayak Adventures (822–5795) has river kayaks for rent—$30 for single kayaks, $60 for doubles. Guided Wailua trips are $85 *per couple*, snacks only.

Kamokila Hawaiian Village (823–0559) is located far up the river, less than 10 minutes from the Fern Grotto and the trail to Secret Falls. They rent kayaks for $35. If you don't want to paddle yourself, you can take a short canoe trip from there for $30.

Kayak Wailua (822–3388) is a no-frills operation. They don't offer you lunch, and you pay extra for seatback upgrade. Their guides have solidified over the years, and it's now mostly a family affair. $47.

Ali'i Kayaks (241–7700) is a local outfit that does tours of the Wailua for

$40. They meet at Wailua Visitor Center at Hwy 580 and Hwy 56.

In addition to standard bus tours, there are other land tours worth considering.

Hawai'i Movie Tours (822–1192) takes people in vans to various locations around the island where movies were filmed. (See page 23 for more on movies that have been filmed on the island.) You see clips of the pertinent movie scenes on monitors in the van while they show you where and how they were filmed. The quality of the tour very much depends on the quality of the guide, and overall the company does a pretty good job. Best seats are right side, middle seat of the van. The half-day trip is $89 and includes lunch. They also have a 4WD van tour of more remote areas for $95. Hawai'i Movie Tours is not the only movie tour, but it's the best one out there.

Aloha Kaua'i Tours (245–8809) provides 4WD tours. Trips include the Kilohana area (which is private and gated), the mountains behind Wailua town (which are open to the public) or a non-4WD road tour of Waimea Canyon area. Prices are $75–$135. The Rain Forest Tour includes a 3-mile hike.

If you're interested in chocolate, **Steelgrass Chocolate Farm** (821–1857) gives 3-hour tours of their 8½ acre farm for $60 (cash); kids 12 and under free. (There's lots of standing around, so kids under 8 may get too antsy.) The tour is about an hour too long and double what it's worth, but it's educational and you'll get to nibble on tons of different gourmet dark chocolates. (Not from here; their plants are too young to be processed.) Once you learn what's involved in making chocolate, you'll wonder why anyone was *ever* able to discover the joys of this plant.

When Hollywood needs a beautiful, remote coastline studded with majestic cliffs and glorious valleys to film movies,

These passengers know what Hollywood knows…Na Pali is mesmerizing.

they often choose Kaua'i's Na Pali Coast. *The Lost World, Six Days/Seven Nights, King Kong* and others have all used a Na Pali backdrop to convey an idyllic paradise. From the sea, this area of the island takes on a magical quality. Many people dream of seeing the Hawaiian Islands by sea. The Na Pali region is surely the most popular area to cruise, but there are others, as well. This can be a fantasy trip. Rough seas are rarely part of the fantasy, but they can be part of reality, depending on conditions.

Seeing Na Pali by boat is an incredible thrill that we highly recommend. Soaking up this coastline and being on a boat are exquisitely relaxing. You can see it by leaving from the west side or the north shore. They are two very different experiences.

If you leave from the **west side** you'll only see half of Na Pali (and not the best

half), and ¾ of the trip isn't even along Na Pali. The boats that leave from Port Allen travel 23 miles along the relatively uninteresting (by sea) Mana Plain, then head up the dry side of Na Pali before turning around at Kalalau. (Boats that leave from Kikiaola Harbor shave 9 miles off the duller part—see map on page 84.) If boats would cruise past Kalalau to Hanakapi'ai, we'd be much happier, because that short stretch has some beautiful sights. But most turn back at Kalalau.

A few companies, however, have permits to leave the **north shore**. Those boats that leave from Hanalei or 'Anini on the north shore have a *far* better and more exciting route, though the return trip is usually into head seas (meaning into the swells) and headwinds, so it can be bumpy.

Some west shore companies switch to south shore tours in October and return to Na Pali in April; others can do Na Pali year-round. Some combine it with a trip to Ni'ihau. If you do Na Pali in winter, expect bigger seas.

There are two main snorkeling spots: *Nu'alolo* (which is pretty good) and a spot near Polihale that the bigger boats often use called *Makole* (which is pretty bad). If you're at *Makole*, the best snorkeling is away from shore, not toward it.

Some of these boating companies give you discounts for booking online.

What & Who

We've spent a lot of time anonymously reviewing these boats, and here's the deal. If it's May through September and you really want to see Na Pali, you want to do this from the north shore—*period*. That means you want **Na Pali Sea Breeze**, **Na Pali Catamaran** or **Captain Sundown**, or if you want no frills, **North Shore Charters**. As mentioned, *nothing*

a west side company can do can compete with the route these four take. They could probably *flog* you on this trip, and they'd still be better than anyone leaving from Port Allen. If you can't book these or it's not these summer months (April and October are borderline), we recommend **HoloHolo** and **Liko Kaua'i**.

Our favorite is **Na Pali Sea Breeze** (828–1285). They have a 34-foot power cat, carrying at most 16 people for $150. Capt. Bob was a resident of the Taylor Camp in 1970 (see page 55) and has over 30 years experience on Kaua'i waters. He's a salty dog with a profound knowledge of the coast that other companies lack. The deli lunch is better than most, with a variety of sandwiches. The boat is comfy even when full. Only thing we don't like is their cheap snorkel gear. Leaving from 'Anini, it takes 10 more minutes to get to Na Pali than the Hanalei guys, but the better amenities are worth it.

Next on our list is **Na Pali Catamaran** (826–6853). Their 34-foot power cat (no sailing) takes up to 16 people. $150 for the 4-hour tour includes snorkeling at Nu'alolo (they're often the first one there for the morning tour) and a cheap deli lunch. There's no shade and no trampoline to lie on with this narrow cat, but we really like how they'll usually go into the sea caves during the trip. Morning is much better than afternoon here. We like them because of their route and their low profile that lets them enter the caves.

Another north shore catamaran, **Captain Sundown** (826–5585), uses a 40-foot sailing catamaran. They'll usually sail part of the way down the coast far from shore, then motor back a bit closer. Because of the tall mast, they don't go into any of the caves, which is a shame. Their narration is not very good (or accurate), but the boat is comfortable and they'll usually only take 15 or so, making it feel nice and roomy. Food is minimal—nothing at breakfast, deli sandwich at lunch and cookies just before you return to your starting point at the Hanalei River. Consider riding the net (trampoline) on the way out. (The way back is much wetter and bumpier.) Although they do go out sometimes in the winter, it's rougher at that time on the part of the north shore that these boats explore. We believe they are flat out *too expensive*, and if they didn't have a north shore launching point we'd probably be talking stink about them. Morning 5–6 hour trip is $199, afternoon (less recommended—no snorkeling) is $150. This includes your *mandatory* gratuity.

All the north shore companies are good about letting you venture away from the boat a bit during your snorkel at Nu'alolo.

Na Pali Coast Hanalei (826–6114) is also out of Hanalei, but their 28-foot boat and $140 3½ hour tours aren't as good as the other north shore companies.

HoloHolo Charters (335–0815) has a large, 65-foot power catamaran. Their trips are distinguished in that they go to the "forbidden" island of Ni'ihau. For $179, the 7-hour trip leaves in the morning from Port Allen and makes a beeline to Kalalau Beach on Na Pali. In light seas they're close to shore; heavier swells call for greater distance. Then they tour part of Na Pali before heading to Ni'ihau where they snorkel. (Clean, clear water and lots of fish, but currents can sometimes make snorkeling there more work.) Continental breakfast and a good deli lunch included. After the snorkeling, the open bar serves drinks, but they refuse to serve cookies until

they're 5 minutes from port. (Maybe they're afraid you'll toss them otherwise.)

There are two large trampolines at the bow for sunning, but they and the entire bow section are off limits most of the time while motoring. Easy steps into and out of the water from the boat. HoloHolo is a good outfit and is easy to recommend. The boat is good, pretty stable, there's plenty of shade available, and the crew is very professional. They have a freshwater shower hose, adequate snorkel gear but no wetsuits available. Our only complaint is that the boat design makes it feel crowded on nice days. Most of the seating is inside, but when it's reasonably calm and sunny most people want to be outside, which is somewhat spartan and lacking in seating, so people tend to crowd around the railings.

Their sunset tour is $99 for appetizers, beer, wine and champagne.

They also have a smaller cat called the Leila, but we don't recommend it as much.

Liko Kaua'i Cruises (338–0333) offers a relaxing 5-hour tour of Na Pali on a 49-foot power catamaran with 34 people. You'll leave from Kikiaola Small Boat Harbor near Kekaha and cruise north up the coast, often going as far as Ke'e Beach if the weather's good. (That's farther than any other west shore power cat goes which pleases us greatly.) On the way back you stop and snorkel at Nu'alolo Kai or sometimes lousy Makole. Liko, a native Hawaiian, narrates with legends and stories. $140 for adults, $95 for keiki (kids), it includes snacks and sandwiches. They do a particularly good job with kids. Afternoon/sunset tours also available in the summer.

Other Big Boats

Captain Andy's Sailing Adventures (335–6833) has 5½ hour Na Pali trips from Port Allen to Kalalau for $150. Snorkeling when conditions permit, but at lousy Makole. Deli lunch with free beer and wine. It would be a better product if they didn't pack up to *49* people on their nice 55-foot catamarans (and it *feels* crowded). You're best off if there's more than 49, because then they'll split the group onto two boats. These are sleek sailing cats, but they only sail a short time and when they *do* raise the sail, it seems to activate the cookie-tossing instinct in some people, especially if they're using the indoor shade. But they are pretty capable sailboats, which will excite sailing enthusiasts. Sunset tours are $139 with a hot buffet and snorkeling. They also have two Zodiac tours for $139 or $159.

Kaua'i Sea Tours (826–7254) leaves from Port Allen for Na Pali trips for $135. They have a 60-foot power/sailing cat called the Lucky Lady, which rides well. Think of this as a power cat, because at best they'll probably only raise the sails *while motoring* downwind. (The sails are more for decoration since this type of vessel sails like a pig.) They also use a 24-foot rigid-hull inflatable that lands at Nu'alolo (in the summer) for $135, but it's not in the same league as Na Pali Explorer's nicer inflatable.

Blue Dolphin Charters (335–5553) has two catamarans called Blue Dolphin I and II similar to the Lucky Lady above. Up to 49 people, continental breakfast (good cinnamon rolls) and deli lunch. They have a slide into the water. $149 for Na Pali trips. You can try SCUBA for an extra $35, which is quite reasonable. (But we've seen them very hesitant to

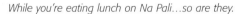

While you're eating lunch on Na Pali...so are they.

give you a wetsuit. Don't believe their ridiculous overestimates of the water temps. You divers *want* a shorty in the summer, and a *full-sized* suit in the winter.) Note that divers and snorkelers usually won't stray far from the boat. Some days they also offer a Ni'ihau trip similar to HoloHolo's for $195. The crew is pretty good and their narrations fair. Plenty of shade, but avoid the inside seats at the front of the cabin. You never sail; at best they'll motor sail downwind. For us, the deal-killer with this company is that they *make* you wear awkward flotation devices, even if you're an Olympic swimmer. If you want to wear one, that's fine, but the mandatory policy is annoying. You won't be able to dive down or get around as easily. Sunset tours are $119.

Rigid-Hull Inflatables (RIBS)

North Shore Charters (828–1379) leaves out of 'Anini Beach *in the summer* with 14 passengers in their 26-foot boat. It has inflatable sides but with a hard hull—amazingly smooth and fast for a Zodiac. No frills, no shade, deli sandwiches, and you'll snorkel at Nu'alolo for $140. The best route of the RIBS.

Na Pali Explorer (338–9999) leaves from the west side and heads north in their 48-foot boat. There is some shade on board. They also have a less impressive 26-foot boat with no shade. $139 for the morning 5-hour Na Pali/snorkel trip. These include continental breakfast and a light lunch. $95 for the 3-hour Na Pali dash, no snorkeling.

Na Pali Riders (742–6331) has a 4½-hour trip, but it's a decidedly mixed bag. Think of them as a low-budget trip. On the positive side they leave from Kikiaola Harbor and, during the summer season, they go all the way to Ke'e on the north

shore, so you'll see all of Na Pali. (Winter is whale watching heading south.) When they encounter dolphins, they get amazingly close. Also, inflatables can be fun on calm seas. But if seas aren't reasonably smooth, it's a rough ride because you'll feel every bump. On the negative side there's no shade or restroom, and they only serve drinks and snacks. Price is $99.

Boating Tips

Many companies offer morning and afternoon trips. Morning trips usually have snorkeling and better food on board. Morning is also when you're more likely to encounter smoother seas and better weather, so that's what we recommend.

Be wary of the information given during narrations. Many boat companies, like their helicopter brethren, are particularly prone to repeating inaccurate nonsense in their attempt to "educate" you, and we've seen some who literally made it up as they went along.

Seasickness can strike anyone. If you're concerned that it will be a problem, strongly consider taking Dramamine or something similar at least an hour *before* you leave. (The night before and morning of are best. It's useless to take it once you're on the boat.) Also, avoid any alcohol the night before. (A *big* no-no.) No greasy foods before or during the trip. And some think that citrus juices are a cause of seasickness. Ginger is a very good preventative/treatment. Below deck or in anything enclosed is a bad place to be if you're worried about getting seasick. Without a reference point, you're much more likely to let 'er rip. Scopolamine patches work but have side effects, including (occasionally) blurred vision that can last a week. (Been there, done that, on a 10-

River trips up and down the Wailua River take you to the Fern Grotto, a fern-lined amphitheater.

day boat trip.) If you're feeling sick, put something cold on the back of your neck. As far as the Ni'ihau trips are concerned, we've had people tell us they were prone to seasickness and ask where they should sit. The answer is...on land. The boats can be mighty rockin' in that channel between the islands, and if you have a history of easy-queasy, that trip might not be for you. Coming back from Ni'ihau is almost always rough.

From the west shore, the best views are off the right (starboard) side going out to Na Pali and off the left (port) side coming back. It's the opposite when you leave from the north shore. Also remember that most boats are a lot smoother in the back than the front, but you may get diesel fumes back there. Just slightly ahead of the back seats is our preferred position.

People come off these trips *toasted*, especially in the summer. Make sure you slather on the sunscreen early and often, or you'll be sorry for the rest of your trip.

Since most trips involve driving early in the morning, consider doing the trip early in your vacation—when your body clock is still on mainland time, and it's easier to rise early.

Overall, we've noticed an improvement in the boating companies' performance. Note, however, that there are a number of smaller boat companies with smaller boats that are crowded and have no shade, and we don't recommend them for these waters.

PARASAILING

Parasailing is outlawed on Kaua'i. Hey, *that* was easy.

Kaua'i is the only Hawaiian island to offer river trips, and there are two ways to do it. You can take a riverboat ride up the Wailua River (often referred to as the only navigable river in all Hawai'i, but this is a relative term) or paddle your own kayak. **Smith's Motorboat Service** (821–6892) goes 3 miles up the Wailua River and stops at the Fern Grotto, a large natural amphitheater with ferns all about. This is a popular place to get married. It's 30 minutes each way with entertainment and interesting information provided throughout. They spend 30–45 minutes at the site. $20 per person, and they leave many times each day in their 100+ passenger boats. If you've heard of the Fern Grotto before and seen photos, be forewarned that those photos, even in current ads, might be *very* old. Hurricane 'Iwa in 1982 thinned out the ferns, and the closing of the nearby sugar company—and its leaky reservoir above the cave that accidentally created the grotto in the first place—has resulted in a greatly diminished attraction. They've tried to rejuvinate it somewhat, but it's still a bit of a letdown.

You can also rent a kayak at any of several places and paddle the Wailua, the Hanalei River, the Kalihiwai River or the Hule'ia Stream. The best thing about kayaking the Wailua River isn't the Fern Grotto. (In fact, they discourage landing kayaks there.) Instead, it's the overall scenery and a hike to a waterfall, if you like. See KAYAKING.

Kaua'i is justly famous for many things: its incomparable lushness, gorgeous beaches and balmy nights. But Kaua'i is not famous for its diving. This is a shame because Kaua'i has some very good dive spots. Turtles are common, and many of them are downright gregarious. Lava tubes, ledges and walls are sprinkled around the island. Fish are abundant and varied. Coral growth is not as good as around the Big Island—at 22° latitude, Kaua'i is on the fringe of the coral belt. Kaua'i's many rivers and streams cut visibility in some areas, but you can still see more than 100 feet on good days.

Dive Operator	Services Available	Price of Dive	Rent Gear For a Day	Boat Size / Passengers	Dive Computer	Ni'ihau 3-Tank Dive	Dive Certification	Rx Masks
Aquatic Adventures 645–0927	Shore Dives	$70–$80 (1 tank)	$40	N/A	No	None	$425–$450	Yes
Bubbles Below 332–7333	Boat Dives & Shore Dives	$125–$150 (2 tank)	No	35' / 8 32' / 6	Included	$295–$320	$450	No
Fathom Five 742–6991	Dive Shop & Boat Dives	$120–$155 (2 tank)	$45	25' / 6 35' / 6	Included	$345–$370	$275–$495	Yes
Mana Divers 335–0881	Boat Dives & Shore Dives	$120–$150 (2 tank)	$40	34' / 6-8	Included	None	$450	Yes
Ocean Quest 822–3589	Shore Dives	$85–$120 (2 tank)	$45	N/A	Included	None	$275–$495	Yes
Seasport Divers 742–9303	Dive Shop & Boat Dives	$120–$150 (2 tank)	$45	32' / 12 48' / 18	Included	$295–$320	$245–$400	Yes

Granted, you might find better conditions on the Kona coast of the Big Island or around Lana'i. It is dryer there and the lava's porous, so the ocean receives virtually no runoff. But this should not dissuade you from enjoying the wondrous underwater sights the Garden Island has to offer.

Kaua'i's ocean pattern is small summer surf on the north shore, larger summer surf on the south shore, and the opposite during winter months, so you should plan your diving activities accordingly. Summer is very popular and the best companies book up early, so call them as soon as you know when you want to dive. The dive boat operators conduct their tours on the south shore year-round since the local government doesn't allow the boats to moor on the north shore. Some also have dives on the west side at Mana Crack and at Lehua Rock off the coast of Ni'ihau. Those dives are generally considered advanced due to the depths and currents involved. The Ni'ihau dive in particular involves at least 1½ hour travel time each way, so those who get seasick (and those who aren't sure) should take Dramamine or Bonine *before* they depart.

Off Ni'ihau, however, you're treated to ridiculously clear water, lots of big life (sharks, rays, dolphins and your best chance at a Hawaiian monk seal) and a close view of the "Forbidden Island." (The Robinsons, who own Ni'ihau, *hate* it when you call it that.) See ADVENTURES chapter for more on this dive. Book in advance to ensure space.

So you'll know **our perspective** when we review companies, we should tell you what we do and don't like when we go on a dive. On a bad dive, the dive master takes the group on a non-stop excursion that keeps you kicking the whole time. No time to stop and explore the nooks and crannies. Good outfits will give you a briefing, tell you about some of the endemic species here, what to look for and will point out various things on the dives, keeping it moving but not too fast. Bad outfits kick a lot. Good outfits explain the unique qualities of Hawai'i's environment. Bad dive masters may tell you what *they* saw (but *you* missed). Good companies work around your needs, wishes and desires. Bad companies keep everyone on a short leash. Good dive masters know their stuff and share it with you. Bad dive masters don't know squat but imply they know it all in order to impress you. As divers, we tend to like companies that wander toward the boat for the latter part of the dive and allow you to go up when you are near the end of your tank, as opposed to everyone going up when the heaviest breather has burned up his/her bottle.

During times when we feel the diving conditions are bad (poor vis or big swells), we like to call around and ask about conditions. We appreciate the companies who admit it's bad, and we hold it against those who tell us how wonderful conditions are. (The company that fails this test the most is **Mana Divers**.)

If You've Never Dived Before

If this is your first dive, the recommendation is a no-brainer. **Fathom Five** wins by default since other companies have poor systems. For instance, **Seasport Divers** soaks up too much pre-dive time since they make you do a pre-dive class in a pool (perhaps the day before) prior to taking you on your boat dive. If you don't do well in the pool, they won't take you on the boat. We don't think

Tunnels Beach sports a fabulous reef, perfect for snorkeling, swimming and SCUBA.

that such measures are necessary. Most first timers in Hawai'i do fine going straight to the ocean, *if* the instructor does a good job, which, fortunately, **Fathom Five** does. They will take you out for an introductory shore dive for $100 (one tank) or $120–$165 (two-tank).

Mana Divers has a one-tank shore intro for $120 and **Aquatic Adventures** has them for $110. Some of the other dive companies encourage you to do your intro off their boat. That's a concept we disagree with since shore dives make beginners *far* more comfortable than jumping from a boat into water over their heads with unfamiliar gear.

If you're interested in getting **certified** or did your book work on the mainland and want an open water referral, **Fathom Five** is your best bet. The open water referral method allows you to do your class work at home, saving your Kaua'i vacation for the *fun stuff*.

Recommended for Certified Divers

As anonymous certified divers (who sometimes pretend to be novices), we are able to experiment with different operators. The outfits we recommend are **Fathom Five** and **Bubbles Below** for boat dives and **Ocean Quest** for shore dives. They are all well-qualified, professional and knowledgeable. **Fathom Five** and their shore dive arm, **Ocean Quest**, is probably the best outfit on the island. We've been impressed at how they run their boat dives, and the personalized service really shows. They use a 25-foot and 35-foot 6-pack, so they're able to keep the groups smaller and respond more to what individual divers want—a nice touch. As for their Ocean Quest arm, we've never seen a better shore dive outfit. Experienced divers will love their shore dives, and beginners will find them perfect for their introduction to the world of

SCUBA. In addition to standard 2-tank dives, they have twilight dives, night dives, premium 3-tank dives and Ni'ihau dives including an extraordinary overnight dive.

Bubbles Below has discovered many of the island's great dive spots, and they are pretty good with customers. During the summer their Mana Crack dives can be exciting. They say they'll take a maximum of 8 on their 35-foot Radon, but you'll want to verify that when you book. They also have a 32-foot power catamaran that takes 6 people.

Sometimes it's tempting to go with the cheapest dive operators. Remember that if you're herded in and out with a cheap company that doesn't know the underwater terrain, you may find that your "better deal" was no bargain at all.

Dive Shops

There are two dive *shops* (as opposed to dive operators) on the island. Although not the biggest, the best is **Fathom Five**. Although their shop is on the small side, they have *two* boats (they tend to use one for more experienced divers, the other for rustier divers), so they don't mix the two unless you *want* them to. (Certifieds will *love* that.) They feed you better than anyone else, get you on the boat quicker and have a good ascent policy. We also like how they'll keep and rinse your personal gear, if you dive on multiple days. They're on Po'ipu Road in Koloa.

Seasport Divers in Po'ipu (with a smaller satellite office in Kapa'a) is the largest shop on the island with the best selection if you're looking to *buy* gear, but we don't recommend their boat dives as much, except perhaps their Ni'ihau trips in the summer.

For **renting gear**, either of the two shops will do fine.

For the heavy breathers among you, **Bubbles Below, Fathom Five,** and **Seasport** have 100s available, so feel free to *suck 'em up.*

Dive computers are available for your own *independent* dives and can only be rented from **Fathom Five**. *Disposable* underwater cameras in a watertight box for snorkeling are available at most grocery stores and sundry shops. **Fathom Five** rents better cameras for SCUBA.

Some of the dive boats on Kaua'i feed you little or nothing between dives. I don't know about you, but I'm tempted to gnaw on the side of the boat after a dive. Bring a package of cookies with you. You'll probably be able to sell them to other hungry divers at prices confiscatory enough to pay for your dive. *I have a bid of $8 for a chocolate chip cookie...Do I hear $9?*

Shorties are usually sufficient for most people *in the summer only*. Surface water temperatures range from a low of 73.4° in February to a high of 80° in October. Any company that will *only* provide you with shorties doesn't seem to care much about your comfort. Or maybe we've just lived here too long and have gotten wussy about the cold.

Between morning and afternoon dives, morning is almost always best.

Nitrox (or enriched air) is available at **Fathom Five, Bubbles Below** and **Seasport Divers**.

Kaua'i has many boat dive spots. Since the more resourceful operators are always finding new spots, and since you basically go where the boat operators go, we'll forgo a detailed description of all boat dive destinations. Suffice it to say that Sheraton Caves, General

Store, Brennecke's Ledge, Turtle Bluffs, Amber's Arches and Fishbowl are all popular. Some sites, such as Sheraton Caves, are nice but a bit over-dived.

Remember not to drive up to Waimea Canyon or the Kalalau Lookout after diving. As far as your nitrogen level is concerned, you're flying.

Below is a list of the best shore dives on the island:

- **Ke'e Beach, north shore**—If the seas are flat on a calm summer day, this area offers interesting shallow relief. The area near the reef drop-off is good, again on calm days.

- **Tunnels, north shore**—Easy access, lots of turtles, reef sharks, lava tubes, caves and nice underwater relief. Tunnels' allure is not its visibility, but the dramatic underwater topography. *If you dive with someone who really knows the reef, this is unquestionably the best shore dive on the island and is often better than a boat dive. Low tide is best.

- **The Hole, north shore**—Located just off the St. Regis Resort. Like the name says, a hole in the reef. Acceptable underwater relief and easy access, especially if you rent your gear from the dive facility just a few feet away, Hanalei Watersports. They will give you precise directions if you call them.

- **Kahala Point, east shore**—Entry and exit is a bugger on the lava rocks with crashing surf. Underwater relief is good, and there are lots of fish. Near Anahola Beach Park.

- **Koloa Landing, south shore**—Easy entry, usually calm conditions year-round and decent coral near the shore. After slightly murky water on entry, the sea is usually quite clear. High tide is best.

Skydiving is available at Port Allen Airport on the west side. You don't need us to tell you whether you should try this or not. It's either, *Yeah, cool. Where do I sign?* or, *Yeah, right. Are you out of your mind?*

The company here, **Skydive Kaua'i** (335–5859), isn't in the same league as those at Dillingham on O'ahu. Skydiving there is a big business, and the reliable onshore breeze on O'ahu's north shore makes it a pretty good place to do tandem jumps. This company is newer and lacks the track record of O'ahu companies. Their plane doesn't exactly inspire confidence, and you're grateful that there are parachutes onboard. And Port Allen isn't an ideal spot to do tandem skydives. It's a peninsula, almost completely surrounded by water, and shifting winds make it more difficult to target your landing area. In fact, during our jump, a solo jumper missed the airport entirely and had to land at a nearby park. You're equipped with an inflatable life vest in case you drop into the water, and the jumpmasters were professional and seemed honest about describing the inadequacies of this jump location. But hey, as long as you understand the risks here, you'll still have the thrill of leaping from a plane at 10,000 feet, the overload of adrenaline that makes things feel like slow motion when you exit the aircraft, and the blissful satisfaction of seeing the parachute inflate above you and your instructor.

It'll run you $229 plus $2 for every pound you weigh over 200 pounds.

You can buy a pretty slick DVD of your jump for $79.

If you have ever looked into a salt-water aquarium and marveled at the diversity of the fish life, snorkeling is an experience you might want to try. Anyone who has ever hovered over hundreds of colorful fish can attest to the thrill you feel being in their environment.

Where to snorkel depends on how good you are and what kind of experience you want. The best place for beginners is **Lydgate Beach Park** in Wailua. There you will find an area protected by a ring of boulders that shields you from the strong ocean. Mornings are best. The intermediate snorkeler will find **Ke'e** or **Tunnels** on the north shore to be fabulous during the calm, warmer months. **Hideaways** is also

Even when the ocean looks angry, Lydgate's protected ocean pool offers relatively safe snorkeling on all but the highest surf days. Morning is best.

Hawaiian Reefs—*Why is it That*...?

What is that crackling sound, like bacon frying, I always hear while snorkeling or diving? For years this baffled people. In the early days of submarines, the sound interfered with sonar operations. Finally we know the answer. It's hidden snapping shrimp defining their territory. One variety is even responsible for all the dark cracks and channels you see in smooth lobe coral. A pair creates the channels, then "farms" algae inside.

Why are there so few shellfish in Hawai'i? It's too warm for some of the more familiar shellfish (which tend to be filter-feeders, and Hawaiian waters don't have as much stuff to filter). But Hawai'i has more shellfish than most people are aware of. They hide well under rocks and in sand. Also, people tend to collect shells (which is illegal), and that depletes the numbers.

Why do coral cuts take so long to heal? Coral contains a live animal. When you scrape coral, it leaves proteinaceous matter in your body, which takes much longer for your body to dispatch.

Why do some of the reefs appear dead? Much of the "coral" you see around Kaua'i isn't the kind of coral you're used to. It's called coralline algae, which secretes calcium carbonate. It's not dead; it's *supposed* to look like that.

What do turtles eat? Dolphins. (Just teasing.) They primarily eat plants growing on rocks, as well as jellyfish when they are lucky enough to encounter them. Unfortunately for turtles and lucky for us, jellyfish aren't numerous here.

Is it harmful when people play with an octopus? Yes, if the octopus gets harmed while trying to get it out of its hole. Best to leave them alone.

Why does the ocean rarely smell fishy here in Hawai'i? Two reasons. We have relatively small tide changes, so the ocean doesn't strand large amounts of smelly seaweed at low tide. Also, the water is fairly sterile compared to mainland water, which owes much of its smell to algae and seaweed that thrives in the bacteria-rich runoff from industrial sources.

Why is the water so clear here? Because relatively little junk is poured into our water compared to the mainland. Also, natural currents tend to flush the water with a continuous supply of fresh, clean ocean water.

Why do my ears hurt when I dive deep, and how are scuba divers able to get over it? Because the increasing weight of the ocean is pressing on your ears the farther down you go. Divers alleviate this by equalizing their ears. Sounds high tech, but that simply means holding your nose while trying to blow out of it. This forces air into the eustachian tubes, creating equal pressures with the outside ocean. (It doesn't work if your sinuses are clogged.) Anything with air between it gets compressed. So if you know someone who gets a headache whenever they go under water...well, they must be an airhead.

great during calm seas. **Po'ipu Beach Park** on the south shore usually offers good snorkeling and calm seas in cooler months on either side of the tombolo. The BEACHES chapter has a description of all the beaches and the different characteristics they possess.

As far as gear goes, there are numerous places to rent gear on the island. We always snorkel wearing reef shoes and divers' fins (which fit over reef shoes). This way we can enter and exit the water without worrying about stepping on anything. Cheap reef shoes can be found at many places, including Kmart. Bootie socks or women's thin, ankle-length socks will keep you from rubbing the top of your tootsies raw. Divers' fins can be rented at most dive shops. If enough people ask snorkel companies about them, they will start to carry them, too.

If you're looking to buy snorkel gear, you can pick it up pretty cheap at Wal-Mart in Lihu'e on the highway or Kmart in Kukui Grove Shopping Center, also in Lihu'e.

Many people prefer to rent gear when they get here and leave it in the trunk, so they may snorkel when the opportunity arises. Your hotel or condo may have gear available. If they don't, try any of the following:

North Shore Rentals

Hanalei Surf Company (826–9000) has pretty good equipment for only $6 per day, $22 per week. *Rx* masks available for nothing extra.

Pedal 'n Paddle (826–9069) in Hanalei rents gear for $5 per day, $20 per week.

East Shore Rentals

Boss Frog (822–4334) on the highway in Kapa'a has decent gear for $2–$8 per day, $9–$30 for the week. *Rx* masks available.

Seasport Divers (823–9222) on the highway in Kapa'a has similar rates, and they also have divers' fins (the kind worn over reef shoes) available.

Snorkel Bob's (823–9433 or 742–2206) has two locations: one on the highway in Kapa'a and the other located on Po'ipu Road past Koloa. You're likely to be drawn by the $2.50 per day gear, but be tempted by the $9 or even *$11* gear. Although the equipment is pretty good, it's not *that* good. $6 gear is your best bet. Weekly rental is $9–$35. *Rx* masks available. You can also rent on Kaua'i and return equipment Snorkel Bob's on another island.

South Shore Rentals

Nukumoi Beach & Surf Shop (742–8019) rents beach equipment, including snorkel gear, boogie boards and the like. A good selection. Convenient, since they are right near Po'ipu Beach Park. $6 per day, $20 per week.

Fathom Five (742–6991) in Po'ipu has gear for $6 per day, $30 per week. Divers' fins available.

See also **Snorkel Bob's** listed above.

Snorkel Tours

If you've never snorkeled before and desire lessons and assistance, **SeaFun Kaua'i** (245–6400) offers guided snorkel tours for $80 per person (children 5–12 cost $60). We once tried to teach a friend to snorkel and were unsuccessful even getting her to put her face in the water (she was terrified). We were very impressed that in only a few minutes they had her snorkeling like an expert. Even *non-swimmers* go out with them. For this price, they'll pick you up at some hotels, take you to a place like Tunnels or

Lawa'i Beach and provide you with gear, wetsuit (which helps you float), lunch and assistance. Prescription masks and video of your trip are available.

Snorkel Tips

- Tropical gloves make snorkeling much more enjoyable. You can grab rocks to maneuver in shallow or surgy areas. (Please don't grab coral, however.)
- Use *Sea Drops* or another brand of anti-fog goop. Spread it *thinly* on the inside of a dry mask, then do a quick rinse. The old-fashioned method of spitting in the mask is not very effective. (It's particularly frightening to see tobacco chewers do this. Yuck!)
- Don't use your arms much, or you will spook the fish. Gentle fin motion. Any rapid motion can cause the little critters to scatter.
- Fish are hungriest and most appreciative in the morning (before their coffee).
- If you have a mustache and have trouble with a leaking mask, try a little Vaseline. Don't get any on the glass—it can get *really* ugly.
- In general, it's not a good idea to feed the fish. It upsets the balance by giving some fish an unnatural advantage over others and has the perverse effect of reducing both fish counts and variety. That said, the fish at **Lydgate** are such longtime people-food junkies that you won't do any harm feeding them there. You can find rabbit or fish food at most grocery stores, Kmart or Wal-Mart. Fill a Ziploc bag and, at the proper time, make a small slit in a corner to let the water fill the bag. You can dispense the food by squeezing the bag and using a slight wiggle motion to attract the fish. Be

careful that the zip part doesn't unzip—a common occurrence. If you can get a few fish interested and they start darting around, others will come. Dispense the food *sparingly*; too much and they will grab a bite and run. If they have to compete, they will increase in numbers. Too much food also makes the water murky—fish don't like murky water and will depart. If you don't want to use rabbit food, a tightly compressed ball of bread works well. Again, dispense *sparingly*. Don't use frozen peas. Although many think that this food is benign, in fact, it can be harmful due to the fish's inability to digest it properly. We cannot stress enough the importance of not losing your plastic bag in the water. If a turtle encounters it, he will surely think it is a jellyfish and choke to death. If you encounter a bag discarded by a thoughtless jerk, please pick it up and wedge it in your suit until you get out of the water.

- Several manufacturers, including Kodak and Fuji, sell disposable waterproof cameras. They are cheap and can provide wonderful souvenirs.

If you've always wanted to see what it's like to SCUBA dive but are a bit worried or don't want to go through the hassle, try SNUBA. That's where you take an air tank and place it on a raft that floats above you. Anyone 8 or older can SNUBA. From the raft there's a 20-foot hose attached to a regulator. There you are, underwater up to 20 feet deep, no tank on your back, no hassle. You'll have some instruction before you go under, and the dive master stays with you the whole time. It can be an exciting way to see the underwater world for the first time. SNUBA **Tours of Kaua'i** (823–8912). They do their thing off Lawa'i Beach on the south shore. $69. It should take a little over an hour.

If you're looking to be pampered, there are several spas on the island worth mentioning, and they're quite different. One of them offer the works and will relax you enough to breeze through the toughest IRS audit.

The grandest by far is **Anara Spa** (742–1234) at The Hyatt in Po'ipu, and their fabulous full-service spa is guaranteed to turn you to jelly. It's the priciest of the lot, but their attention to detail and overall surroundings makes it worth the splurge. (You'll love their lava rock showers.)

Waipouli Beach Aveda Salon & Spa (823–1488) at the Waipouli Beach Resort in central Kapa'a is your next best bet. The facilities are nice (though there are no day spa facilities), and after your treatment, you can access their incredible meandering pool with its waterfalls. Good shower and locker room facilities and professional staff. Our only gripe is that although they have tons of hair-related products to use, most of the other lotions and potions you'd like to have are absent.

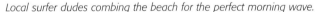

Local surfer dudes combing the beach for the perfect morning wave.

Princeville Health Club & Spa (826–5030) in Princeville is also highly recommended. Their prices are cheaper than Hyatt and it's not as snazzy, but it's a pretty good deal, and, like the Hyatt, you get free access to their day spa with any treatment. (And if you don't want a treatment, it's only $20 to access it and their killer view from the fitness room.)

Alexander Day Spa (246–4918) in the Kaua'i Marriott also has spa treatments, but they come in third for us. After paying for your massage (or whatever else you want from the spa), you don't get access to day spa facilities. Think of it as a no-frills experience but with prices similar to the frillier Princeville.

Ho, braddah, da shreddin's da kine! (Just trying to get you in the mood.) Surfing is synonymous with Hawai'i. And why not? Hawaiians invented *da bugga*. Learning isn't as hard as you may think. Depending on conditions they may put you on a large, soft board the size of a garage door (well…almost), so it's fairly easy to master, at least at this level.

Hanalei Bay is justly famous island-wide as one of the best and *most challenging* in Hawai'i. The chapter on BEACHES can assist you in picking beaches with surfing possibilities. **Cannons**, **Hanalei Bay**, **Kalihiwai**, **Kealia**, **Kalapaki**, **Infinities (Pakala Beach)**, are all well-known surf spots. If you want lessons, the best teacher we've seen on the south shore is **Learn to Surf** (826–7612). For $40 they'll spend 90 minutes with you at whichever beach has the right conditions. Good attitude and good place to rent a board.

Most of the companies on the south side teach at Kiahuna Beach. They might seem distracted and disinterested, but that's only because they're distracted and disinterested. But you'll probably eventually ride a wave here. Companies there include **Margo Oberg Surfing School** (332–6100) and **Garden Island Surf School** (652–4841).

Titus Kinimaka Hawaiian School of Surfing (652–1116) teaches out of Hanalei Bay, and you won't have the same crowd issue as on the south shore. With the sandier bottom at Hanalei (the south shore is reefier) it might be worth the higher price ($55 for 90 minutes).

Hawaiian Surfing Adventures (482–0749) has 2-hour group lessons for $65, $95 for private. We found them patient and eager to get you riding your first wave. They mostly go out of the north shore, too.

If you just want to rent a board, contact your hotel activity desk or any of the following: **Progressive Expressions** (742–6041) and **Nukumoi** (742–8019), both in Po'ipu, **Hanalei Surf Company** (826–9000) in Hanalei, or **Kaua'i Waterski, Surf & Kayak** (822–3574) in Kapa'a.

Contrary to what you see in the movies, beginners should look for crumbling waves, not the picturesque, breaking waves that slap the water.

By the way, a collection of surfboards is known in surfing lingo here as a *quiver*. A little kid surfer who doesn't have a job or car yet is called a *grommet*. Double *overhead* is when the waves are really big, and double *overtoes* is when they're *not*. If someone says your girlfriend is *filthy*, it's a compliment. And a *landshark* is someone who says he surfs…but doesn't.

TENNIS

If you are into tennis, Kaua'i has no shortage of courts. Many hotels offer free courts for their guests. (Check our resort reviews.) If your hotel doesn't have one, you may contact the courts listed below to arrange court time. Kaua'i County has 10 separate municipal courts scattered around the island, some lighted. They won't be as pristine as the private courts, but they are free to the public. You can call the county at 241–4463 to get the location of the court nearest you. **Kaua'i Lagoons** (241–6000) has a stadium court if you brought your own crowd.

Other places to rent a court include **Princeville Tennis Club** (826–3620), **Grand Hyatt** (742–1234) and **Kiahuna Tennis Club** (742–9533).

Tubing is where you sit in an inner tube and slowly drift along an old irrigation ditch. It's actually quite relaxing and calls for so little physical expenditure that you'll be tempted to look for your remote control and a can of beer while you're sitting there. Overall, however, we're kind of lukewarm on this. It's semi-lame, and there doesn't seem to be enough bang for your buck.

Kaua'i Backcountry Adventures (245–2506) does their tubing in an old sugar cane field between Lihu'e and Kapa'a. They'll pick you up in Hanama'ulu and drive you out to the area, narrating along the way. Then they'll put a helmet and gloves on you (wetsuits are extra), plunk you and 11 other people in inner tubes and off you go. This is *not* a whitewater adventure. Builders of these ditches didn't want to give up precious elevation quickly. So you'll putt-putt along at about 2 miles an hour. The best parts are the five tunnels, which represent about half your trip. They're dark, and the sounds of you and your fellow tubers bounce around in there.

Overall, the company does a pretty good job with what they have to work with, though you won't see much in the way of views—the ditch banks block most of that. Deli lunch is included, but you'll be forgiven if you think the price—$100 per person—is pretty darned steep considering you're only in the water an hour. People with bad backs might not like the posture they're in for the ride. They also have kid-size tubes, but they'll ride at the adult-sized price.

At **Kaua'i Waterski, Surf & Kayak** (822–3574), you can waterski the Wailua River. They rent a ski boat for $140 per hour, $75 for half hour. This includes the boat, driver, ski equipment and lessons, if you wish. Since you pay for the boat and not for skiing, non-skiers come along for free, up to 5 customers in the boat. If you've never skied before, it's *much* more tiring than it looks, but it's gobs of fun.

Whale Watching

Although Maui sees more whales than Kaua'i, they are still very common here. Whales work in Alaska in the summer, building up fat, then vacation here from December or January to March or April, when the females give birth and the males sing the blues. Only the males sing, and they all sing the same song, usually with their heads pointed down. Humpbacks don't eat while they're here and may lose ⅓ of their body weight during their Hawaiian vacation. (I doubt that many *human* visitors can make that same claim.) These gentle giants are very social and have been known to come right up to boats to check out the sightseers. Regulations prohibit the boat companies from initiating this kind of intimacy, but they get close enough to enjoy the whales. If you want to go on a whale watching boat tour, see OCEAN TOURS for a description of the tour boat operators.

Windsurfing

If you want to try windsurfing (formerly known as sailboarding), you'll find that

A kitesurfer soars overhead. Though Kaua'i waters are difficult for beginners, more advanced kiters can snag as much as 50 feet of air.

your options are limited on Kaua'i. Higher winds and more reefs mostly favor the experienced. A notable exception is 'Anini Beach. Celeste at **Windsurf Kaua'i** (828–6838) specializes in lessons for beginners on the north shore. Rates are $100 per person for 3 hours of lessons and practice. $25 for an hour for rental. Since county laws prohibit renting boards at the beach, you will probably have to pick up a board at another location if you don't want any lessons. Take it to Maha'ulepu or Salt Pond on the south shore, if you like. The west side just south of the Pacific Missile Range Facility can also be very exciting for the experienced. There the winds that wrap around Na Pali can create ideal conditions.

Kiteboarding/Kitesurfing

We're hesitant to give this sport its own section because so many people still don't know what it is, and because it's an offshoot of windsurfing. It's all the rage here in Hawai'i and is called **kitesurfing** or **kiteboarding**. Imagine a modified surfboard, shorter and boxier than a normal board, with fins at both ends and straps for your feet. Then let a special, controllable, two-line kite drag you along. Like windsurfing, you don't have to go the direction the wind takes you, you have control (though not as much as on a windsurf board). It's harder to learn than windsurfing, but *oh*, what fun it is! More fun than windsurfing, if you can get over the steeper learning curve.

The problem for Kaua'i visitors is that it takes a big investment of time and money to learn, and there's no reliable source for lessons. If you have your heart set on kitesurfing, you're better off doing it on Maui where there is a larger learning infrastructure.

Ever seen movies where military commandos don a harness, hook a pulley onto a steel cable and zip down into the action? This is similar—without the hostile fire at the end. You'll need to weigh between 80 and 280 pounds.

There are three companies doing this. Our favorite is **Princeville Ranch Adventures** (826–7669). Unlike the others, you don't need to hold on to the strap you're riding. The longest of the 9 lines is 1,200 feet. Their scenery isn't as nice as the others, but the zipping is more diverse, separated by a mile of hiking. They also have the best swimming hole. (Swimming at a waterfall and lunch in addition to the zipping for $145.)

Kaua'i Backcountry Adventures (245–2506) has 7 lines, the longest of which is 940 feet. But they're all over the same valley and they seem so preoccupied with "safety" that it takes some of the fun out of it. It's $125, which includes lunch and swimming in a stream.

Just Live (482–1295). Their concerns about safety seem more justified since they literally keep you in the trees—a big grove of Cook Island Pines—the whole time, so you'll need to stay clipped in. Think of it more like a ropes course with seven zips. You also have to cross two challenging bridges that will spook some of the less adventurous. Too bad their zips are shorter—the longest is about 800 feet. The waiting is longer between zips since they have more safety procedures to do up in the trees. They are the cheapest at $120. No lunch and no swimming.

OK, so 16 miles is a long way to paddle, whether over one day or several. But the wind, current and luscious scenery help propel you along.

The activities described below are for the serious adventurer. They can be experiences of a lifetime. We are assuming that if you consider any of them that you are a person of sound judgment, capable of assessing risks. All adventures carry risks of one kind or another.  Our descriptions below do not attempt to convey all risks associated with an activity. These activities are not for everyone. Good preparation is essential. In the end, it comes down to your own good judgment.

NA PALI KAYAK TRIP

If you really want adventure, consider a kayak trip down the Na Pali Coast. June through August are normally the only months where ocean conditions permit kayak transit. Kayakers put in at Ke'e Beach on the north shore, exiting at Polihale Beach on the west shore, a total of 16 miles. Along the way you'll encounter incomparable beauty, innumerable waterfalls and sea caves, pristine aquamarine seas, turtles, flying fish and possibly dolphins. If you're doing this as a maverick trip (below), at night you can camp on beautiful beaches, sleeping to the sound of the surf. The experience will stay with you for a lifetime.

There are two ways to do this trip—either on a guided tour or on your own. Guided tours do the entire trip in one day, offering a more structured—though less leisurely—way to see the coast.

These trips, usually led by experienced guides, offer the *relative* safety of an expert. The drawbacks to this method are a lack of independent movement, a more brisk paddling pace (it can be *tough* to do in one day) and the lack of an opportunity to camp. Na Pali Kayak (826–6900), Kayak Kaua'i (826–9844) and Outfitters Kaua'i (742–9667). Of the three, we like Na Pali Kayak for their slower pace and their service. Expect to pay around $205. They bring the gear, food and know-how; you bring the muscles.

If you want twice as much cost and hassle but *ten times* the gratification, you can do a maverick trip. Na Pali Kayak and Kayak Kaua'i will give you a personal guide who will travel with you to Kalalau and then make a judgment call as to whether you're up to continuing on your own. You'll need a permit with a kayak landing stamp for Kalalau before even applying for this service. See page 190 for info on permits.

Doing it on your own allows *you* to set the pace and the schedule. You go when you like, how you like, where you like and at the speed you like. You can rent a two-person kayak, if you desire. Consideration of this method necessitates a dispassionate evaluation of your skills, abilities, strengths and weaknesses. Although you don't need to be an expert kayaker, it doesn't hurt to have experience. Though we try to do this trip every year, when we *first* did it on our own, our only kayaking experience had been a 3-hour trip up the Wailua River. On that first trip we experienced ideal conditions, which don't always occur, even during the summer. Please bear in mind that this trip is not for everyone. The Na Pali Coast is wild and unpredictable, and you are exposing yourself to the ocean's caprice. The usually calm June through August seas can become difficult with surprising suddenness. Most of the Na Pali boat companies can tell

Sunset from the caves of Kalalau is your rich reward for a morning's paddle.

you stories about kayakers who had to be rescued when they got in over their heads (so to speak).

If you decide to do it on your own, here are a few things to keep in mind:

- Learn as much as you can about kayaking. (*Paddling Hawai'i* by Audrey Sutherland was our main reference when we made the first trip.) Proper paddling and loading techniques are *vital*.
- In addition to other essentials, make sure you bring waterproof sunblock, a hat, sunglasses, Chapstick and possibly Dramamine.
- Apply for camping permits *well in advance* (as much as 6–12 months in advance might be needed for Na Pali campsites), and *make sure* you get a kayak landing stamp on the permit.
- Think through your food requirements. (You *won't* be living off the land.)
- Any water source you utilize along the way will require water treatment pills to avoid possible contraction of leptospirosis. Water filters that don't use chemicals are not considered reliable due to the corkscrew shape of the leptospirosis bacterium. Fresh water is present at the following beaches along the route: Ke'e, Hanakapi'ai, Kalalau, Honopu, Miloli'i and Polihale, as well as some waterfalls that fall right into the ocean.
- Normal June through August conditions mean that the wind and currents are both pushing you in the direction you want to go, but *normal* doesn't mean *always*. Monitor ocean conditions by calling Hawaiian Waters (245–3564) and the National Weather Service (245–6001) for weather.
- Paddling in the early morning usually offers the calmest seas (sometimes like glass, if you're lucky) and easier launchings.
- Unless you spring for pick-up service, you'll have to rent an extra car for a couple days and leave one at Ke'e Beach and one at Polihale.

Here's some of what you can expect…

From Ke'e, Hanakapi'ai Beach is slightly over a mile. With campgrounds and a freshwater stream, Hanakapi'ai is a favorite place for hikers to camp (but the campsite was closed by bureaucrats at press time). Past Hanakapi'ai, you will start to see caves and waterfalls to your heart's content. Some of the caves are horseshoe-shaped, with separate entrances and exits. Explore 'em all if conditions are safe.

Keep an eye out for dolphins and turtles, which become more plentiful as you get farther down the coast. At Kalalau, you have paddled 6 miles. If you're on your own, this is a good place to camp with half a mile of sand, fresh water and portable toilets. We like to pitch our tents in the caves (hoping rocks won't fall on us) at the far end of the beach and walk a few minutes to a waterfall to shower. Kalalau is as far as hikers can go, so from here on you are in exclusive company.

Less than a mile past Kalalau is Honopu Beach. Landing crafts of all types, including *surfboards,* are prohibited. The only legal way to visit Honopu Beach is to swim there from Kalalau Beach (which can be hazardous if there's surf), or you can anchor your craft offshore and swim in (which can also be hazardous).

In all the Hawaiian Islands, and perhaps in all the world, you'll never find a more glorious, moving and mystical beach. Unspoiled Honopu is only accessible by sea. It is actually two beaches, separated by a gigantic arch carved into Na Pali by Mother Nature's furious waves. During the summertime when the pounding Na Pali surf weakens,

Honopu is reclaimed from the sea. As you approach by kayak, you're left speechless by the sheer majesty of what unfolds before you. *Vertical* walls 1,200 feet high are the first characteristics you see from the sea. If you're lucky enough to visit here, the giant arch draws you toward it like a magnet. As you approach it, you can just make out the cascading waterfall around the bend. This is no mere trickle. This immense cataract can knock you down with its force. The stream continues through the arch and out to sea, providing a superb way to rinse off the saltwater. The southern beach of Honopu actually makes a better kayak landing than its northern counterpart, but the northern beach is the most dramatic, and its unfolding vista will surely stay with you forever.

Past Honopu, listen for goats. Although considered pests by island officials, it's charming to hear them from your position on the water. At 9 miles you come to a pair of reefs fringing a beach called Nu'alolo Kai. The waters inside the reef offer good snorkeling during calm seas (and you wouldn't be here if the seas weren't calm, right?). From your kayak, when the two signs onshore are aligned, you're heading toward the deeper channel and to shore.

In times past the Hawaiians mostly lived in the hanging valley above the beach. Access required scaling the vertical wall (actually, it's worse than vertical; it leans outward!) up a ladder and along a "trail" in the cliff, which was often nothing more than cubbyholes for your feet. Worse yet was a large rock in the "trail" that was very difficult to get around. The Hawaiians even had a name for this dangerously placed immovable rock. They called it "fat man's misery."

Next, Miloli'i is 11 miles into your journey. Camping and fresh water make Miloli'i an inviting respite. There is a reef all along the beach and the same system to mark the channel as at Nu'alolo. You need a permit to camp at Miloli'i.

After Miloli'i, you will see a radio transmitter on top of a mountain belonging to Pacific Missile Range Facility. From the radar transmitter (helicopter pilots avoid getting too close to it, claiming they can feel their *da kines* cook), it's only 3 miles to Polihale. After your surf landing there, you can look forward to dragging your kayak through 500 feet of sand in searing heat, a task that would make a Himalayan Sherpa weep. (Good thing you were smart enough to spring for pick-up service from your kayak company.)

Congratulations—you have now joined an elite club of adventurers who have braved the Na Pali. A not-so-quick shower at Polihale Beach, and you are ready to dance all night. Or maybe not.

An open-ceiling cave along Na Pali is one of the many places to poke your kayak into during your voyage.

THE KALALAU TRAIL

So you don't like paddling or the surf is raging. You can still see Na Pali. Because the ultimate hike is also the most famous hike in all Hawai'i—11 miles of switchbacks, hills and beautiful scenery. See map below. Much of the trail is narrow and not without hazards. The trail calls for several stream crossings (some flip-flops are handy for this). Don't cross if the water is too high. Don't go if overnight hikes are a problem. To get the proper permits, contact: Hawai'i DLNR, State Parks, 3060 Eiwa St., Room 306, Lihu'e, HI 96766-1875, (808) 274–3444.

Our map is an accurate, computer-generated, shaded relief map drawn at a 45° angle to give you a perspective of when and how much climbing is involved—altogether about 5,000 feet.

The first 2 miles of the trail leads to Hanakapi'ai Beach (sandy in the summer, bouldery in the winter). There are plenty of slippery and muddy sections, and the second mile is steep downhill (and tough coming back up). It's tricky in spots if you're a beginner hiker, but it's worth it. The views along the coast are exceptional. Hanakapi'ai is a beautiful but treacher-

ous beach to swim, and it takes most people 1½–2 hours to hike each way. From here there is a fairly tough 1⁸∕₁₀-mile side trip near the stream to Hanakapi'ai Falls, one of the more spectacular falls and pools on the north shore. Many people like to reward themselves by swimming in the pool under the falls. Watch out for falling rocks.

This is as far as you can go without a permit. The authorities assume anyone going past Hanakapi'ai will be camping. If this is your plan, and you have your state camping permit, keep going. *Only* 9 miles to go from here. At Hanakoa, you have the choice of either camping *(if it's open)*, continuing to Kalalau or taking the ½ mile side trip to Hanakoa Falls, which is even lovelier than Hanakapi'ai. You'll cross the Hanakoa Stream and take a left at the trail near a shelter. After 50 yards take the left fork for 15 minutes. Watch for falling rocks at the falls. If you've come as far as Hanakoa, go see the falls. It's worth the walk.

Back on the trail, your toughest stretch is the last. From here to Kalalau Beach you'll find lots of switchbacks and a narrow trail at times. The stretch 7–8 miles

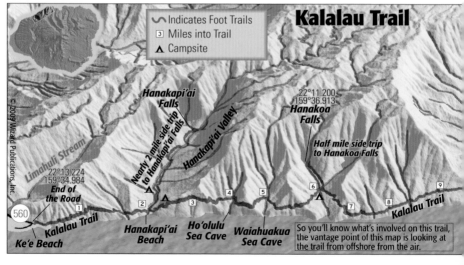

Kalalau Trail

Indicates Foot Trails
3 Miles into Trail
Λ Campsite

Hanakapi'ai Falls

Hanakapi'ai Valley

22°11.200
159°36.913
Hanakoa Falls

Half mile side trip to Hanakoa Falls

Nearly 2-mile side trip to Hanakapi'ai Falls

Limahuli Stream

22°13.224
159°34.984
End of the Road

560
Ke'e Beach

Kalalau Trail

Hanakapi'ai Beach

Ho'olulu Sea Cave

Waiahuakua Sea Cave

Kalalau Trail

So you'll know what's involved on this trail, the vantage point of this map is looking at the trail from offshore from the air.

© 2009 Wizard Publications, Inc.

Wild, raw and unforgettable—the Kalalau Trail.

into the trail has a couple of dicey spots, but they're not as bad as they used to be. The views are stunning. Persevere and you will be richly rewarded. Wow! This is the glorious valley you see from the top of Waimea Canyon Drive at the Kalalau Lookout. The beach, the valley and the isolation all make Kalalau a magic place. There is a 2-mile trail inland, which takes you to "Big Pool," a large natural pool in the stream.

Have you ever read *Ko'olau the Leper* by Jack London? It's based on the true story of Ko'olau, who fled to Kalalau in the 1880s after authorities refused to let his wife accompany him to the Kalaupapa leper settlement on Moloka'i. On July 2, 1893, a ship carrying 12 police, 14 soldiers, the sheriff, many rifles and a howitzer came ashore to capture Koolau and the other lepers who had joined him. After Ko'olau shot two of the soldiers dead and a third accidentally shot himself in the head (oops), the authorities decided to leave Koolau alone. He died in Kalalau in 1896 from his affliction.

As you stand on the beach at Kalalau, it's amazing to think that the entire valley was once populated. It was only in 1919 that this isolated valley was finally abandoned as people sought the life available to them in Lihu'e and other towns.

This is as far as you can go. A half mile farther down the coast is the most beautiful beach in all the islands, maybe

Kalalau
Lookout

Kalalau
Valley

550

Map continued on page 145

22°09.903
159°38.079
**Big
Pool**

**Honopu
Valley**

22°10.289
159°39.572

Falls

Kalalau Beach   **Caves**

**Honopu Beach   Open Ceiling
& Honopu Arch   Cave**

E   S

N   W

in all the Pacific—Honopu Beach. There is none finer. Period. The only legal way to visit the beach is to swim there. If you do this, beware that the current is against you coming back. Only during calm seas, only with fins and only if you're a strong swimmer. In late summer Kalalau Beach snakes its way closer to Honopu, and people walk on the rocks and sand most of the way. Beware of unexpectedly large waves if you do this. For more information on Honopu, see NA PALI KAYAK TRIP above.

Kalalau has composting toilets. The waterfall provides fresh water, which should be treated before drinking as should your en route sources at Hanakapi'ai and Hanakoa streams. In fact, *all* fresh water in nature should be treated to avoid possible bacteriological contamination from animals or people polluting the stream.

NI'IHAU SCUBA DIVE

For SCUBA divers looking for clean, clear, virgin waters, several dive operators offer three-tank dives near the privately owned island of Ni'ihau, mostly off Lehua Rock north of the island. (For more information on Ni'ihau, see INTRODUCTION chapter.) Since this island is in the rain shadow of Kaua'i, there are no permanent streams on the island (and consequently, no run-off). So visibility is often *well* over a hundred feet. This is possibly the best diving in the state. Between dives we've found ourselves snorkeling with dolphins. *Very* cool.

The waters are rich in critters, arches, caves and pelagics. There's a good chance you will share the water with sharks, so be prepared. The dive requires a 70-mile round trip (if you leave from Port Allen) boat ride and involves drop-offs, currents and sometimes rough seas. This is not for the inexperienced diver. Dives are usually deeper here. The table in the SCUBA section of the ACTIVITIES chapter tells which companies offer Ni'ihau trips, mostly around the summer months. We like Fathom Five and Bubbles Below the best. It's a very good idea to book a month in advance to ensure space.

HIKE TO THE BLUE HOLE

The term Blue Hole is widely used on Kaua'i yet is oddly ambiguous. Some use it to refer to Wai'ale'ale Crater. Some for the dam at the end of the dirt road that marks the trailhead. And others say Blue Hole is the pool at the end of an arduous hike. Let's go with the latter.

Getting to the trailhead can be difficult if you don't have 4WD. Read the directions to the Jungle Hike on page 154. Instead of looking for that trailhead, keep walking on the road until it ends at a concrete diversion dam. If the water is turid and nasty, it's an indication that heavy rains have occurred and the river might be getting ready to flood. (Of course, *any* river can flash flood at *any* time.)

Walk across the dam. The trail *up* the river starts out strong and quickly becomes vague. After it dumps you out into the river, another trail begins close by. This is the pattern these trails follow and many people have so much trouble

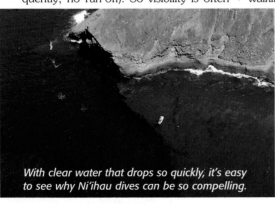

With clear water that drops so quickly, it's easy to see why Ni'ihau dives can be so compelling.

It takes time, a 4WD and wet feet to get to the so-called Blue Hole.

spotting them they spend the whole time in the river. The trails are only along the right (north) side of the river, and you can make good time by searching them out. They'll be narrow, muddy and overgrown, but it's easier than walking on slick river boulders. Flagging tape is an obvious sign that a trail is near. Even if you see an unmarked open swath in the trees, it's worth checking out. You'll be gaining 440 feet of elevation, and the boulder parts can be tiring. Tabis (described on page 137) are *strongly* recommended.

It takes 3 hours round trip for good hikers, twice that long or more for sketchier trekkers or if you can't find the trail segments.

At last you arrive at your goal. Three streams come together with two of them forming a glorious split waterfall. It's like a scene from heaven. You've been in the river and on the trail for less than 1½ miles, but you'd *swear* it's more than that. (We're positive about that number, we promise.) Soak it all in (easy to do since your already wet to the bone) and return the way you came.

For those who are tempted to continue into the crater, you should pass on that idea. The hiking gets harder, and it can't be done in a single day. If you insist on trying, you're going beyond adventure and working your way toward crazy since it involves scaling waterfalls ahead. Anyway, the correct direction is the stream to the left (not up the waterfall), and stay to the right at the next intersection. Stop when you come to a 3,000-foot wall in front of you at the back of the crater.

Hike through bamboo, cross the stream several times, step in mud, walk on wet rocks. All this just to marvel at Makaleha. It works for our hiker friend pictured here.

MAKALEHA HIKE

This hike is in the ADVENTURES chapter because it is only for the advanced hiker. The trail goes along a beautiful stream, through a bamboo grove and offers lush scenery. There are a number of places along the way to bathe in the stream, which can be deep in spots. Past the end of the trail are waterfalls just for you. The problem is that the trail is a trail-of-use and is not officially maintained. As a result, it is splendid in some parts, wretched in others. Some big steps up and down and mud spots keep it interesting. You will have to walk in the stream in some places, so we usually bring tabis (fuzzy mittens for your feet that work well on slippery rocks). Even without the waterfalls, you will get a real Indiana Jones feel for this part of God's country.

The trail starts at the end of Kahuna Road in northern Kapa'a. (See top of map on page 58 to get there.) From here, you walk past the water tank to the trail. At one point, the trail on the right (northern) bank veers away to a water tunnel. Don't go there, but instead cross the main stream at the remains of an old concrete dam. (The area just below the dam makes a dandy swimming hole.) Follow the trail close to the stream until it seems to end. From here, backtrack 20 feet and enter the bamboo. You'll see three large trees; behind the one on the far right is a trail that ascends into the bamboo grove, skirts the cliff edge and gives some opportunities (take the second one) to return to the river below. Remember that place for your return hike. From here, it can be muddy if it's been raining (and it probably has been). This is the real Kaua'i—lush, wet and beautiful.

At one point the trail dumps into the stream, and you'll have to cross it onto an island in the river. Walk the length of

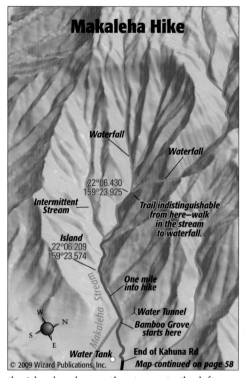

Makaleha Hike

Waterfall

Waterfall

22°06.430
159°23.925

Intermittent Stream

Trail indistinguishable from here—walk in the stream to waterfall.

Island
22°06.209
159°23.574

One mile into hike

Makaleha Stream

Water Tunnel
Bamboo Grove starts here

W N S E

Water Tank   End of Kahuna Rd

© 2009 Wizard Publications, Inc.   Map continued on page 58

the island and cross the stream to the left and pick up the trail again. Follow it until you come to some large boulders that form a wall. Go over the wall and cross the stream. The trail gets difficult from here. Look for machete marks in the annoying hau trees that cross the trail, sometimes forming a jungle gym of limbs. You should always be able to hear the stream, but if you get into trouble, there probably won't be anyone combing along to help. Bring mosquito repellent or don't go. Footwear should include hiking sandals or boots and tabis for stream walking. Bring water. You'll have to walk in the stream the last 50 yards before you come to a fork (where three streams converge at a stunning vista). A waterfall is up the left-most stream. *If you're feeling lucky*, a better waterfall is 20–30 minutes to the right.

Sometimes it's hard to capture the immensity of what you're seeing on film. The boat offshore and the helicopter (the light blip above our friend's hat) are testament to the grandness of what awaits you on the Honopu Ridge.

It's an easier walk in a tall, narrow canyon, and the falls are two beautiful tiers with good swimming at the base. But that narrowness opens you up to the possiblility of getting hammered by falling rocks, if one lets loose above you. Regardless, allow ample time to get back. In all, it's only 1½ miles each way, but the going is pretty slow in many spots, and it *can* take much of the day.

4WD MILOLI'I RIDGE ROAD

The southern, dryer part of Na Pali is defined by a series of ridges. The map on page 84 shows roads such as Ka-uhao and Ka'aweiki that wind their way along the ridges to the edge of Na Pali. Unfortunately, these are hunter roads, always closed during the week, and you're supposed to get a hunting permit to drive on them on weekends. But Miloli'i Ridge Road (see same map) is open all week long and, if you have a 4WD and it's not raining, you can probably drive to the end where you'll get a beautiful view of this part of Na Pali. Once at the road's end, look for a trail to the left that goes around and up a hill.

Intrepid hikers might want to brave the ridge as long as their nerve takes them. (The ridge ends rather conclusively—right above Miloli'i Beach a dramatic 1,400 feet below you.)

Here's the deal: The road is maintained by State Parks, which means it may be rutted, nasty, impassible or even closed if they feel like it. Or it might be fine. Either way, when you get to some picnic tables (shown on the map), you've come to the last part you should consider driving if it's *been* raining or you *think* it will. Because after that the road gets steeper, and you might have problems returning if it's too slippery. All told it's just over 5 miles of 4WD each way. You access Miloli'i Ridge Road ³⁄₁₀ mile into the paved Makaha Ridge Road between the 13 and 14 mile markers on Hwy 550 (Waimea Canyon Drive).

HONOPU RIDGE TO A DROP-DEAD VIEW

Imagine a trail that cuts through forest, ventures down a ridge and culminates in perhaps the most inspirational view on the island. Until recently that's exactly what you had to do...*imagine* it. Back in 1982 one of Kaua'i's most delicious trails was damaged by a hurricane. The State Park, ever grumbling about budgets, decided not to put in the effort to reopen it. Over the course of more than two decades it became unrecognizable. But volunteers have spent the time to bring it back to life. Today Honopu Trail is available to ambitious hikers. Why ambitious? Because, although it's only about 2 miles each way, there's opportunity to wander off the trail if you're not careful. Most of the trail is obvious, but there are a few hunter trails that might lead you astray. (See maps on pages 145 and 140.)

Located on the west side, you take Hwy 50 to Waimea Canyon Drive (550). At ⁴/₁₀ mile past the 17 mile marker (not far from the end of the road at Kalalau) there's a turnout on the curve about 100 feet past a telephone pole. Park there and the trail heads left toward the coast. After just 120 yards you come to your first confusing intersection. The trail to the left is the correct path. (Don't go straight.) At ²/₁₀ mile the trail comes to a T intersection at a tree whose branches all point to the right. Turn right. (The incorrect left leads down to a stream bed.) From here you'll *really* be grateful for long pants, because the native Pacific false staghorn ferns tend to claw at your legs. (Jeans can feel heavy—we've become fond of light pants with zip-off legs.)

It's mostly the first ½ mile that has the confusing intersections. Tips to staying on the correct trail include following the most beaten path, looking for logs or other barriers placed to block side trails and staying on the trail that has the most tags (ribbons) on trees.

Soon most of your 1,000 feet of elevation loss will occur. (You actually climbed a bit until now.) Always stay on the most worn path. About 1 mile into the trail (it will seem like more) you'll be on a wide ridge that will eventually get narrow enough to see Honopu on one side and Awa-'awapuhi on the other. Eventually the trail comes to a glorious lookout presided over by an 'ohi'a tree on a dirt bluff. The vista into Honopu Valley is so magnificent that it defies description. The entire heavenly valley is before you. Honopu Beach and the Pacific are to your left 3,000 feet below. The scene is so intense that it literally looks unreal. If clouds are in the valley, wait a while. They tend to come and go. The trail continues another 15 minutes, terminating at a point where the ridge takes a drop down to a razorback spine (which you *don't* want to visit). From the end you're treated to a tasty view of Na Pali coast.

While on the trail, if you take a wrong turn, keep track of where you've been and backtrack. Nothing's worse than being lost in the forest. Our first time in (when the trail was more vague than it is now) we made two wrong turns, realized our mistakes, and returned to the intersection to find the right way. Also, make sure you're back at your car *at least* 1½ hours before sunset. It will take most people 1½–2½ hours each way, and the trip back up is fairly strenuous. Bring gobs of water down, suck 'em up at the overlook, and bring only what you need back up. The trail has a few areas where there's opportunity to fall or twist an ankle. One short stretch is on the side of a dirt hill that may make some nervous. This hike is in the ADVENTURES chapter because of the poor trail conditions in a few scattered areas and because of the potential to get off the trail. Coming back, the ¼ mile closest to your car seems to present new opportunities to wander off the same trail you already took on the way down.

MOUNTAIN BIKE/HIKE THE OTHER SIDE OF WAIMEA CANYON

There's a trail in Koke'e called Kohua Ridge Trail that leads 2½ miles to a dazzling view of Waimea Canyon *from the other side*. Problem is, the trailhead is 3⁹/10 miles from where most cars can go. But bring along a mountain bike to get you there, and you have an afternoon adventure. See map on page 140 and take Mohihi-Camp 10 Road to where the map indicates 4WD only (1⁶/10 miles from Hwy 550). The bike ride to the trailhead is along a dirt road through the forest. The sights are beautiful along the way. The biking is fairly strenuous due to the rolling nature of the road. Get a decent bike with shocks and low gears.

At the trailhead, stash your bike in some bushes and proceed. (Be sure to repeatedly refer to the map so you can anticipate the easy-to-miss trailhead sign.) The trail crosses Mohihi Ditch via a small bridge, then heads down to Mohihi Stream. It's usually a boulder hop across the stream. (Don't cross if it's raging.) Then comes the toughest part—¼ mile of steep trail, a slight leveling and then a shorter steep part before the saddle where it veers southwest. (Remember this point for your return.) At the end of the trail is a stunning view of Po'omau Canyon to your right, Koai'e Canyon to your left, with Waimea Canyon in front of you. You're at the apex of all of them. Across the canyon is the Waimea Canyon Lookout, where mere mortals view the spectacular canyon. *You,* on the other hand, have earned the right to see it from a more exclusive perspective. It's been pretty strenuous getting to this point, but it's soon forgotten in the glory of your own personal overlook.

Take your time, but be back to your car before dark.

SECRET TUNNEL TO THE NORTH SHORE

Imagine that you're in an east shore valley. You come upon a tunnel that's a *mile* long. From the moment you enter, you can see the light at the other end. When you emerge, you're in the virtually inaccessible back of the north shore's Hanalei Valley, surrounded by nearly vertical mountains, a perfect river and no people. Aside from a few hunters, almost no one on Kaua'i had even *heard* of this tunnel until we revealed it. Those who had heard of it considered it one of those urban legends, a myth. Well, it's no myth.

In the 1920s a sugar company was seriously coveting the abundant water flowing out the Hanalei River. They needed the water for their east shore sugar. So for $300,000 they cut this tunnel and diverted 28 million gallons of water a day under the mountain and into a series of ditches to quench their thirsty crops. But times change. As sugar production dwindled on the east shore, they found that they no longer needed the north shore's water. So, years ago, they stopped diverting the water and abandoned the dam. The flume to divert the water is no longer there. They couldn't divert water into this tunnel even if they wanted to without doing major reconstruction on the dam. But the tunnel, blasted out of solid rock, remains.

Getting there can be a sloppy affair. It involves walking 2½ miles along a trail through fairly muddy conditions. (It rains about 160 inches annually here, spread fairly evenly throughout the year.)

A Few Basics

Driving to the trailhead means taking a dirt road (see map). A regular car can usually go past the sign that says 4WD only, but you *may* have trouble on the last part of the road. You'll have to see. This road is sporadically improved, and it depends on your timing. 4WDs are a sure thing. See directions to the Jungle Hike on page 153 and stop *just before* the first gate. Hiking boots are recommended on this trail. Tabis (described on page 137), water socks or old tennis shoes work best *in* the tunnel. (The latter cushion the bottoms of your feet the best.) Tabis the whole way might be desirable if it's real muddy. Long pants are also recommended. Ferns have a habit of sticking out in the trail, scratching at your legs. Jeans are OK, but they get heavy and stick to your legs, making it harder. Lighter pants are preferred. Look for delicious red thimbleberries along the way. (The redder, the better.) Bring a flashlight (or two) for the tunnel. Also bring water and snacks.

The trail to the tunnel is a hunters' trail and it's usually muddy. The first 100 yards are very muddy with a permanent puddle near the place where you park. Several short stretches are on uneven terrain, and caution needs to be taken. In the first 5 minutes you'll have to cross the Wailua River. *Usually* it's done by hopping across a couple of rocks. If it's too deep and you aren't comfortable, don't go. If it's been raining a lot, don't go. During very heavy rains you may find that the river isn't crossable coming back, presenting you with a dilemma. Just after the crossing, look for a trail in the bamboo thicket that heads upstream. Bamboo is the best natural material there is for walking sticks, and it's a good idea to have one on this hike. (It makes a good spider stick in case there are webs across the trail.) Cut it so that a knuckle is near the bottom, acting as a

Tunnel & Jungle Hikes

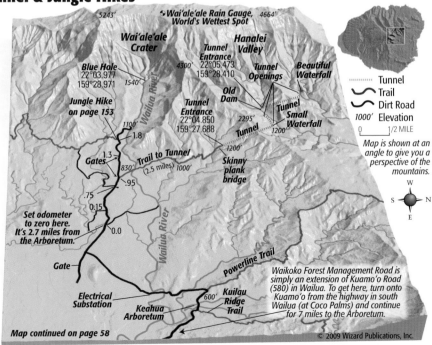

Waiʻaleʻale Rain Gauge, World's Wettest Spot

5243'   4664'

Waiʻaleʻale Crater

Hanalei Valley

Blue Hole
22°03.977
159°28.971

Tunnel Entrance
4300'   22°05.473
159°28.410

Tunnel Openings

Beautiful Waterfall

1540'

Jungle Hike on page 153

Old Dam

Tunnel Entrance
22°04.850
159°27.688

Tunnel Small Waterfall

2295'

1100'
1.8

Tunnel   1200'

1200'

Gates   1.3

Trail to Tunnel

830'   (2.5 miles)   1000'

Skinny plank bridge

.95

.75

0.15

Set odometer to zero here. It's 2.7 miles from the Arboretum.

0.0

Wailua River

Gate

Powerline Trail

Electrical Substation

600'   Kuilau Ridge Trail

Keahua Arboretum

.... Tunnel

∿ Trail

∿ Dirt Road

1000' Elevation

0   1/2 MILE

Map is shown at an angle to give you a perspective of the mountains.

W
S   N
E

Waikoko Forest Management Road is simply an extension of Kuamoʻo Road (580) in Wailua. To get here, turn onto Kuamoʻo from the highway in south Wailua (at Coco Palms) and continue for 7 miles to the Arboretum.

Map continued on page 58

© 2009 Wizard Publications, Inc.

natural stopper, preventing dirt or mud from filling the hollow tube.

The trail is intermittently "paved" with 'ohi'a tree logs looking like railroad ties from long ago. Avoid false trails. Remember, you'll never go more than 15 minutes without seeing the 'ohi'a logs. You've gone almost a mile when you see your first old abandoned wooden power pole. Just after this you come to a flat muddy area and a trail to the left. We've walked through the flat part and sunk three feet into a bog. Take the

A hiker marvels at the richness of Kaua'i, which is ever-present on this trek.

side trail around unless you want to lose a shoe. You'll cross a couple of smaller streams (a foot wide) and a slightly larger stream.

After 1½ hours or so, when the trail encounters a large stream again, it seems to end. This is where people get lost. It actually veers slightly left, away from the stream and over some rocks. Look for muddy stains on the rocks and they will lead you to the trail in the tall grass ahead. It crosses the stream where the stream makes a right turn. Once you cross, pick up the trail *directly* on the other side, and it's not far before you walk on a skinny plank bridge over a ditch. There are two trails here, one straight and one to the left. *Take the left trail*. It goes to the gauging station and tunnel. It takes us 1¾–2½ hours *to* the first tunnel, and about 45 minutes *in* the tunnel. Coming back is a bit faster. You'll gain about 600 feet with all the ups and downs.

Once in the tunnel you notice that there's water standing in it. That's from the small amount of water that drips from the ceiling. It's just the right amount to keep about four inches of water fresh. The tunnel is about 6 feet wide and 7–10 feet high with an occasional need for a head duck on the straight portion. The bottom is flat and lined with small rocks, which makes for fairly straightforward walking. The tunnel reverberates with the ever-constant sound of the splashing of your feet in the ankle-high water. About 900 feet above you is the ridge that the ancient Hawaiians used to walk on to reach the summit of

Wai'ale'ale where the remains of their altar, at the wettest spot on Earth, may still be found. As you approach what appears to be the end, you see an odd sight: railroad tracks in the shallow water, probably used to haul the debris out of the tunnel during construction. At the light at the not-quite-end of the tunnel, you can step outside momentarily to visit a small waterfall waiting for you. Then it's back in the tunnel for the remaining ¼ mile. That latter portion is partially lined with cement and shorings, requiring anyone 6 feet tall or more to duck for a bit. At the real end you need to get up on the dike and take the overgrown trail near the tunnel exit. It goes down for about a minute to the Hanalei River. During good weather the scenery is magnificent. The mountains tower all around you. Wai'ale'ale plateau is above and to your left, its side etched with waterfalls. The river, with some impossibly large boulders, makes a perfect place for lunch.

Hikers entering the tunnel.

Most will be more than satisfied with this destination. But if you started early (hiking by 7 or 7:30 a.m.), there is one more challenge for the intrepid. You've been through a mile of tunnel already and are at the river. Directly across from the giant boulder and pool (you'll see it), there's a *very* faint trail on the other side of the river that leads 5–10 minutes upstream to *another* ⁷⁄₁₀ mile-long tunnel. It's more dicey. Follow the trail until it meets an old diversion dam. From the top of the dam look upstream then turn to your right. You should see a vague trail going directly uphill. It will take you to a cement wall (part of the next ditch). The next tunnel entrance is to the right.

Once inside the tunnel (known to hunters as Ka'apoko Tunnel), there's lots of head ducking, and it has a more rickety feel. When the tunnel ends, there's an offshoot to the left. Not far from there, you come to an incline with water gurgling down. Scoot up and you'll emerge in a Shangri-La that will make you giddy with joy. A cathedral of 200-foot sheer walls are so steep they actually lean *inward*. Water drips from above, creating an exotic backdrop. To the left is a pounding waterfall. The setting is unbelievable and worth all the effort you went through to get here.

Needless to say, you'll have the opportunity to get muddy, slip on your 'okole, bump your head, twist your ankle, etc., on this adventure. Use your best judgment. This tunnel is not maintained for this purpose, so please don't complain to *anybody* if you have any problems. This is a strenuous, exciting and memorable adventure with absolutely *no* guarantees. *That's* why it's an adventure.

First a day at the beach, then a romantic evening at the Sheraton Kaua'i.

By their very nature, restaurant reviews are the most subjective part of any guidebook. Nothing strains the credibility of a guidebook more. No matter what we say, if you eat at enough restaurants here, you will eventually have a dining experience directly in conflict with what this book leads you to believe. All it takes is one person to wreck what is usually a good meal. You've probably had an experience where a friend referred you to a restaurant using reverent terms, indicating that you were about to experience dining ecstasy. And, of course, when you go there, the food is awful and the waiter is a jerk. There are many variables involved in getting a good or bad meal. Is the chef new? Was the place sold last month? Was the waitress just released from prison for mauling a customer? We truly hope that our reviews match your experience. If they don't (or

even if they do), please drop us a line. Readers help us *tremendously* in keeping tabs on the restaurants, and we read and digest (so to speak) every e-mail.

We often leave out restaurant hours of operation because they change so frequently that the information would be immediately out of date. These decisions are usually made quite capriciously in Hawai'i. If you're going to drive a long way to eat at an establishment, it's best to call first. Restaurants that stand out from the others in some way are highlighted with this ONO symbol.

In some restaurants around the island you'll see guidebook recommendation plaques, guidebook door stickers and signed guidebooks, but you won't see ours. The reason? We *never* tell them when we're there. We review everything on the island *anonymously*. We're more interested in being treated like everyone else than in copping a free meal. How could you trust our opinion if the restaurant *knew* who we were?

By their reviews, many guidebooks lead you to believe that every meal you eat in Hawai'i will be a feast, the best food in the free world. Frankly, that's not our style. Kaua'i, like anywhere else, has ample opportunity to have lousy food served in a rotten ambiance by uncaring waiters. In the interest of space, we've left out some of the dives. We did, however, leave in some of the turkeys just to demonstrate that we live in the real world.

For each restaurant, we list the price *per person* you can expect to pay. It ranges from the least expensive entrées to the most expensive, plus a beverage and usually an appetizer. You can spend more if you try, but this is a good guideline. *The price excludes alcoholic beverages since this component of a meal can be so variable.* Obviously, everyone's ordering pattern is different, but we thought that it would be easier to compare restaurants using actual prices than if we used symbols like different numbers of dollar signs or drawings of forks or whatever to differentiate prices between restaurants.

When we give **directions** to a restaurant, *mauka side* of highway means "toward the mountain" (or away from the ocean). The shopping centers we mention are on the maps to that area.

Very few restaurants care how you dress. A few discourage tank tops and bathing suits. Some of the fancy resorts like the St. Regis Princeville, Sheraton or Hyatt have dress codes. Their dress codes require **resort wear**, meaning covered shoes and collared shirts for men (nice shorts are *usually* OK), dressy sportswear or dresses for women.

It's legal to bring your own alcohol to restaurants in Hawai'i, and many restaurants, especially inexpensive ones, have no objections to letting you BYOB.

Local food can be difficult to classify. Basically, local food combines Hawaiian, American, Japanese, Chinese, Filipino and several other types and is (not surprisingly) eaten mainly by locals.

Pacific Rim is sort of a fusion of American and various countries around the Pacific, including Hawaiian and Asian. It's a fine (and subjective) line between American and Pacific Rim. We don't have a separate **Seafood** section because nearly every restaurant on Kaua'i serves some kind of fish.

Below are descriptions of various island foods. Not all are Hawaiian, but this might help if you encounter dishes unfamiliar to you.

ISLAND FISH & SEAFOOD

Ahi–Tuna; raw in sashimi or poke, also seared, blackened, baked or grilled; good in fish sandwiches. Try painting ahi steaks with mayonnaise, which *completely* burns off when BBQ'd but seals in the moisture. You end up tasting only the moist ocean steak. Generally plentiful April through September.

Lobster–Hawaiian spiny lobster is quite good; also called "bugs" by lobster hunters. Maine lobster kept alive on the Big Island are also available.

Mahimahi–Deep ocean fish also known as a dolphinfish; served at lu'aus; very common in restaurants. Sometimes tastes fishy (especially if frozen), which can be offset in the preparation.

Marlin–Tasty when smoked; otherwise, can be tough; the Pacific Blue Marlin (kajiki) is available almost year round.

Monchong–Excellent tasting deepwater fish, available year-round. Usually served marinated and grilled.

Onaga–Also known as a ruby snapper; excellent eating in many preparations.

Ono–(Wahoo); *awesome* eating fish and can be prepared many ways; most plentiful May through October. Ono is also the Hawaiian word for delicious.

Opah–(Moonfish); excellent eating in many different preparations; generally available April through August.

'Opakapaka–(Crimson snapper); great tasting fish cooked several ways. Common October through February.

'Opihi–Using a specialized knife, these must be pried off rocks at the shoreline, which can be hazardous. Best eaten raw mixed with salt.

Poke–Fresh raw fish or octopus (tako) mixed with seaweed (limu), sesame seed and other seasonings and oil.

Shutome–Swordfish; dense meat that can be cooked several ways. Most plentiful March through July.

Hanalei Dolphin (826–6113) buys from the fishing boats and has a fish market that sells fresh, locally caught fish. Other places include **Foodland** (822–7271) and **Safeway** (822–2464) in Kapa'a, **Fish Express** (across from Wal-Mart) in Lihu'e and the **Koloa Fish Market** in Koloa.

LU'AU FOODS

Chicken lu'au–Chicken cooked in coconut milk and taro leaves.

Haupia–Coconut milk custard. Tasty, but too much will give you the… *ahem*.

Hawaiian sweet potatoes–Purple inside; not as sweet as mainland sweet potatoes but very flavorful.

Kalua pig–Pig cooked in an underground oven called an imu, shredded and mixed with Hawaiian sea salt (outstanding!).

Lomi salmon–Chilled salad consisting of raw, salted salmon, tomatoes and two kinds of onions.

Pipi kaula–Hawaiian-style beef jerky.

Poi–Steamed taro root pounded into a paste. It's a starch that will take on the taste of other foods mixed with it. Consider dipping your pipi kaula in it. (Now *that* sounds bad if you don't read it right.) Visitors are encouraged to try it at least once so they can bad-mouth it with authority.

OTHER ISLAND FOODS

Apple bananas–A smaller, denser, smoother texture than regular (Williams) bananas and a bit tangy.

Barbecue sticks–Teriyaki-marinated pork, chicken or beef pieces barbecued and served on bamboo sticks.

Bento–Japanese box lunch.

Breadfruit–Melon-sized starchy fruit; served baked, deep fried, steamed or boiled. Definitely an *acquired* taste.

Crackseed–Chinese-style spicy preserved fruits and seeds.

Guava–About the size of an apricot or plum. The inside is full of seeds and tart, so it is rarely eaten raw. Used primarily for juice, jelly or jam.

Hawaiian supersweet corn–The finest corn you ever had, even raw. We'll lie, cheat, steal or maim to get it fresh.

Huli huli chicken–Hawaiian BBQ style.

Ka'u oranges–Big Island oranges. Usually, the uglier the orange, the better it tastes.

Kim chee–A Korean relish consisting of pickled cabbage, onions, radishes, garlic and chilies.

Kona coffee–Grown on the Kona coast of the Big Island. Smooth, mild flavor. Better than Kaua'i coffee.

Kulolo–Steamed taro pudding. (Tasty.)

Laulau–Pork, beef or fish wrapped in taro and ti leaves, then steamed. (You don't eat the ti leaf wrapping.)

Liliko'i–Passion fruit.

Loco moco–Rice, meat patty, egg and gravy. A hit with cholesterol lovers.

Lychee–A reddish, woody peel that is discarded for the sweet, white fruit inside. Be careful of the pit. Good, small seed (or chicken-tongue) lychees are so delicious, they should be illegal.

Macadamia nut–A large, round nut.

Malasada–Portuguese donut dipped in sugar. Best when served hot.

Manapua–Steamed or baked bun filled with meat.

Mango–Bright orange fruit with yellow pink skin. Distinct, tasty flavor.

Manju–Cookie filled with a sweet center.

Methley plums–A wild fruit harvested with a permit at Koke'e State Park during the summer months.

Musubi–Cold steamed rice, often with sliced Spam rolled in black seaweed.

Papaya–Melon-like, pear-shaped fruit with yellow skin; best eaten chilled. Good at breakfast. Kaua'i has varieties called sunrise and strawberry papaya.

Plate lunch–An island favorite as an inexpensive, filling lunch. Consists of "two-scoop rice," a scoop of macaroni salad and some type of meat, either beef, chicken or fish. Sometimes called a box lunch. Great for picnics.

Portuguese sausage–Pork sausage, highly seasoned with red pepper. Tastes weird to some people.

Pupu–Appetizer, finger foods or snacks.

Saimin–Noodles cooked in either chicken, pork or fish broth. Word is peculiar to Hawai'i. Local Japanese say the dish comes from China. Local Chinese say it comes from Japan.

Sea salt–Excellent (and strong) salt distilled from seawater. Much of our sea salt comes from Salt Pond Beach Park.

Shave ice–A block of ice is "shaved" (*never* crushed) into a ball with flavored syrup poured over the top. Best served with ice cream on the bottom. Very delicious.

Smoothie–Usually papaya, mango, frozen passion fruit and frozen banana, but almost any fruit can be used to make this milkshake-like drink. Add milk for creaminess.

Taro–Found in everything from enchiladas to breads and rolls to taro chips and fritters. Tends to color foods purple. Has lots of fluoride for your teeth.

NORTH SHORE AMERICAN

Bar Acuda
5-5161 Kuhio Hwy • 826–7081

ONO A pretty unusual concept, it's called tapas food. (Yeah, we didn't know what that meant, either. It's Spanish food served in small, communally shared portions.) In this case, you order lots of small entrées and share them. The menu changes weekly and seasonally, so you'll have to explore it on your own. Expect to see items such as smoked trout, braised short ribs, mesclun salad, garlic green beans or chorizo sausage with chickpea stew *(particularly* good). The food is pricey (and the drinks seriously overpriced), but the flavors are unusual and very effective, and you'll sample a number of them. The molten chocolate cake is incredibly earthy and wonderful—tiny but ONO. And the atmosphere, sort of a contemporary jazzy feel, works for us. **$20–$45** for dinner. In Located in Hanalei, in Hanalei Center. Closed Monday.

CJ's Steak & Seafood
5-4280 Kuhio Hwy • 826–6211

Princeville's version of a typical steak house. They have a salad bar (rare in these parts), and the prime rib isn't bad. The nightly fish specials are worth a try. Avoid sitting at the bar, where you might get rude service. The menu is pricey considering you're in a shopping center without a view. Dinner is shrimp for $30, lamb for $31 and $24 for an 8-ounce prime rib. In Princeville Shopping Center. **$8–$12** for lunch, **$25–$40** for dinner.

Foodland Deli
5-4280 Kuhio Hwy • 826–9880

Though the Foodland grocery store in Princeville Center will *never* be considered a bargain (their grocery prices are confiscatory), the deli is a good deal. For **$5–$8** you can pick up a fairly decent sandwich (either packaged or custom made) and be on your merry way to the beach.

Hanalei Dolphin Restaurant
5-5016 Kuhio Hwy • 826–6113

(ONO) This is a north shore tradition that often has great seafood and steak in a pleasant, open-air atmosphere. They have some outdoor tables on a lawn next to the Hanalei River—very nice at lunch or while waiting for your indoor table at dinner. They are often busy and don't take reservations—so if waiting bothers you, arrive early or you're out of luck. The seafood chowder is usually great, and their seafood selection is excellent. Pick a fish and pick a side item. They have a seafood market, a good place to pick up fish for cooking back at the condo. **$9–$14** for lunch, **$20–$35** for dinner. On the highway in Hanalei; can't miss it.

Hanalei Gourmet
5-5161 Kuhio Hwy • 826–2524

Burgers, sandwiches and salads for lunch, steak, seafood, pastas and burgers for dinner. The food and service have improved, and we might have given 'em an ONO, but their prices are a bit too high for what you get. **$10–$14** for lunch, **$20–$30** for dinner (less if you want a burger). In the Old Hanalei School across from Ching Young Village, Hanalei. Live music some nights.

Java Kai
5-5183 Kuhio Hwy • 826–6717

A good place to stop for coffee and baked goods on the north shore. The drink selection is vast (love the spicy chai latte), but the hot breakfast items are small and overpriced. Their $8 bagel sandwich is pathetic compared to the $5 equivalent at their Kapaʻa location. **$5–$12**. In the Hanalei Center next to Bubba's Burgers.

Kalypso Island Bar & Grill
5-5156 Kuhio Hwy • 826–9700

Items are hit or miss but rarely rise above acceptable. Decent mac nut-crusted fish, unremarkable shrimp and chicken, horrible calamari or artichokes. The menu is mostly a single selection of fish, steak, pasta and chicken. And they have an awesome chocolate suicide cake. **$13–$30** for lunch and dinner. Located in Hanalei; can't miss it.

Lighthouse Bistro
2484 Keneke St. • 828–0480

First of all, you can't see the Kilauea Lighthouse from here. (Sorry to burst your bubble.) Although dinner is *very* overpriced ($34 for a steak, and it's served à la carte!), lunch is our favorite, and it works fairly well with items such as fish tacos, fish burritos and burgers. Dinner is mainly fish, shrimp, chicken and pork. Pretty good food at lunch, but way too high for dinner. **$10–$16** for lunch, **$20–$40** for dinner. In Kilauea in Kong Lung Center off Kilauea Road.

Mediterranean Gourmet
5-7132 Kuhio Hwy • 826–9875

(ONO) There is a long and distinguished list of failed restaurants at this location, so call ahead if you're coming. Their greatest asset, an awesome oceanside location, is also their biggest curse since most people have made their dining decisions before they drive west of Hanalei. The view of the ocean is wonderful as long as they keep the plants trimmed. (A sin some of their predecessors have committed.) The food is pricey and the portions small. But the food is good and the flavors can be pretty strong, like the stuffed grape leaves. The owner's background is Lebanese, and you'll find items like hummus, tabouleh and babaganush. Most of the items we've had here we'd never heard of, but we liked most of them. Service can be scant. Lunch is several tasty wraps and a few other items for **$13–$20**. Dinner is **$25–$45**.

North Shore Grindz
5-4280 Kuhio Hwy • 826-1122

ONO It's pretty rare that we give an ONO to a *gas* station. (Especially one with *their* prices.) Using quality lean Princeville Ranch beef, these guys make one of the best burgers around. If you're into BBQ sauce, onion rings and bacon, try the Braddah's BBQ burger. A burger with fries is $7–$9, a deal that can't be beat in this town. They also make pizza, Mexican and fish-n-chips at equally competitive prices. Their breakfast sandwiches are tasty for only $5. They come with a hash brown patty that works best when you put it *in* the sandwich. Only a few stools outside, so be prepared to take it to go. In the Chevron gas station at the Princeville Center. Breakfast **$5–$8**, lunch and dinner **$7–$14**.

Paradise Bar & Grill
5-4280 Kuhio Hwy • 826-1775

One of the few places in Princeville that's easy on your wallet. The service is uninterested, the food underwhelming and the experience unremarkable. Breakfast is **$5–$15**. Burgers, sandwiches and fried stuff at lunch for **$6–$13**. Dinner has

more expensive options for **$10–$30**. In back of the Princeville Center.

Polynesia Café
5-5190 Kuhio Hwy • 826-1999

Breakfast is kind of sketchy on the north shore, and this is probably your best bet. For lunch and dinner it's a mix of American, Mexican, Asian and local food served on paper plates *(without,* however, the paper plate prices). Some tables outside or take-out. **$5–$10** for breakfast, **$10–$20** for lunch and dinner. In Hanalei in Ching Young Village.

Postcards
5-5075A Kuhio Hwy • 826-1191

A vegetarian restaurant that also serves fish. The food is distinctive and can be fairly well prepared. They use organic ingredients and have creative selections. Taro fritters make a good pupu, and the fresh fish is recommended. Ambiance is homey. The two areas that need work are the service (often slow), and the food too often isn't served hot. **$20–$35** for dinner. On mauka side of the highway in Hanalei. Reservations required for parties of 6 or more.

NORTH SHORE CHINESE

Panda's Kitchen
5-5190 Kuhio Hwy • 826-7388

If you want something fast to take to the beach or have a hankering for take-out quality Chinese food, this might do. Fairly good ingredients, prepared well with items like orange chicken, lo mein, sweet & sour pork and the like. Portions are more than acceptable. Add to that really fast service if you order from what you see in front of you. Don't bother asking; if it looks good, it probably is. Grab it and head to the beach. Lunch and dinner are **$7–$11**. The 1, 2 & 3 choice combos are a good deal until they stop serving them at 3 p.m. In Ching Young Village in Hanalei.

NORTH SHORE ITALIAN

Kilauea Bakery & Pau Hana Pizza
Kong Lung Center • 828–2020

(ono) Delicious baked goods and breads. (Try the macaroons or macadamia shortbread cookies.) The pizza is pricey, but the unusual fresh ingredients and the flavor combinations of the whole pizza specials work well. An example: Their island-style pizza is ham, pineapple, roasted garlic and chipotle peppers—much more interesting than traditional Hawaiian-style. More typical pizzas by the slice. As you'd expect from a bakery, the crust is very good. And the Big Kilauea Salad is particularly good. Service is either very friendly or shamefully indifferent—they sometimes seem to pride themselves on their surliness. But the food outshines the attitude. They have a dozen tables split indoors and out. **$10–$18** for meals. Bakery is reasonably priced. In Kilauea in Kong Lung Center off Kilauea Road. Open 6:30ish a.m. to 9 p.m.

NORTH SHORE JAPANESE

Bouchons Hanalei
5-5190 Kuhio Hwy • 826–9701

(ono) A popular spot in Hanalei that's always hopping. The entrées are good here, but the sushi is the star. The specialty rolls are fresh and filling. We really like the crunchy roll, the grasshopper and the spider roll. Their crab cakes are absurdly good. All their martinis are served with a full shaker that fills your glass 3 or more times. Do yourself in with the deadly chocolate suicide cake. Reservations recommended. Nightly entertainment on weekends. Upstairs in the Ching Young Village. **$22–$55.**

NORTH SHORE LOCAL

Hanalei Wake-up Café
5-5140 Kuhio Hwy • 826–5551

Hanalei restaurants tend to open late for breakfast, if they open at all. This place opens at 6:30 a.m. Very small menu and less-than-pristine surroundings. Service is fast but the food is hastily assembled. Decor is an homage to all things surfing. **$7–$14** for breakfast. In Hanalei on ocean side of road. Can't miss it. No credit cards.

Kilauea Fish Market
4270 Kilauea Rd. • 828–6244

Besides the usual fresh seafood, they carry some pricey free-range beef. If you don't want to cook at home, we suggest their ahi fajita burrito or the fish tacos. They also have salads, plate lunches and unique specials. The outdoor seating is covered, so if you want some sun, take it to the beach. It's pricier because you're in Kilauea. Behind the Kilauea Plantation Center, kitty-corner from the Kong Lung Center. **$10–$15** for lunch and dinner. Closed Sunday.

Tahiti Nui
5-5134 Kuhio Hwy • 826–6277

A legendary local establishment whose reputation is far grander than the present reality. Now it's basically a watering hole with overpriced food, spotty service and a dark atmosphere. (Pretty good mai tais, though.) People watching is the main reason to come here. A rainbow of colorful local characters keeps it interesting. Foodwise, it's burgers and uninspiring pizza. **$10–$20.**

Village Snack & Bakery Shop
5-5190 Kuhio Hwy • 826–6841

(ono) Their baked goods are *excellent* and very reasonably priced. Ambiance is...well, they don't have any. But if you want a place that sells lunch, cake and sometimes jewelry, this is the place for you. Hearty, cheap food. Try the apple cobbler—*very* ono and only $2. **$4–$8** for breakfast and lunch. Not bad food for the price. Simple, homey and cluttered. In Ching Young Village in Hanalei town. Open at 6:30 a.m.

NORTH SHORE MEXICAN

Neide's Salsa & Samba
5-5161 Kuhio Hwy • 826–1851

Our ONOs have come and gone with them. Currently the food's reasonably good, but it's too bland to recommend strongly. Though they're Brazilian (with some Brazilian dishes), the Mexican items like the burritos and enchiladas work best, *if* you use some of their salsa. Service is friendly and laid back. For the price, it's a reasonable place to go if you're sandy from the beach and don't want a lot of pretense. In Hanalei Center, Hanalei, at the back of the center. **$10–$22** for lunch and dinner. When they say the plate's hot, what they *really* mean is that you could bake a raw pizza on it.

Red Hot Mama's
5-6607 Kuhio Hwy • 826–7266

ono Literally a hole-in-the-wall take-out window past the 6 mile marker before the end of the road on Hwy 560 next to the Last Chance Store in Ha'ena. Simple, hearty Mexican food, mostly burritos and tacos with some salads and tuna wraps. Their "small kine" burrito is pretty good-sized for $7, and the "fat mama" will do most bigger eaters for $9. The hot sauce is fairly spicy and tasty. Lunch is **$7–$12**, and they close promptly at 5 p.m or *before*, if they run out of food. Buy your drinks next door and take it all to the beach. Cash only. Closed Saturdays.

Tropical Taco
5-5088 Kuhio Hwy • 827–8226

If you're wondering why there's a likeness of a green truck inside this location, it's because the owner operated Tropical Taco out of one for over 20 years. Located in the green Halele'a Building on the ocean side of the highway in Hanalei, the food is pretty good (though a bit expensive and the portions could be bigger), and it's not a bad place to grab a bite when you're on the run on the north shore. Lunch and dinner are **$8–$13**. No credit cards.

NORTH SHORE TREATS

Kilauea Video, Ice Cream & Candy
4270 Kilauea Rd. • 828–0128

ono This is the only place on the island to get the coveted, Big Island-made, Tropical Dreams ice cream. They use a higher percentage of milk fat than most ice creams, and their flavors are outstanding. Tropical Dreams previously wouldn't ship to Kaua'i for fear of their ice cream being stored or served incorrectly. Now Kilauea Video is an official distributor with around 20 flavors for $3.75 per scoop. In the Kilauea Plantation Center, kitty-corner from the Kong Lung Center in Kilauea. Opens at 2 p.m.

Shave Ice Paradise
5-5161 Kuhio Hwy • 826–6659

Good shave ice, but they are inconsistent on the syrup. Sometimes too much, sometimes too little. On expensive side. Across from Ching Young Village in Hanalei. Try Wishing Well instead.

Wishing Well Shave Ice

ono In a truck on the ocean side of the road in Hanalei, their shave ice is excellent; get it with ice cream on the bottom. Service is strangely moody—sometimes nice as can be, sometimes amazingly snippy—but the quality of the shave ice is excellent. Squirrely, seemingly random hours. Closed Monday. And they don't let you choose your flavor combinations. Take their combos or hit the road.

EAST SHORE AMERICAN

Bubba's Burgers
4-1421 Kuhio Hwy • 823–0069

(ONO) Funky place to get decent (but *small)* burgers, chili rice, etc., with a limited choice of burger toppings. If it weren't for their sassy attitude, we probably *wouldn't* give them an ONO. Their motto is, "We cheat tourists, drunks and attorneys." So if you are a drunk attorney visiting the island, you're on your own, counselor. **$5–$10**. On highway in Hanalei and highway in north Kapa'a; can't miss 'em. Nothing stands out individually, but overall the place works fairly well at the Kapa'a location. We can't recommend the Hanalei location because it's not run as well. We should point out that our reader e-mail seems more negative than positive on Bubba's, so maybe we're being too generous with the ONO even for the Kapa'a location.

Bull Shed
4-796 Kuhio Hwy • 822–3791
Dinner only, quite popular with both locals and tourists, known for hearty beef and seafood and moderate portions. The food *might* be good, but they really rely on their location to keep you happy. They seem to strive for mediocrity and usually succeed. The window seats are particularly close to the water (we've been there when the waves actually splashed against the glass), but arrive 10–15 minutes before they open (they start serving dinner at 5:30 p.m.) to get one. All entrées come with a

choice of salad or...salad. Sorry, no soup. (With a dependably pathetic salad bar, too.) The service can be slow and decidedly unenthusiastic. And if I may rant, you only get rice with entrées. If you pay extra and get a baked potato, they take the rice away. Hey, I'm *paying* for it. Leave it alone! (Whew, I feel better already.) **$15–$30**. Limited desserts such as mud pie and a pretty good and reasonably priced wine list. In Kapa'a on the ocean side of highway across from Kaua'i Village. Reservations only for six or more.

Caffé Coco
4-369 Kuhio Hwy • 822–7990

(ONO) Tucked away and hard to find, they serve some very delicious food along with some unusual recipes. Sort of a vegetarian/Pacific Rim/fish menu with other items, as well. Specials and regular items change on a whim—you may hear them debate or invent what to fix on the spot. But many items are clever and tasty, such as the fish with a mango grilling sauce on organic greens and spaghetti noodles with killer potstickers filled with tofu and chutney. Or try the various vegetarian items or the seafood gumbo. Flavor combinations seem well-chosen here. Relaxing ambiance with tables sprinkled about on gravel under various umbrellas and awnings with plants all around. (Sometimes mosquitoes are a problem.) Service is so relaxed that it's easy to feel ignored or unwelcome at first. You're not; it's just that they're profoundly laid back. But once you order your food, you are served well. **$17–$27** for dinner. Across the street from Kintaro Restaurant on Hwy 56 in Wailua (north of 6 mile marker); head toward the back. Closed Monday. Still for sale at press time, so things may change. B.Y.O.B. with a $5 corkage fee.

Deli & Bread Connection
2600 Kaumualii Hwy • 245–7115

ONO An absolutely dandy place to get sandwiches (although you'll often have to wait a while at lunch time). Large selection of traditional meats and veggies, plus some extras. Try the TOPS sandwich. $6–$9. In Kukui Grove next to Macy's. Some effective baked goods (though sometimes stale).

Duane's Ono-Char Burger
4-4350 Kuhio Hwy • 822–9181

ONO Duane's Ono-Char Burger is an institution on Kaua'i. Now into their third decade, Duane's still serves some of the best burgers on the island (though the burgers are on the small side). Though a bit too pricey, their specialty burgers, such as the teriyaki burger and the mushroom burger, are delicious. Their milkshakes (especially the marionberry shake) are outstanding. Most opt to eat at the cement outdoor tables, complete with shade from a large tree. Marauding wild chickens and cats usually compete for your jettisoned french fries. Or consider taking your food down Anahola Road (south of Duane's) to Anahola Beach Park, where picnic tables at the beach make for a pleasant atmosphere. (Weekends at that beach, however, are a bit crowded.) $7–$14 for lunch till 6 p.m. On the highway in Anahola; can't miss it. You may want to call in your order because you'll never wait less than 20 minutes, often way longer, if you order at the counter.

Duke's Canoe Club
3610 Rice St. • 246–9599

ONO Before we talk about the food, we should mention that this is one of the better places on the island to have a cocktail, downstairs outdoors overlooking Kalapaki Bay. We also like the indoor table by the small indoor waterfall. The pupu (hors d'oeuvre) selection includes pizzas, ribs, burgers and sandwiches and can easily serve as a meal and is not as overpriced as most resort foods. Service there is only fair and prices are $8–$17. Now as for the restaurant upstairs, the beef and seafood are very good. Consider the fresh catch prepared Duke-style. The prime rib is huge (it's hard to believe it came from just one cow) and delicious, and their salad bar is probably the best on the island. Lanai tables at the railing are best, offering a nice view of the bay. $18–$30, which is fairly reasonable for the quality of the surroundings. Located at the Marriott. (You can park in their lot or next to Anchor Cove at the beach parking lot.) The also have free valet parking from the road next to Anchor Cove, but it often fills up.

Fish Hut
4-484 Kuhio Hwy • 821–0033

ONO The fish burgers are excellent here, even when they don't come on focaccia bread like the menu says. You choose from fresh ahi, mahi mahi or ono. (Wish they had better fries, though.) Items from the fryer aren't as fresh, and don't bother with the clam chowder. The shave ice is outstanding, and they claim to have over 80 flavors. (But we didn't see nearly that many syrup bottles.) In the Coconut Marketplace, Kapa'a. $7–$13 for lunch and dinner.

Gaylord's Restaurant
3-2087 Kaumualii Hwy • 245–9593

ONO Gaylord's is one of those restaurants that seems to go in cycles from giving great experiences to resting on their laurels. They're up right now. Tables are arranged around a courtyard, and evenings can be very romantic. Lots of specials plus an eclectic assortment of entrées, including fish, pasta, venison, lamb, prime rib, etc. At lunch nearly all sandwiches are served on onion rolls.

$12–$20 for lunch, $30–$55 for dinner. Reservations recommended. In Kilohana just south of Lihu'e on the way to Po'ipu.

Harley's Tropical BBQ
4-484 Kuhio Hwy • 822–2505
Their namesake tropical BBQ sauce can best be described as a novelty. It's sweet and gimmicky. Prices are good considering the size, but the ribs are merely OK, so stick with the sandwiches. **$7–$12** for lunch and dinner. In the Coconut Marketplace, Kapa'a.

Hukilau Lanai
520 Aleka Loop • 822–0600
(ONO) Fish is their specialty, and they do it very well. (They're less talented with prime rib and other non-seafood items.) The atmosphere and views of the courtyard are peaceful and romantic. Try the Hukilau Mixed Grill—a tasty selection of seafood items. Portions are on the small side. At Kaua'i Coast Resort, Kapa'a, next to Coconut Marketplace. **$18–$30** for dinner. Closed Monday.

Hula Girl
4-484 Kuhio Hwy • 822–4422
This was two separate restaurants that combined into one location. Breakfast is served till around 2 p.m. Service can be unresponsive. The signature item, eggs Benedict, may not live up to your expectations, but the banana pancakes are the fluffiest you'll find. All in all, it's an OK pick for breakfast (though portions could be a bit bigger). For dinner, the steak and seafood have slipped and the portions on some items inexcusably small. For appetizers, consider the crab cakes or the imu pork tacos. Otherwise, it's a forgettable meal. **$7–$14** for breakfast, **$20–$35** for dinner. Lunch is a bit overpriced sandwiches and plate lunches for **$11–$17**. At the northern end of Coconut Market-

place between the 6 and 7 mile markers. Hawaiian music and simple hula some nights. Open for breakfast every day, open for dinner Wednesdays though Saturdays.

Java Kai
4-1384 Kuhio Hwy • 823–6887
A small coffee place on the ocean side of Hwy 56 in northern Kapa'a that serves lots of tasty coffee concoctions and other drinks. (Good chai latte; ask them not to make it too sweet.) You're better off with their baked goods than ordering from their 3-item menu. (Avoid the premade breakfast burritos.) Coffee by the pound. **$4–$8**. On highway in north Kapa'a. Open at 6 a.m.

JJ's Broiler
3416 Rice St. • 246–4422
(ONO) A longtime steak and seafood landmark. The menu selection is good, but the food is only a bit above average, and portions on some of the items are inexcusably small. So why the ONO? Their location adjacent to Kalapaki Beach makes lunch (which is downstairs) at the outdoor/indoor tables taste better. (Locations can do that.) Lunch features sandwiches, fish and chips and several pretty good salads. Their specialty at dinner (which is upstairs) is Slavonic steak (dipped in butter, wine and garlic sauce), but it's not their best item. Many of the other dinner items are good but overpriced, and the seaside setting isn't as much of an asset because the sun sets behind you. The ice cream pie is wonderful. With a grand view of Kalapaki Bay, large glass windows (upstairs) and sailboats hanging from the ceiling, JJ's sports a nice atmosphere. The lounge/lunch area downstairs often has live music and weak drinks at night. (Sometimes it's a bit loud.) **$12–$20** for lunch, **$27–$40** for

dinner. In Anchor Cove, Nawiliwili. All in all, JJ's is best for lunch (hence the ONO), overpriced at dinner.

Kalapaki Beach Hut
2474 Rice St. • 246–6330

ONO Gourmet burgers such as mahi-mahi, veggie burgers...*even beef.* This roadside stand has a counter and some upstairs tables with nice views. $4–$7 for breakfast, $6–$12 for lunch or early dinner. They're friendly and do it well. Next to Anchor Cove Shopping Center in Nawiliwili. Open at 7 a.m.

Kountry Kitchen
4-1485 Kuhio Hwy • 822–3511

ONO Dandy place to get breakfast (served till 1:30 p.m.) with pretty good breakfasts. Hence the ONO. Lunch also available. You may have to wait during peak times. Large selection of omelette ingredients. (Omelettes are hit or miss; the pancakes are very fluffy.) Be sure to check the board for specials (which, strangely, *never* seem to change). Simple American and local food in a small, diner-style atmosphere. $10–$18 for breakfast, $9–$15 for lunch.

Kukui's
3610 Rice St. • 246–5171

ONO Buffets are the specialty here, and they do them very well. Breakfast is $24. Dinner is $18–$35 off the menu, $41 for the Fri. and Sat. king crab and prime rib buffet—add $5 for champagne. (Lunch is off the menu for $12–$20.) Their pricey Sunday brunch ($38) is wonderful. In addition to the usual suspects, they have prime rib, Japanese dishes, muffins, omelettes and an outrageous roster of desserts. This is a good place to experience the old Hawaiian adage, "Don't eat till you're full; eat till you're tired." Next to the pool at the Marriott

in Lihu'e. Service is only fair, but if it's a buffet, it's no big deal.

Lihu'e Barbecue Inn
2982 Kress St. • 245–2921

ONO Steak, seafood and sandwiches with some Asian dishes served in a simple, clean atmosphere. Breakfast is great. Their French toast creations deserve a medal. We also liked the breakfast burrito and the benedict. They tend to run out of basic, core items. This place is very popular with locals who appreciate the good food and usually large portions. Tasty homemade bread and pies. Teriyaki pork chops, sandwiches, fish, great kalua pig and cabbage—they do most things well. (Avoid the ribs, though. Local style and very fatty.) A good value all around. How nice when you find out your beverages and desserts are included with many meals for $10 or less. An *excellent* deal. Kress is a side street off Rice in Lihu'e. $7–$10 for breakfast, $10–$16 for lunch, $12–$27 for dinner. Closed Sunday.

Market Street Diner
3501 Rice St. • 246–1100

Comfort food served in a '50s-themed diner. Lunch is a solid deal with burgers or fish & chips for $9. Dinner is also thrifty, but most side items taste canned except for the mashed potatoes. Their chicken fried steak is actually chicken fried chicken, and they top it with brown gravy (an absolute *sin* in any Southern home). The meatloaf isn't bad, and the burgers can also be had at dinner. In Lihu'e at the Harbor Mall. $8–$12 for breakfast and lunch, $12–$20 for dinner.

Mermaids Café
4-1384 Kuhio Hwy • 821–2026

They strive for a healthier meal here and often succeed with their tiny menu.

You're best off with the ahi wraps, the fish tacos or the curry plate. They have a number of tasty and unusual drinks, such as hibiscus lemonade. Just a few outdoor tables. In Kapa'a, on Kuhio Hwy near 581. **$10–$13** for lunch and dinner.

Olympic Café
4-1354 Kuhio Hwy • 822–5825

The menu here is vast and most portions are bulky. Breakfast scrambles are tasty, and the burritos and burgers work well at lunch. Dinner adds some more expensive items like steak, pasta and fajitas. For dessert, the Kaua'i Pie has nearly a half-gallon of ice cream and can easily satisfy a table of 4. Fridays they have a free taco bar during happy hour (3 p.m. to 7 p.m.), which can get really busy. It's a weird night, and you should stay away from the fish. **$10–$15** for breakfast and lunch, **$10–$30** for dinner. Across from ABC store in downtown Kapa'a.

Ono Family Restaurant
4-1292 Kuhio Hwy • 822–1710

(ono) A wonderful breakfast selection and fairly reasonable prices. One of the reasons for reviewing a restaurant multiple times is to discern patterns. This is a good example. We may come here one day and be seated by a grumpy greeter and receive bad food. Another two times we'll arrive and get good food (but with the same grumpy greeter). Most of the breakfasts are good (though the hash browns need work, as does the sausage—consider the sweet Chinese sausage for a different experience). The tropical stack of pancakes is also good. The ONO is for the breakfast. Lunch is average burgers. **$8–$13** for breakfast and lunch. On the ocean side of Hwy 56 in Kapa'a south of 581.

Papaya's Natural Foods
4-831 Kuhio Hwy • 823–0190

A good health food store that also serves mostly veggie items, such as veggie lasagna, tofu and falafels and perhaps some sandwiches. Basically you fill a plate once for about $6.50, and results are mixed. We've had some good meals here…and we've walked away with our inedible plates still full. Hard to say what you'll get. **$5–$9** all day. If you eat at the tables, be forewarned that you are likely to be dining with individuals who consider bathing an unnecessary and decadent ritual. Located in Kaua'i Village in Kapa'a.

Scotty's Beachside BBQ
4-1546 Kuhio Hwy • 823–8480

(ono) First things first. Since the initial edition of this book, we've reviewed every company from a dispassionate and unbiased view. We've never had a stake in *any* company. We now have a singular exception, and we want be upfront and tell you why. For years people wrote to us saying, *I want to move to Kaua'i. What does the island really need?* And for years we gave the same response—*You can't get good* BBQ *on Kaua'i.* Much to our surprise, nobody ever took our advice. We missed good BBQ, and with a hugely talented partner we decided to open *Scotty's* at the ocean in Kapa'a. You won't find us working there (our partner, Scotty, is da man), but you will find some of the things we learned after reviewing hundreds and hundreds of eateries in the islands, and we tried to fix the things that always bugged us about restaurants, from the design of the building to the design of the mai tais. (Lots of selfless research went into the recipe for *that* one.) For the first year it was open, we *didn't* give it an ONO because it felt unseemly given our ownership. After a year of getting pretty vocal e-mails from readers telling us it deserves an ONO, we relented, but given our interest you are allowed to feel skeptical. *We* believe in it, but we're biased in this case. The menu includes ribs, BBQ shredded pork and beef brisket sandwiches (we always request the sauce be mixed into the meat) and also includes steak and seafood, fish and chips, etc. It's right next to the ocean and built in a series of tiers so every table has an unobstructed, open-air ocean view. On the highway at the north end of Kapa'a, north of Hwy 581, ocean side. **$10–$18** for lunch, **$16–$30** for dinner.

Small Town Coffee
4-1495 Kuhio Hwy • 821–1604

An artsy, hodgepodge café with personality. Their coffee is consistently good and organically grown. Powerful espressos, homemade hot chocolates and lattes. Their breakfast bagels are fantastic with amusing names like the Italian scallion, the El Guapo and the We Found Nemo (bagel and lox). Diehard regulars usually occupy the outside tables where they solve the world's problems among themselves. It tends to take awhile to get your breakfast. Open 5:30 a.m. (food starts at 7 a.m.). Free WiFi. **$3–$8**. On mauka side of Hwy 56 north of Lehua Street but before Kojima's Store. (Just keep your eyes peeled.)

TNT Steakburgers
Kuhio Hwy • 651–4922

At the north end of Kapa'a in Kojima's parking lot on the mauka side of Hwy you may see a trailer that serves up some surprisingly good burgers. They grind their own steak and the buns are made specially for them. Sizes range from small to their 1-pound slab served on a bun large enough to serve as a flotation device. The fries are soaked in vinegar before cooking, giving them a distinct flavor that will either wow ya or turn you off. (Most people love them.)

Prices ain't cheap, but not as pricey as a more fixed location. (For that, we hope they *don't* follow through on their musings of building a larger location.) **$7–$12** for lunch and dinner. They may move around, so call them for a current location.

EAST SHORE CHINESE

Garden Island Barbecue
4252 Rice St. • 245–8868

Despite the name, it's a Chinese restaurant with a local twist, *not* a BBQ. The selection is dizzying—over 150 items! (And no, we haven't tried every one.) Portions are good and the price is reasonable. There will almost certainly be something that interests you. Service is lightning fast. Although the food's not the greatest, you ain't paying for the greatest. You're paying for a large selection, large portions, and you want to get in and out fast. So you're getting what you pay for; hence the ONO. **$7–$11** for lunch and dinner. In Lihu'e at Rice and Hardy. Closed Sunday.

Hong Kong Café
4-361 Kuhio Hwy • 822–3288

Fairly typical Chinese menu with plate lunch combos the least expensive option. Quality of food is about right for the price. Not great, not bad. (Tasty duck.) Very clean and tidy inside. **$8–$15** for lunch and dinner. In Wailua Shopping Plaza in south Wailua off Hwy 56.

Ho's Chinese Kitchen
3-2600 Kaumualii Hwy • 245–5255

Hideous Chinese food in unclean surroundings. Any questions? **$7–$12** per person. In Kukui Grove Center, Lihu'e.

Pacific Island Bistro
4-831 Kuhio Hwy • 822–0092

A difficult one to classify. Basically Chinese with a

Pacific Rim twist. The menu has lots of compelling choices, including the tasty Peking duck. Other items include flaming satay New York, pot roast chicken and pork tenderloin. In the Kaua'i Village Shopping Center, Kapa'a. **$10–$25** for lunch and dinner.

EAST SHORE ITALIAN

Aloha Kaua'i Pizza
4-484 Kuhio Hwy • 822–4511
In the Coconut Marketplace. One of those places that is strikingly consistent. Too bad it's consistently mediocre. We think the pizza is a bit wet and greasy and lacking taste. Their menu says, "Voted Best Pizza in Hawai'i." Lucky them. **$7–$12**.

Café Portofino
3481 Hoolaulea Way • 245–2121
(ONO) Their view alone creates a very tasty atmosphere for those fortunate enough to get a railing table. Kalapaki Bay waves creates a background hum that can enhance any food. The owner is Italian, and some of the flavors smack of the real Italy, for good and bad. (After spending a month in Italy, we came to expect good wine and bad bread—just like this restaurant.) Some items may disappoint, but on the whole, the overall experience gets them an ONO. At the Kaua'i Marriott. **$25–$50** for dinner.

Kaua'i Pasta
4-939B Kuhio Hwy • 822–7447
(ONO) A pretty easy place to like. There will only be a couple of pastas and four sauces, plus the specials. But the quality is good for the price and portions ample. Their salads are very large and they are happy to split them, so consider ordering only one per couple. You can add chicken breast to any pasta for $4, but the portion is sur-

prisingly small. Well chosen wine and beer list, and they'll ding you for $15 if you BYOB. Dinner only for **$10–$20**. On Kuhio Hwy in Kapa'a behind Taco Bell. No reservations, and the small dining room fills quickly. They also have a location in Lihu'e at 3-3142 Kuhio Hwy that is equally as good.

Pizzetta
4-1387 Kuhio Hwy • 823–8882
Formerly great, now terrible. It's sad when a place that you liked goes downhill so far. Bad food and appallingly bad service. Believe it or not you're better off at Pizza Hut. On Kuhio Hwy north of the intersection at Hwy 581. **$10–$20** for dinner.

EAST SHORE JAPANESE

Hanama'ulu Café,
Tea House & Sushi Bar
3-4291 Kuhio Hwy • 245–2511
Japanese and Chinese served in a *delightful* atmosphere. There are gardens out back, a koi pond and individual tea rooms (if you reserve one with a group). The food here isn't the highest quality, but portions are good considering the price. $7 will get you a heaping plate of their famous crispy fried ginger chicken. On the main highway (56) just outside of Lihu'e in Hanama'ulu. Hours can be squirrely; call to verify. **$8–$12** for lunch, **$10–$25** (more if you go nuts on the sushi) for dinner. Reservations recommended. Mosquitoes can be a problem at times. Closed Monday.

Kintaro Restaurant
4-370 Kuhio Hwy • 822–3341
(ONO) You will be happy with this selection. *Excellent* sushi bar (try the Hanalei rolls), large teppan yaki section (that's where the food is prepared in front of you by a talented, knife-wielding chef), full bar and

a very pleasant atmosphere. The food is expertly prepared using only the freshest ingredients. The service is outstanding. Fun but not stuffy. Filet mignon for those who don't want Japanese food. In fact, they have the best steak and lobster on the island. It's cubed and cooked in front of you, and it melts in your mouth. A bit pricier than others, but worth it. (Occasionally they get overenthusiastic with the salt.) Just north of Kinipopo Shopping Center not too far from the Wailua River on Hwy 56. Dinner only, **$18–$40**. Reservations recommended for the teppan yaki. (They don't take them for the sushi bar.)

Sushi Bushido
3416 Rice St. • 632–0664
From the back of Anchor Cove Mall, you can watch people surf in Kalapaki Bay. You're better off doing that than eating here. The sushi is overpriced, and the specialty rolls have some strange combinations that just don't work for us. Almost every roll comes topped with shredded dried fish that blankets the item with a fishy taste. (Good sushi shouldn't taste fishy.) Their tempura is their best item. Pretty tasty. **$15–$40** for dinner.

EAST SHORE KOREAN

Korean Bar-B-Q
4-356 Kuhio Hwy • 823–6744
(ONO) A good place to try some Korean food with a local twist. The combo plates are the best deal. One or more meats—teriyaki beef, chicken katsu, kalbi (short ribs), etc.—plus plenty of side dishes—rice, mac salad, kimchee and Korean miso soup, which is excellent, but make *sure* you finish it before the meats arrive. Miso tastes terrible if you eat it with the meats. Overall, consistently good. **$8–$15** for lunch and dinner. In

the Kinipopo Shopping Village in the south part of Wailua on Hwy 56.

EAST SHORE LOCAL

Dani's Restaurant
4201 Rice St. • 245–4991
Clean, cheap and reasonably good. Breakfast is very popular and your best bet here. Lunch is kalua pig, tripe stew, lau lau, pork chops, etc. Service is totally dependent on who your waitress is. It's *very* loud inside and crowded, but this isn't a bad choice if price is important. **$7–$10** for breakfast (coffee is included with meal) and lunch. Open at 5 a.m. Closed Sunday.

Fish Express
3343 Kuhio Hwy • 245–9918
(ONO) A long-time local favorite, this is the place to get your seafood fix to go. Along with lu'au foods and salads (both very good), they make some wicked fish specials. Seven different preparations are paired with a fresh fish that changes daily. You can't go wrong with macadamia nut crusted fish with liliko'i, or have it sautéed with garlic and herbs. Get brave and try some of the unusual but tasty seafood creations at the deli counter. The ahi poke is a good place to start. **$8–$12**. Across from Wal-Mart on Hwy 56 in Lihu'e. Open 10 a.m. to 6 p.m. Closed Sundays and no grilled items on saturdays.

Hamura's Saimin Stand
2956 Kress St. • 245–3271
(ONO) Universally loved by locals and forewarned visitors alike, they have *some of the best saimin on Kaua'i.* (See page 206 for definition of saimin.) It is wildly popular, and people come from other parts of the island to eat here. Their selection is scant, but the food is excellent and cheap. Consider the "special" saimin, which has more ingredients

and is tastier. Their only dessert—liliko'i pie—is light and pretty good but sells out early. Food is served lunch-counter style. Though dumpy, it'll be here forever unless the sodium police raid the place. Makes for good takeout, but it's so hot that transporting it almost necessitates a hazardous materials permit. (Spill any on you, and you may burst into flames.) They have good shave ice. (That part of the business is called **Halo Halo Shave Ice**, and they ignore it when they're busy (and sometimes when they're not). Try ringing the bell. Make sure to get the shave ice with ice cream on the bottom. **$5–$8** for lunch and dinner. Kress is off Rice Street in Lihu'e. See map on page 65.

House of Noodles
4-1330 Kuhio Hwy • 822–2708
Diverse menu of saimin, sandwiches, battered lobster and burgers. Items are hit or miss. In general, stick with noodle items like the saimin and won ton soup. The sandwiches are small and unimpressive, and the ambiance is a bit third world. Kuhio Hwy in Kapa'a south of Hwy 581. **$8–$18** for lunch and dinner.

Kawayan
1543 Haleukana St. • 245–8823
A hard-to-find place that serves good local/Filipino/American food. Plate lunches, burgers and hot dogs. They also have sweet chili chicken (which is pretty good) and a good pork and peas. The food will never be confused with health food (super salty). In Puhi, take Puhi Road, right on Hanalima, left on Haleukama. It's on the right side. Food is noticeably better at peak eating times. Lunch and dinner are **$4–$11**. Closed weekends. Cash only.

Mark's Place
1610 Haleukana St. • 245–2722
One of those places that you'd never know was here

if someone didn't tell you about it. They probably serve the best local food on the island. The prices are reasonable and the portions ample. Consider the mixed plate with chicken katsu, teriyaki beef and beef stew for around $7.75. That's the most expensive meal. Or try the loco moco, Korean chicken, or one of the specials, such as the occasional kalua pig and cabbage. This is local-style food, so don't expect low calorie or low cholesterol. And don't expect to eat in; everything's to go. But if you want to eat what many locals eat and don't want to spend much, this is the place for you. **$6–$8** for lunch. From Hwy 50 in Puhi, take Puhi Road, right on Hanalima. Closed weekends.

Pono Market
4-1300 Kuhio Hwy • 822–4581
The friendly folks here serve a great plate lunch with lots of aloha. If you don't know what an item is, they take the time to explain. It's the perfect place to try some local dishes like lau lau or kalua pork. Their ahi poke is arguably the best on island. It can get busy around lunch, but they run it like a well-oiled machine. **$6–$12**, cash only. On the ocean side of Hwy 56 in downtown Kapa'a.

Tip Top Café
3173 Akahi St. • 245–2333
This place is recognized by locals as an outstanding bargain for breakfast and lunch. The menu includes some non-traditional breakfast items, such as beef stew and oxtail soup served first thing in the morning. Banana and macadamia nut pancakes come large, fluffy and light, but hardy and filling. Or try the pineapple pancakes—very tasty. Good coffee. Great cream puffs and pastries in the morning (pass on the cookies, though.) Eggs are their weak spot. Clean, unpretentious hardiness, less-than-bubbly service.

$5–$10 for breakfast, $7–$10 for lunch. (We think you'll like breakfast over lunch.) In Lihu'e. Closed Monday.

Waipouli Restaurant
4-771 Kuhio Hwy • 822-9311

ONO A good place to have some reasonably priced and flavorful (if not particularly healthy) local food. Lunch features items like teriyaki steak, shrimp tempura (which is good), beef sukiyaki, saimin, liver & onions, chopped steak, tofu or burgers. Portions are large, and the place is simple but utilitarian. $6–$10 for breakfast, $8–$12 for lunch, $10–$17 for dinner. In Waipouli Town Center, Kapa'a, near Foodland on Hwy 56. If they don't bring your check, take your money to the counter. They're *real* informal here. Cash only. Closed Monday.

EAST SHORE MEXICAN

La Bamba
3-2600 Kaumualii Hwy • 245-5972
In the large Kukui Grove Shopping Center in Lihu'e. The food can be flavorful, but it's on the oily side, and other items like stale chips and stale service bring 'em down. The chile relleno is probably their best bet. Don't go here if you're in a hurry. It takes a *long* time to get your food. $9–$18 for lunch and dinner.

Mariachi's
3501 Rice St. • 246-1570
The menu here is vast and nothing we've tried has been bad (except maybe the taco salad). It's not exactly authentic, but it's good Mexican comfort food. The portions are disappointing on some items. Service isn't as quick as you'd expect from Mexican cuisine, but they've put a disclaimer on the menu stating that it takes time, so we can't

rightly scold them for it. We like to get the burritos *enchilada* style. The combination plates are a good deal if you get them "as is," otherwise they'll nickel and dime you with extras. For dessert, try their homemade sopapillas. $8–$11 for breakfast, $11–$25 for lunch and dinner. Upstairs in the Harbor Mall.

Monico's Taqueria
4-356 Kuhio Hwy • 822-4300
They make an admirable effort in the presentation department and the food is fresh but bland. (And they must keep the hot sauce in the safe, because you'll be hard pressed to have them part with any.) Some portions are ample, like the giant burritos. The café is loud inside with some quieter tables next to the highway. $11–$20 for lunch and dinner. In the Kinipopo Shopping Center, Kapa'a.

Norberto's El Café
4-1373 Kuhio Hwy • 822-3362
Fairly poor Mexican food. All items come as a meal or à la carte, regular or vegetarian. They try to compensate by adding bean soup or a tiny cheese enchilada to the meals. At least their rum cake is fairly tasty. Funky Spanish decor. Overpriced at $17–$25, dinner only. Located on the main highway in downtown Kapa'a near 581. Closed Sunday.

EAST SHORE PACIFIC RIM

The Eastside
4-1380 Kuhio Hwy • 823-9500
ONO Great food and good service make this a no-brainer to recommend. We've kind of gotten into a rut here, usually ordering the mochiko dusted calamari for appetizer and the potato crusted mahi mahi

entrée. But they also have great ceviche and excellent filet mignon. The atmosphere is fairly simple and there's no view other than the highway. *But da grinds work here, brah.* Live music some nights. **$25–$38** for dinner.

Lemongrass
4-885 Kuhio Hwy • 821–2888

An interesting and eclectic menu featuring Asian, local and American items, plus pasta, fresh fish and steak. Food can be good here, but usually isn't and is overpriced. Service has a tendency to be pretty bumbling. **$20–$40** for dinner. On Hwy 56 in Kapa'a north of Kaua'i Village.

Wahooo Seafood Grill & Bar
4-733 Kuhio Hwy • 822–7833

ONO A strongly seafood-oriented menu with some steak and pasta, as well. Atmosphere is subdued—nice without too much hype—and the service is responsive. The food is flavorful, so it's a good place to go to fill that yearning for some seafood. We wish that they'd spend a bit less energy on the flair and presentation in favor of larger fish cuts. **$20–$50** for dinner. Avoid the strawberry bread pudding for dessert. In Kapa'a on Kuhio Highway just south of Foodland.

EAST SHORE THAI

King & I Thai Cuisine
4-901 Kuhio Hwy • 822–1642

A formerly good restaurant that has been slowly running out of steam. The flavors just aren't as bursting as they used to be. Their mango fish special (which they usually have) is very good, but the curries and pad thai are lacking. Located in Waipouli Plaza, mauka side of highway in Kapa'a. **$10–$20** for dinner. They burn incense as an offering to the Buddha when they open, so

wait a bit longer if the smell of *strong* incense bothers you.

Mema Thai Chinese
4-369 Kuhio Hwy • 823–0899

ONO A great selection of Thai and some Chinese dishes, and though not great, it's the best Thai on the east shore. Consider the pad Thai, house curry or one of the vegetable items. On mauka side of Hwy 56 just north of Haleilio Road. **$13–$30** for lunch and dinner. (Lunch during the week only.) It's BYOB, which you can buy from the *flower* store next door.

Sukhothai
4-1105 Kuhio Hwy • 821–1224

An endless menu of fairly mediocre food. It's listed under Thai, but they also serve Chinese, Vietnamese, vegetarian and Asian BBQ. The food *can be* well prepared, the restaurant pleasing and service friendly. But not always…If you want it spicy, stress it strongly. They seem afraid of giving you the heat. **$10–$20** for lunch and dinner. In Kapa'a Shopping Center near Big Save on mauka side of highway.

EAST SHORE TREATS

Cold Stone Creamery
4-831 Kuhio Hwy • 823–9099

ONO Part of a growing national chain. The name refers to the frozen slab of granite they use to mix whatever your little heart desires into their homemade ice cream—mixes like candy bars, berries, brownies, etc. Outrageous dipped waffle cup liners. Price is steep. You can easily spend **$6** for a medium cup, but that's for a *ton* of ice cream. In Kapa'a near Safeway in the Kaua'i Village Shopping Center and at Kukui Grove Shopping Center in Lihu'e. At press time one was planned at Po'ipu Shopping Village.

Halo Halo Shave Ice
2956 Kress St. • 245-5094

ono Good shave ice, poor service. Located in Hamura's Saimin on Kress Street in Lihu'e; see map on page 65. They'll ignore you if the restaurant's busy. If that's the case, don't take it personally.

Hanalima Baking Co.
4495 Puhi Rd. • 246-8816

On the corner of Puhi Road and Hwy 50 in Puhi, they serve pretty tasty malasadas (a Portuguese donut) 3 for $1. They have decent blueberry scones and cocoa puffs. $2-$3. Open at 6 a.m. Closed Sunday.

Hawaiian Blizzard
4-1105 Kuhio Hwy

ono This is simply a shave ice stand in front of Big Save in Kapa'a at the Kapa'a Shopping Center on Hwy 56 near the 8 mile marker. Though selection is limited and they don't offer ice cream on the bottom (our preferred way), they keep their ice blade especially sharp, creating extraordinarily fine shave ice. $3. Flexible hours means they're not always there.

Kaua'i Bakery & Cinnamons
3-2600 Kaumualii Hwy • 246-4765

ono Located in Lihu'e's Kukui Grove Shopping Center, they have a sparse selection but outstanding quality on some items. Their apple turnovers are the best on the planet. (Pretty strong words, Andy!) Other items not as stellar. They open at 6 a.m. and may run out of many things by 11. You won't find bubbly service, but da grinds broke da mouf, brah.

Kaua'i Fruit & Flower
3-4684 Kuhio Hwy • 245-1814

On Hwy 56 near the airport. $9 for a pineapple! Need we say more?

SOUTH SHORE AMERICAN

Beach House Restaurant
5022 Lawai Rd. • 742-1424

ono A longtime south shore landmark. Steak and seafood with exceptional ocean views—they are right next to the water. Nice sunsets from here. Tables are reasonably spaced. The food quality is usually very good. (Steak is probably their weakest offering—stick with the seafood.) Vast wine list. Dinner, with entrées like lamb, fresh fish, steak and the like, will run you $28-$45. On Lawai Road in Po'ipu on way to Spouting Horn. Almost always a memorable meal, this is one of the best restaurants on the south shore. Reservations *strongly* recommended days in advance.

Brennecke's Beach Broiler
2100 Hoone Rd. • 742-7588

Their motto is "right on the beach" (actually they're across the street from Po'ipu Beach Park, but the view is still awesome) and "right on the price" (which is, unfortunately, dead wrong). We think they rely too much on the view. Reader comments are consistently two to one against this long-time landmark, and that matches our experience. Sometimes good service, but not usually. Sometimes good food, but too pricey. Brennecke's is still *capable* of great seafood and steak memories, but they need to stop resting on their laurels and get more consistent. They still pour some of the better drinks on the south shore (with legendary mai tais), and their chowder is pretty tasty. $12-$22 for lunch, $20-$35 for dinner. Next to Po'ipu Beach Park.

Downstairs and next door, their **Brennecke's Deli** has breakfast items before 10 a.m., sandwiches, hot dogs and bad shave ice. Though the food's certainly not gourmet, it's amazing how much better it'll taste if you take it across the street to one of the beach park tables and gaze at the delicious scenery. **$5–$9**.

Ilima Terrace
1571 Poipu Rd. • 742–1234

ONO Located at the Hyatt in Po'ipu, they offer good food in a beautiful, open-air setting near a Hyatt waterfall. Breakfast is overpriced (how else can you describe $15 pancakes or $18 loco moco?). And at lunch you have burgers or a cobb salad for $18 or pricier dinner-style entrées for more. They also have a fairly good daily breakfast buffet for **$28**. A bargain? No. But the location helps take the sting out of it and garners them the ONO. The setting is fantastic—ask for the table next to the waterfall. Reservations recommended.

Joe's on the Green
2545 Kiahuna Pl. • 742–9696

On the Kiahuna Golf Course next to the driving range, the open-air feel and views of mountains give it a pretty and relaxing atmosphere. Breakfast is your best bet. Lunch is sandwiches (love the Bruddah Reuben and the Marta's Melt), salads and fish and chips. Service is friendly. **$8–$15** for breakfast and lunch. From Po'ipu Road take the road into Po'ipu Shopping Village, drive past it into Kiahuna Golf Course.

Kalaheo Café & Coffee Co.
2-2560 Kaumualii Hwy • 332–5858

ONO Quality breakfast choices and a large list of coffee drinks make this a good spot to stop on your way to a boat tour on the west side. We like the bonzo burrito and the bagel benny. Their cinnamon knuckles are deadly and best eaten hot. Sandwiches and salads at lunch. Dinner offers an eclectic menu. We like the open-face enchilada, but the coconut shrimp will have us coming back. **$6–$11** for breakfast, **$14–$30** for dinner. On highway in Kalaheo. Open at 6:30 a.m.

Keoki's Paradise
2360 Kiahuna Plantation • 742–7534

ONO This is a special sort of place that people either love or hate (we love it). The ambiance is the story here with plants everywhere, a large fish lagoon, waterfalls and thatched roof booths (try to say *that* three times fast). It's the South Pacific that never really existed except in movies. The exotic bar area serves burgers, sandwiches and ribs at lunch and dinner for **$8–$14**. Some people wait there for a table while others make a meal of it to save money. The tables in the main area are arranged on several levels. Purists will sniff that the ambiance is not real—so what?! It's still exotic inside. If you are in the right mood, this is the sort of place you will remember for a long time. As for the food, it's a steak and seafood restaurant with above average food and service. Quite good, but not great. Several of the entrées, such as the prime rib, are only served as long as they last. They have a 26-ounce prime rib for those who swam here from O'ahu. The hula pie is equally large. The place can get pretty busy, which can have an effect on the service. Reservations strongly recommended. **$20–$35** for dinner. Located in the Po'ipu Shopping Village in Po'ipu.

Plantation Garden
2253 Poipu Rd. • 742–2121

ONO A very relaxing tropical cactus garden setting with mostly outdoor tables (which are preferred). Dinner is a fairly small selection of steak and seafood, but flavors are well-conceived. The kalua pork lettuce wrap is a tasty appetizer if you can get past the inherent saltiness. The seafood lau lau is great if a bit generous with the scallops at the expense of the fresh fish. They don't do as well with steaks. They seem to lean toward slightly undercooking, so order with this in mind. Their bartending skills really stand out, and they have an amazingly refreshing cucumber mojito. **$25–$40** for dinner. At the Kiahuna Plantation in Po'ipu. Reservations recommended.

Po'ipu Beach Broiler
1941 Poipu Rd. • 742–6433
Reader comments to us are universally negative and we definitely side with them. Overpriced and underperforming food. The fish and chips should be called batter and fries with a hint of fish. Sandwiches and burgers at lunch, lots of steak and seafood at dinner. Staff is less than professional for cloth napkin service. In Po'ipu Kai condos on Po'ipu Road. Lunch (from 2 p.m.) is **$11–$15**, dinner is **$25–$40**.

Po'ipu Grill
2827 Poipu Rd. • 742–1707
Literally a hole in the wall in Po'ipu Plaza next to Seasport Divers. Burgers are their thing, and there's nothing magic about them. (Not even the magic mushroom burger.) Fries are extra and the wait for your food is long, so blow on by if you're in a hurry. **$7–$12**.

Po'ipu Tropical Burgers
2360 Kiahuna Plantation • 742–1808
An unexpectedly large menu for a burger joint. In addition to the *many* half-pound burgers combinations (which start at $8 and include fries), there's spaghetti, fish and chips, sandwiches, lots of salads, veggie items, and lots of cold drinks like smoothies, freezes and floats. They are very reluctant to cook burgers less than what *they* call med/well (which seems well done to us), citing "Board of Health regulations." Plus the burgers aren't very good. **$8–$13** for breakfast and lunch, **$10–$22** for dinner. Back of Po'ipu Shopping Village.

Puka Dogs
2360 Kiahuna Plantation • 742–6044
ONO Hard to believe we'd give an ONO for a $6 hot dog. Granted, it's overpriced. But these are very good hot dogs served in an unusual way. The dogs are roasted (giving them the slightly crunchy skin), then embedded in a wraparound bun served with a choice of sauces inside. Get some of their mango relish to smear on the tip each time you bite. Only two dogs—a Polish sausage and a veggie dog. But with their sauces and fixin's you'll be pleased. For a beverage get their lemonade...or bring your drink. In the Po'ipu Shopping Village. **$7–$9**.

Shells *come early*
2440 Hoonani Rd. • 742–1661
ONO The most delicious thing about this restaurant is the view, one of the best you will find on the south shore. It's at the water's edge overlooking the beach with lots of windows and some outdoor tables. At breakfast they have an expensive buffet ($20), but it's memorable for this reason. Off the menu also available. Shells dinner features fish, pasta, beef, crab, etc., most prepared very well. Since part of the price you are paying is for the view, dinner, especially late dinners, aren't such a good deal since it's too dark to see. Resort wear requested. **$35–$50** for dinner. At the Sheraton Po'ipu.

Tidepools ✕
1571 Poipu Rd. • 742-1234

(ono) Located at the Hyatt Po'i-pu, their best feature is a very romantic atmosphere. A thatched roof, a stocked freshwater lagoon next to your table and flickering tiki torches outside provide a calm, quiet dinner environment. The limited menu concentrates on fresh fish, with some beef and vegetarian items. (Good ahi sashimi.) **$30–$45.** Service is adequate. Reservations recommended. Dinner only.

Tomkats Grille
5402 Koloa Rd. • 742-8887

A fairly large menu of burgers, plate lunches and grilled sandwiches for lunch, steak, seafood and chicken for dinner. All served in a decidedly feline atmosphere. The ambiance is relaxing with an open-air feel next to a small fish pond and garden. But the food isn't good enough and the service is closer to a hiss than a purr. (Sorry, couldn't resist.) Lunch is your best bet. Some of their specialties are rather inventive. Not a bad place to bring the kittens, though they also feature a full bar and a huge selection of catnips (beer and tropical drinks) for the adult cats. It can get a bit warm under the hot tin roof. **$10–$17** for lunch, **$18–$30** for dinner. In Koloa town. Look for the sign near Pizzetta.

SOUTH SHORE ITALIAN

Brick Oven Pizza
2-2555 Kaumualii Hwy • 332-8561
4-4361 Kuhio Hwy • 823-8561

(ono) We have a lot of affection for this place and we eat here often, but we have to admit that it's overpriced. The pizza is the best on Kaua'i, bar none. Though not baked in a real brick oven, they pride themselves

on making their own sauce, sausage and other ingredients. (Inexplicably, though, the mushrooms are canned.) The crust is thin with scalloped edges and brushed with garlic butter with tasty results. The sauce is simply perfect Simple Italian atmosphere, attentive, friendly service and excellent pizza. But the prices—they've gone from pretty pricy to almost insane. It's just shy of *$40* for a large 4-topping pizza. It's still a great place for pizza and sandwiches, but they only reason we keep the ONO is because the pizza can't be beat. Prices are **$9–$25.** No reservations. Kids are given a wad of pizza dough to play with—nice touch. (And fitting, since adults will *spend* a wad of dough.) Located on mauka side of highway as you enter Kalaheo or the mauka side as you enter Kapa'a from Lihu'e. Closed for lunch on Monday.

Casa Di Amici
2301 Nalo Rd. • 742-1555

(ono) Good food in a hard-to-find location. Items include standard pastas plus things like Tuscan pork loin and some island-inspired dishes and a killer crabcake. Service can be brusk, and we've had bad experiences here, but not often. **$25–$40** for dinner. In Po'ipu, take Hoowili to Hoone, drive past Brennecke Beach, and when the road goes mauka and changes names to Nalo, look for it on a corner.

Dondero's
1571 Poipu Rd. • 742-1234

(ono) Regional Italian food. Entrées change too often to recommend a specific one here. Pastas, veal, fresh fish and lamb, usually expertly prepared. Outstanding wine list. Elegant dining; their dress code requires casual resort wear, meaning covered shoes, collared shirts for men, etc. Dinner is **$30–$50**. In the Hyatt Po'ipu. Reservations recommended.

Pizzetta
5408 Koloa Rd. • 742-8881
Similar to the Pizzetta in Kapa'a. Not too good.

Pomodoro Ristorante Italiano
2-2514 Kaumualii Hwy • 332-5945
ono Upscale Italian food in small, pleasing surroundings. The owners of the former Casa Italia opened this place when their restaurant in Lihu'e literally blew away. Excellent food quality, attention to detail and great service. The lasagna is *highly* recommended. So are the raviolis. The baked penne is a bit too cheesy and their pestos are disappointing, but overall, this is the best Italian food on the island. Dinner is **$20–$30**. In the Rainbow Plaza in Kalaheo. (Ocean side of highway.) Closed Sunday.

SOUTH SHORE JAPANESE

Naniwa
2440 Hoonani Rd. • 742-1661
ono A beautiful view highlights the wonderful sushi (though not authentic Japanese in preparation). Scrupulous attention to freshness and presentation, and they have a good variety. Overlooking Kiahuna Beach in Po'ipu. Tempura and other cooked items for non-sushi lovers. Price is **$30** on up to the sky. At the Sheraton Po'ipu. Reservations strongly recommended.

SOUTH SHORE LOCAL

Koloa Fish Market
5482 Koloa Rd. • 742-6199
Ordering can be intimidating. You're standing at the counter with locals who *know* what they want. You, however, are trying to figure out what the items are. They serve plate lunches like lau lau, kalua pig, etc. Small selection but decent quality. **$7–$10**. In Koloa. Closed Sunday. Cash only.

Sueoka's Snack Shop
5392 Koloa Rd. • 742-1112
ono Probably the cheapest food on the south shore. Prices top out at around **$5**. Burgers, beef curry, fish burgers, chili rice and plate lunches. It's been popular forever with locals. Remember, since it's local style, items may be different than you think. For instance, the teriyaki burger isn't ground beef—it's strips of teri beef on a bun. On Koloa Road near Po'ipu Road beside Sueoka's Market. No credit cards.

SOUTH SHORE PACIFIC RIM

Roy's Po'ipu Bar & Grill
2360 Kiahuna Plantation • 742-5000
ono Well known throughout the islands for having the midas touch, Roy Yamaguchi has a knack for combining flavors very successfully. You won't get huge portions here, but the food is extremely well prepared and well presented with prices commensurate with the quality. Atmosphere is somewhat elegant but busy, with a large, glass, sound-proof wall showcasing the kitchen. (Ask for a table in the patio room for a less busy atmosphere.) The service is efficient, attentive and friendly, but they sometimes rush you a bit. If they do, just tell them to slow down. Fresh fish, pasta, chicken, beef and a host of nightly specials, all skillfully created. The fish is usually incredible. The signature dessert, baked chocolate soufflé, is obscenely delicious—order it à la mode

to actually *counter* the richness. You can BYOB *only* if they don't sell that particular wine, and they charge a hefty $18 corkage fee. Located in Po'ipu Shopping Village. Dinner is $30–$40. Reservations strongly recommended.

SOUTH SHORE TREATS

Lappert's Ice Cream
5242 Koloa Rd. • 742–1272

They have locations in Koloa, Princeville, Kapa'a and Hanapepe. All offer locally made Lappert's Ice Cream, which has slipped over the years and gotten too expensive. Two people can get one scoop each and a chocolate cone and spend *$10*. Open at 6 a.m. for pastries and coffee.

WEST SHORE AMERICAN

Grinds Café
4469 Waialo Rd. • 335–6027

Standard breakfast fare, hot and cold sandwiches plus pizza for lunch at this former Dairy Queen. Pretty ordinary stuff except for the mean cinnamon rolls. Service can be oddly inept. $7–$10 for breakfast, $8–$14 for lunch, $9–$17 for dinner. In 'Ele'ele Shopping Center on Hwy 50 near Hanapepe. Open at 6 a.m.; good if you're doing a boat trip nearby.

Koke'e Lodge
3600 Kokee Rd. • 335–6061

Hearty. That's the word that comes to mind. They classify themselves as local soul food. Consider the cornbread and chili. Their coconut pie is excellent. Lunch only for the most part. $7–$12. Located *waaaay* up the road in Koke'e on Waimea Canyon Road past the 15 mile marker. This is the road you take to get to Waimea Canyon and

the Kalalau Lookout. Open 9 a.m. to 3 p.m.

Shrimp Station
9652 Kaumualii Hwy • 338–1242

A good place for a plate of shrimp with rice or fries. Some items, like the sweet chili garlic shrimp (very tasty), you'll have to peel. Others, like the coconut shrimp, are peeled. Most items are $12, though some are less. On the ocean side of Hwy 50 in Waimea just before Waimea Canyon Road. Just some outdoor picnic tables. Service is slow.

Waimea Brewing Company
9400 Kaumualii Hwy • 338–9733

The beer is a bit too hoppy for our tastes. And the food is...well, who cares? It's a brewpub with bad beer. Anyway, the food's reasonably good—not great. Burgers, sandwiches, plus some steak and seafood. $11–$30. At Waimea Plantation Cottages, Waimea.

Wrangler's Steakhouse
9852 Kaumualii Hwy • 338–1218

Well, with a name like Wrangler's, you ain't a' lookin' for no Mongolian food, and you ain't a'gonna find it here. (Cowboy accents are hard to do in print.) The dinner menu is steak, which they do *very* well (the steak pulehu rocks!), and seafood. All entrées come with soup and a trip to the tiny salad bar. Lunch is burgers, steak and some specials. (Try the Kau Kau Tin.) Some outdoor tables in sunny Waimea can make for a pleasant meal. Good food with reasonable service. $9–$15 for lunch, $20–$40 for dinner. On the ocean side of the highway in Waimea; can't miss it. Avoid the horrible mai tais. Saturday is dinner only, closed Sunday.

WEST SHORE ITALIAN

Hanapepe Café
3830 Hanapepe Rd. • 335–5011
They classify themselves gourmet vegetarian Italian. Since they only do dinner once a week (Fridays—by reservation only), consider it a lunch-only place. Soups, lots of salads, sandwiches and burgers. That description makes the food sound less interesting than it really is. Actually, it's pretty good. They also have some tasty and creative entrées such as lasagna. **$7–$14** for lunch. Open Monday through Friday. In Hanapepe town.

Pacific Pizza & Deli
9852 Kaumualii Hwy • 338–1020
(ONO) A surprisingly good pizza place on the ocean side of Hwy 50 in Waimea next to Wrangler's. In addition to the typical ingredients, they have innovations such as teriyaki chicken, shrimp, spicy Thai sauce, salmon, etc. The crust is crunchy on the bottom—very tasty—and their sauce complements things well. They could use a bit more toppings on some, but the pizza is very flavorful. Consider having them go easy on the cheese—sometimes they're *too* generous. They have other items such as calzone (cheesy, greasy and tasty). Your options are limited on the west side. It gets a bit warm inside, but you can always take it to the beach. **$10–$20** for lunch and dinner. Closed Sunday.

WEST SHORE THAI

Toi's Thai Kitchen
4469 Waialo Rd. • 335–3111
(ONO) Amazingly good Thai food. Prices are probably too high, but Toi's food is excellent. Try it with cold Thai tea. Their curries are quite memorable and come with a green papaya salad and a drink. Their signature dish is Toi's Temptation. On mauka side of highway in 'Ele'ele Shopping Center, just before Hanapepe. **$13–$28** for lunch and dinner. Closed Sunday and Monday.

WEST SHORE TREATS

Kaua'i Chocolate Company
4341 Waialo Rd. • 335–0448
Homemade chocolates, fudge and ice cream. None are great; none are bad. It's solidly mid-level quality. In Hanapepe in the Port Allen Marina Center. **$3–$6**.

Jo-Jo's Clubhouse
9734 Kaumualii Hwy
(ONO) *Sometimes* the best shave ice on the island. Expertly prepared, large portions (piled twice as high as the cup), very reasonable prices and an outrageous selection of over 60 flavors. What else is there? Across from the 23 mile marker. Great place to stop on your way to or from Waimea Canyon (we usually do). Some problems can kill the experience, however. They sometimes let the blade get too dull lately (resulting in more of a snow cone-type product), and it's sometimes too crowded and understaffed, so there may be a long wait. Also, we wish they had a way to keep the syrup chilled before pouring onto the ice. When this is done, it keeps hard ice from forming on the bottom of the shave ice. The surroundings aren't so good and service often poor. If you catch 'em on a bad day, we don't vouch for them. But we gave them an ONO because we wanted to call your attention to them, and it's a cheap gamble. **$3–$6**. Not to be confused with **Jo-Jo's Anuenue** around the corner. Their ice isn't quite as fine.

ISLAND NIGHTLIFE

I know what you're thinking. "Gee, this section sure is small." True. Let's face it—

Kaua'i won't be confused with Las Vegas when it comes to nightlife. That's part of our charm. But hey, it's not like we spend *all* of our nights rearranging our sock drawers. (Usually just Fridays, and *oh, what a crazy time that* is!) Besides, if you did most of the things in the previous two sections, you're too pooped to party.

That said, there is probably enough nightlife on Kaua'i to satisfy *most* people's needs. Many of the restaurants feature entertainment at night, but the schedules are always changing. You can select a restaurant from the listings above and inquire as to their entertainment.

People have different desires when it comes to nightlife. Here we simply try to describe what's available and let you pick what you want.

Po'ipu

Stevenson's Library at the Hyatt is designed to appeal to anyone who ever wanted to visit the private library of one of the Rockefellers. Richly decorated, bookcases filled with the classics, pool tables (not billiards), large aquarium, chess tables and a terrace. The bar is the center attraction and is beautifully crafted out of strips of koa and monkeypod. Some of the staff can be a bit snotty, but otherwise, it's a nice place to have a drink. Things can get surprisingly lively. The Hyatt's **Seaview Terrace** commands a fabulous view of the resort and can be a relaxing place to have a drink after a long day. Nightly music.

The bar at the **Sheraton** is a smashing place for an early evening cocktail overlooking the beach. Live music available on some nights.

Keoki's Paradise at 742-7534 in the Po'ipu Shopping Village has entertainment in the lounge most nights. Hula demonstrations in the shopping center's courtyard many nights.

Lihu'e

Duke's Barefoot Bar at the Marriott is a great place for a drink; sporadic music offered. **Rob's Good Times Grill** (246-0311) on Rice Street offers entertainment every night. Mostly a local spot; sometimes a bit rough. **Nawiliwili Tavern** (245-1781) is very visible near the harbor and has pool tables and bar food.

Moviegoers can call **Kukui Grove Cinemas** at 245-5055 for a listing of their features.

Kapa'a

Trees (823-0600) behind Coconut Marketplace in Kapa'a is currently *the* place to go on the east shore for live music, pupus and cocktails. Most of the local musicians featured are pretty good, and the food is better than you'd expect at a lounge. **Cook's Landing** at the Kaua'i Beach at Maka'iwa (822-3455) is a decent place for a beverage while you listen to music near the pool. Some like to grab a drink here and stroll along the beach. **Tradewinds, A South Seas Bar** in the Coconut Marketplace is a small but sometimes lively little bar, often getting busier when Trees closes at 11 p.m. Dancing some nights. Hula shows are held nearby several nights a week. **Caffè Coco** has offbeat music most nights 7 p.m. to 9 p.m.

The **Poolside Bar** at Islander on the Beach is a favorite place to pick up a mai tai before walking over to the beach, plopping down and watching the waves.

North Shore

Hanalei Gourmet (826-2524) across from Ching Young Village usually has music but is only recommended for those on the prowl. It's a bit seedy there. **Tahiti Nui** (826-6277) in Hanalei is famous for its...colorful characters. **Bouchons Hanalei** (826-9701) has music nightly Thursday through Sunday.

The Happy Talk Lounge in the Hanalei Bay Resort has always been one of the best places in Princeville to have a drink and appreciate the night air.

West Shore

Find a bright light bulb and watch the geckos eat the mosquitoes—you crazy party animal, you.

LU'AUS & DINNER SHOWS

If you've ever seen a movie that takes place in Hawai'i, odds are there was a lu'au scene. This is where everyone stands around with a mai tai in one hand and a plate of kalua pig in the other. There's always a show where someone is twirling a torch lit at both ends, and, of course, the obligatory hula dancers. And the truth is, that's not far from reality. The pig is baked in the ground (called an imu) all day and is absolutely delicious. Shows are usually exciting and fast moving. Although the lu'aus on O'ahu can make you feel like cattle being led to slaughter, Kaua'i's lu'aus are somewhat smaller and much more pleasant.

All in all, lu'aus can be a real blast. If your time allows for one, it is highly recommended. We have two favorites, Kalamaku and Smith's.

Lu'au Kalamaku at Kilohana (245–9593) is one of the largest lu'aus in the state. Their 20,000-square-foot pavilion can hold nearly 1,000 people. You may not see it at maximum capacity, as some nights are cruise ship-only performances. Instead of waiting in line at the entrance, you're encouraged to roam their manicured grounds, visit the vendor booths and grab a drink while the line diminishes. They also offer carriage rides for $8 and a 30-minute train ride for $18 (leaves the station at 5:15 p.m.).

Seating is assigned and there's hardly a bad table in the house, with the inexplicable exception of one behind a column that we're told is only used when they sell out. Considering the cost of this lu'au, we expected the food to be better. The main dishes are simple, and there's little variety in the side items. Dessert is very weak, and waiting in line for 20 minutes to get it (as has happened to us) makes it worse. At least the bar is accommodating, but it closes at 7:30 p.m., just as the show begins. The show is energetic, captivating and highly entertaining. Instead of the traditional Polynesian revue, they offer a theatrical production of the Polynesian migration to Hawai'i. There is a plot to the show and each element is presented with quality sound, inventive lighting and a level of intensity that remains constant throughout the show. The fire knife dance is especially exciting. Call to see which days are open. **$95**.

We also like **Smith's Tropical Paradise** (821–6895). Lu'aus are Mon., Wed. and Fri. The food is not the star; it's the marvelous setting. (And they need more desserts.) Smith's is surrounded by a huge garden area. Though the garden could use a little polishing, the site works perfectly for a lu'au. After dinner, you move to a separate show area where a small pond separates the audience from the stage. The show is the most dazzling on the island. While not authentic by any means, it's well choreographed and is quite entertaining, complete with an erupting volcano. **$75**. Free open bar, but it closes at 7:30. Allow 30 minutes for a garden tour before the imu ceremony. You can also attend the show alone, without the food, for $15.

Next on our list is the **Grand Hyatt Kaua'i Lu'au** (742–1234). The food is well-prepared. When they have the lu'au in their Ilima Garden, it's a nice setting. But when it's in the courtyard or ballroom, it suffers. It has a more comfortable dining experience than Smith's but an average show. Free, open bar all night, plus table service for drinks, and there's no annoying lounge lizard hogging the stage. Sundays and Thursdays for **$94**.

Surf to Sunset Lu'au at the Sheraton Po'ipu (742–8200) has lu'aus on Fridays for **$75**. The show's location is so close to the beach that casual beachgoers could get a free show if they wanted to. The food is pretty good overall, and the open bar is there for you all night. The grounds don't seem to have been designed with lu'aus in mind, and traffic at the buffet table can get awkward. They offer a $12 upgrade that includes table service, if you like. The MC can get a little corny, but he's entertaining. The stage, however, is too small.

Although this isn't a lu'au, we didn't know where to put it. Every Wednesday night the Hilton Kaua'i Beach Resort (245–1955) hosts a performance of Rodgers & Hammerstein's 1949 Broadway musical, **South Pacific**. Wednesday also happens to be a big cruise ship day. Coincidence? Don't expect the excited atmosphere of a lu'au here. There is no audience participation, and you're not encouraged to drink and cut loose. (The bar makes bad $8 mai tais.) This is true dinner theater, and the audience tends to be older and much more subdued than lu'au audiences. The show is very well rehearsed, and the actors are as talented as the program describes. If you're familiar with *South Pacific*, or just enjoy theater, you'll like their presentation. If not, you might find yourself sleeping through the second act. The buffet is not spectacular, but the desserts are good. **$86**.

DINNER ON A BEACH

How about a romantic dinner by the ocean? For around $350–$500 per couple, the **Sheraton Kaua'i Resort** (742–1661), the **Grand Hyatt Kaua'i Resort** (742–1234) or the **Kauai Marriott Resort & Beach Club** (245–5050) will serve you near their beach. What a perfect way to make up for forgetting your anniversary.

ISLAND DINING BEST BETS

Best Pizza—Brick Oven Pizza
Best Cheap Mexican Food—Red Hot Mamas
Best View—Beach House Restaurant in Po'ipu
Best Phony but Exotic Ambiance—Keoki's Paradise
Best Shave Ice—Jo-Jo's Clubhouse—*usually*
Best Saimin—Hamura's Saimin
Best Hamburger—TNT Steakburgers, or Duane's Ono-Char Burger
Best Lu'au—Smith's Tropical Paradise
Best Pancakes—Tip Top Café
Best Sushi—Kintaro
Best Sandwich—Deli & Bread Connection
Best Ice Cream—Kilauea Video, Ice Cream & Candy
Best Sunday Morning Buffet—Kukui's
Best Inexpensive Baked Goods—Village Snack Shop
Best Live Music With Your Cocktail—Trees
Best Lasagna—Pomodoro's
Best Place for a Romantic Dinner—Tidepools or Dinner on a Beach
Best BBQ—Scotty's Beachside BBQ
Best Local Food—Mark's Place
Best Place on South Shore for Drinks and Pupus—Sheraton

Hotels shown in this color. Condominiums shown in this color.

Rental Agents

Ahh! Aloha. . . . . (866) 922-5642
B & B Kaua'i (bed & breakfast referral service). (800) 822-1176
Hanalei Aloha Rental Management. . . . . (800) 487-9833 or (808) 826-7288
Kaua'i Vacation Rentals . . . . (800) 367-5025 or (808) 245-8841
Na Pali Properties (north shore home listings) . . . . . . (800) 715-7273 or (808) 826-7272
Oceanfront Realty . . . . (800) 222-5541 or (808) 826-6585
The Parrish Collection Kaua'i . . . . (800) 325-5701 or (808) 742-2000
Prosser Realty. . . . . (800) 767-4707 or (808) 245-4711
Po'ipu Connection Realty . . . . (800) 742-2260 or (808) 742-2233
R & R Realty and Rentals . . . . (800) 367-8022 or (808) 742-7555
Regency Pacific Realty. . . . . (800) 826-7782 or (808) 826-9775
RE/MAX Kauai . . . . (877) 838-8149 or (808) 826-9675
Suite Paradise. . . . . (800) 367-8020 or (808) 742-7400

Wanted: Visitor seeking room with a view. Must be willing to burn your return airline ticket.

Your selection of where to stay is one of the more important decisions you'll make in planning your Kaua'i vacation. To some, it's just a place to sleep and rather meaningless. To others, it's the difference between a good vacation and a bad one.

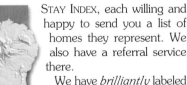

There are four main types of lodging on the island: hotels, condominiums, bed and breakfasts, and single family homes. The vast majority will stay in one of the first two types. But B&Bs and single family homes are often overlooked and can be very good values. If your group or family is large, you should strongly consider renting a house for privacy, roominess and plain ol' value. There is a list of rental agents in the WHERE TO

STAY INDEX, each willing and happy to send you a list of homes they represent. We also have a referral service there.

We have *brilliantly* labeled the four main sections of Kaua'i as North Shore, South Shore, East Shore and West Shore and listed the resorts geographically within in each section. **Hotels are in green** and **condominiums are in blue**. Hotels usually offer more services, but smaller spaces and no kitchens. Condos usually have full kitchens, but you won't get the kind of attention you would from a hotel, including daily maid service. There are exceptions, of course, and we will point them out when they come up.

See all Web reviews at: www.wizardpub.com

You can find their locations on the various maps.

All prices given are RACK rates, meaning *without any discounts*. Tour packages and travel agents can often get better rates. Most resorts offer discounts for stays of a week or more, and some will negotiate price with you. Some won't budge at all, while others told us *no one* pays RACK rates. Also, these prices are subject to taxes of nearly 12%.

The gold bar indicates that the property is exceptionally well priced for what you get.

SOLID GOLD VALUE

A REAL GEM

The gem means that this hotel or condominium offers something *particularly* special, not *necessarily* related to the price.

These are subjective reviews. If we say that rooms are small, we mean that we've been in them, and they feel small or cramped to us. If we say that maintenance is poor, we mean that the paint might be peeling, or the carpets are dingy or it otherwise felt worn to us.

HOTELS

All hotel rooms described **(shown in this color)** have air conditioning, an activity or travel desk, telephones, small refrigerators, lanais (verandas), cable TV and have cribs available upon request. None have room service unless otherwise noted. If you are a smoker, call about smoking policies because most hotel rooms in Hawai'i are designated non-smoking.

CONDOS

One of the confusing aspects about renting a condo **(shown in this color)**, cottage or house on Kaua'i is the fact that there's no central rental source for many individual properties. Most condo complexes, whether large or small, consist of individually owned condominiums. Individual owners have the prerogative of renting their units through any rental agent they choose. Consequently, a 50-unit condo resort might be represented by many rental agents. Usually (but not always), prices for comparable units within a given resort are equivalent through different agents. When we describe a particular resort, we will often give the names or phone numbers of one or two companies that dominate the rental pool. But realize that this does not always do justice to the *entire* property. When we describe rates, it is for the larger rental agents. Different agents have different policies for the same complex.

Once you have decided where you want to stay, you can contact the resort. You may also want to contact some of the rental agents on page 232 to determine if they represent any units from the property you have chosen.

Also realize that condominium owners usually have complete autonomy in how they furnish their individual units. Consequently, a resort that we describe as a good deal might have individual units that are not as hot. (Notice how we neatly cover our 'okoles, so that if you get a less-than-charming condo in a resort we recommend, we can always say you got one of the few duds there.)

Many condos have minimum stays—usually three nights. We don't always list this because it changes with different rental companies. More and more rental agents are also requiring you to pay *all* of your condo rental costs before you arrive. It may make you nervous, but you might not have a choice if you're intent on staying at a particular place.

Three bedroom/two bath units are described as 3/2, two bedroom/one bath

See all Web reviews at: www.wizardpub.com

units are described as 2/1, etc. Differentiation between half baths and full baths is not made. The price spread for rooms of a given size is due to different views, different locations within the resort and seasonal fluctuations. So when you see that a 2/2 unit rents for $140–$180, you should figure that $180 units have a better view or are closer to the water. The terms Oceanfront, Ocean View and Garden View are used rather capriciously in Hawai'i, so you should be skeptical of them.

Unless otherwise noted, all rooms come with telephones, complete kitchens, washer/dryers in unit, coffee makers, lanais (verandas), cable TV, ceiling fans and have cribs available upon request. Maid service is usually not available, and none have air conditioning unless otherwise noted. (On Kaua'i, trade winds often make a/c unnecessary, and few opt for it.) Most condos also have an additional cleaning fee and charge more at Christmas. If you are a smoker, you will want to check policies before you book. Most condos don't allow smoking in the units, and some even restrict you from smoking on the lanai and property, too.

BED & BREAKFASTS

Rather than describe the countless B&Bs scattered about the island, you're better off calling **Hawai'i's Best B&B** (800) 262–9912. We have lots of links to B&Bs on our website, but it's not practical to personally review them the way we do other accommodations.

RENTAL AGENTS

Nearly all the rental agents on the list on page 232 also represent private home vacation rentals, as well as condominiums in various resorts. Contact them in advance to obtain lists of rentals available or hit their websites. (We have links to all of them from our site.) Many great bargains can be found this way.

WHERE SHOULD I STAY?

What part of the island you want to stay on will dictate, to a degree, what kind of vacation you have. Although Kaua'i is small enough to do a driving tour in one day, where you stay will dominate certain activities.

The **north shore** is probably the prettiest part of the island and is dominated by one large hotel and lots of condos and vacation rentals. The weather is usually great in the summer and can be quite a bit wetter in the winter. Though the scenery is incomparable, the down side is the remoteness you'll feel when you want to venture to other parts of the island.

The **east shore** is the most geographically convenient. Trips to the north or south shore don't feel as daunting. There are plenty of hotels and condos and the most dining and shopping options. The down side is traffic in Kapa'a (especially heading south on Hwy 56) and the scenery and beaches aren't as good as the north shore.

The **south shore** has better weather year round and some great beaches. Several big hotels and lots of condos dominate. But the backdrop isn't as nice as the north or even east shores and there aren't as many dining or shopping choices as the east shore. Also, construction of new condos will be ever-present.

Finally there's the **west shore**. It's nearly always sunny, it's the hottest and driest part of the island and has only one resort plus a few vacation rentals to choose from. If you plan to spend all your time hiking in Koke'e and Waimea Canyon, it's convenient. Otherwise, it's isolated and remote.

See all Web reviews at: www.wizardpub.com

WHERE ARE THE REST?

You'll notice that some of the resorts listed here don't have full reviews. When we review a place to stay, we don't just want to list bare bones information on them. After all, you can get that kind of info on the Internet. We wanted to tell you what we really *think* about a place, and that takes space. Also, we wanted to include aerial photos of the resorts. After all, a picture speaks a thousand words (and a thousand words takes too long to read, anyway). But in the end we only have so much space we can devote to accommodations.

We had a choice—give you *less* info on *all* of them or do *detailed* reviews on only a *portion* of them. Neither choice seemed palatable.

So we came up with a *third* way: List minimal info on all (including if they are GEMS or SOLID GOLD VALUES), print detailed reviews on *most,* and post full reviews of all on our website, **www.wizardpub.com**. After all, most people use this section before they come to the islands. And with the Web (which has infinite space), we can do more, like post larger aerial photos of the resorts with specific buildings labeled when appropriate, provide constant updates when necessary, and put links to the various rental agents or hotels right in the review, allowing you to go to their sites and get more photos of the rooms. You should remember, however, that resorts post photos to lure you in, and some aren't above posting modified or overly flattering shots when they were new and sparkling. Our aerials don't lie and are designed to give you a feel for their ocean proximity (does oceanfront *really* mean oceanfront?), so you'll know what kind of view to expect from a given location within the resort. Resorts whose review is posted *only* on our website are identified with WEB REVIEW

Please remember that all these reviews are *relative to each other*. This is important. Even staying at a dump right on the ocean is still a *golly gee!* experience. In other words, *Hey, you're on the ocean on Kaua'i!* So if we sound whiny or picky when critiquing a resort, it's only because their next door neighbor might be such a better experience. It doesn't mean you'll be miserable, it just means that *compared to another resort*, you can do better.

NORTH SHORE

Hanalei Colony Resort
(800) 628–3004 or (808) 826–6235
7130 Kuhio Hwy

52 units, pool and spa, BBQs, coin-op laundry room, small day spa, restaurant, free Wi-Fi in restaurant with computers available, maid every 3 days, wedding coordinator. No telephones, no TV. Kitchens lack dishwashers. This is the only beachfront resort on the north shore. Some of their units are as close to the water as you will get on Kaua'i *(25 feet)*. We especially like units in A, F, G, I and the front J units. The resort is secluded and somewhat isolated, near the end of the road on the north shore. All units are two bedroom (although the bed-

A REAL GEM

See all Web reviews at: www.wizardpub.com

rooms aren't completely walled off and second rooms have twins). Rooms are nicely kept and were remodeled in 2007. Their location on Kepuhi Beach is outstanding, and the attention to detail is admirable. We like how they clean the windows every 3 days and include fresh flowers and fruit in each room. While the lack of room telephones might make arranging your day slightly awkward, others will welcome it. Cell phone coverage may be spotty, depending on your carrier. (You can use the phones by the pool, which is also where the laundry facilities are, so you won't be bored between loads.) 2/2 units (850 sq. ft.) are $240–$420. Garden views are quite nice. Seventh night free and other packages.

Hanalei Inn
(808) 826–9333
5-5468 Kuhio Hwy
WEB REVIEW

St. Regis Princeville
(877) 787–3447 or (808) 826–9644
5520 Ka Haku Rd.
WEB REVIEW ◆

Hanalei Bay Resort & Suites
(800) 827–4427 or (808) 826–6522
(800) 826–7782 or (808) 826–9775
5380 Honoiki Rd.
WEB REVIEW

Pu'u Poa
(866) 922–5642
(800) 222–5541 or (808) 826–6585
5454 Ka Haku Rd.
56 rooms, tennis court, pool, BBQ. Units are large (2,079 sq. ft.), comfortable and most are very nice. Most units (especially higher floors) have commanding ocean views. Units vary depending on the care of the particular owner, but most we saw were nice. The great ocean bluff causes

lots of seaspray-induced maintenance headaches. Many bathrooms have deep, round Japanese-style tubs or Jacuzzis next to the shower. Note that some of the unit owners have converted their lanai into a separate room (which they call an atrium). It's nice, but your upstairs neighbors will be able to see you through the glass...so behave yourself. 2/2 units from the first phone number (which is an off-island rental agent) are $295–$375 and have a 3-night minimum. The second numbers has less pricey units mostly of similar quality and no minimum stay. Regency Pacific Realty and Kaua'i Vacation Rentals also have units here. Marc Resorts has some, too, but we don't recommend them.

Hanalei Bay Villas
(800) 222–5541 or (808) 826–6585
5451 Ka Haku Rd.
WEB REVIEW

Hale Moi
(800) 367–5004 or (808) 826–9066
5301 Ka Haku Rd.

See all Web reviews at: www.wizardpub.com

40 units. Cheap. No, not the price, but the quality. Duplex units share a lanai. Inside, the construction feels...cheap. The sound of passing traffic is a given if you leave the jalousie windows open (which you'll want to do). And the mountain views are mixed but generally poor. Top this off with Castle Resort's ridiculous rates of $230–$260, depending on if you want both sides (one of which has a kitchen). Either way, the bed is in the main (only) room. In short, you can do better almost anywhere.

Pali Ke Kua
(800) 826–7782 or (808) 826–9775
(800) 367–5004 or (808) 826–9066
5300 Ka Haku Rd.

98 units, pool and spa, BBQs, hi-speed Internet access in some, restaurant. Some nicely furnished units from the second set of numbers, private path to eastern part of Hideaways Beach below the cliffs (which is otherwise only reachable by swimming from the western part of the beach). Nicely tucked away, offering quiet privacy. Many units have very fine ocean bluff views, but it's a bit pricey at rates listed below. Some of the layouts are a bit strange, and the bedrooms feel small to us. Try to get an upstairs unit for a better ocean view. Avoid units 1–16 whose poor views demand a steep discount. 1/1 units

(763–993 sq. ft.) are $198–$220, 2/2 units (1,100 sq. ft.) are $145–$303. The second set of numbers is for Castle Resorts whose units are even more expensive. You should check with other rental agents such as Kaua'i Vacation Rentals, RE/MAX, Oceanfront Realty or Ahh! Aloha. (See list page 232.)

Emmalani Court
(800) 826–7782 or (808) 826–9775
(877) 838–8149 or (808) 826–9675
5200 Ka Haku Rd.
WEB REVIEW

Villas of Kamali'i
(800) 367–5025 or (808) 245–8841
4141 Lei O Papa Rd.
WEB REVIEW

Alii Kai I
(866) 922–5642
(800) 222–5541 or (808) 826–6585
3780 Edward Rd.

63 units, BBQ, pool, many units have free hi-speed Internet access. Most of the buildings are perched on the sea cliffs (except #s 1 & 2). **SOLID GOLD VALUE** Bldgs. 3, 4 and 5 have the best views and can be quite dreamy, though the mountain views from 1 & 2 are pleasing. Layouts of these 2/2 units are good with even the second bedrooms often having ocean views. Sounds do carry in these buildings. Don't confuse this

See all Web reviews at: www.wizardpub.com

resort with Alii Kai II next door. Units (1,086 sq. ft.) are $110–$195. 3-night minimum from first phone number. Decor varies a lot here from unit to unit—some feeling more dated than others. It's worth it to splurge for the ocean view here. Regency Pacific Realty and Hanalei Aloha also have units here. See list on page 232.

The Cliffs
(800) 367–8024 or (808) 826–6219
(800) 222–5541 or (808) 826–6585
3811 Edward Rd.
WEB REVIEW

Nihilani at Princeville Resort
(877) 838–8149 or (808) 826–9675
4919 Pepelani Loop

102 units, pool, spa, a/c, BBQ, free Wi-Fi, 2-car garages. These 34 triplex buildings were completed in 2008. The close proximity of the buildings, lack of any decent views and roads on three sides of the grounds give the property a very claustrophobic feel. If you can get past all that, the interiors were pretty nice. Big bathtubs and separate showers in many of the bathrooms. Very pleasing layouts on the single-story 2/3 units, which at 1,972 sq. ft. make them very livable. We liked the large den and separate living room. The 2-story 2/3 (1,406 sq. ft.) units were our least favorite layout here. They show Bali Hai views on their property map, but the views of it are not great and only a few units can see Bali Hai, mostly buildings 16–19. (Even in some of those we had to walk out onto the second floor lanai to see it.) 2/3s are $175–$250, 3/3s (1,874 sq. ft.) are $195–$275. 3-night minimum.

Plantation at Princeville
(877) 838–8149 or (808) 826–9675
(800) 367–5025 or (808) 245–8841
4771 Pepelani Loop
WEB REVIEW 🔲

SeaLodge
(866) 922–5642
(800) 585–6101
3700 Kamehameha Rd.
WEB REVIEW 🔲

Kamahana
(800) 826–7782 or (808) 826–9775
3800 Kamehameha Rd.

30 units, pool, BBQs, hi-speed Internet access in most. Although the units are reasonably sized, they have an enclosed feel. The awkward design and poor use of angles makes you wonder if the architect stayed with the craft. At least the kitchens are large. 2/2s (1,200 sq. ft.) are $138–$200. Lots of long-term rentals. If you're forced to stay here, get an upstairs unit.

The Westin Princeville Ocean Resort Villas
(800) 937–8461 or (808) 827–8700
3838 Wyllie Rd.
WEB REVIEW

See all Web reviews at: www.wizardpub.com

Puamana
(800) 222–5541 or (808) 826–6585
(800) 487–9833 or (808) 826–7288
3880 Wyllie Rd.
WEB REVIEW

Mauna Kai
(800) 826–7782 or (808) 826–9775
3920 Wyllie Rd.
WEB REVIEW

Villas on the Prince
(866) 922–5642
(800) 367–5025 or (808) 245–8841
4141 Queen Emma's Dr.
WEB REVIEW

EAST SHORE

**Hotel Coral Reef Resort
on the Beach**
(800) 843–4659 or (808) 822–4481
4-1516 Kuhio Hwy

19 rooms, pool, fitness room, sauna, free Wi-Fi in lobby, free room safes, BBQ, a/c, refrigerators in king bed oceanfront units only, free room safe, coin-op laundry, lanais on all. Renovations in 2006 added upgrades, including a new pool, sauna, fitness room, coffee makers with free coffee daily (in all but garden rooms) and phones in the rooms. (No Internet access, though.) They did a nice job upgrading the resort and giving the rooms a fresh tropical feel. The oceanfront units have new bathrooms with deep Jacuzzi tubs. We used to label them a SOLID GOLD VALUE, but the price increase that came with the renovations, especially on the oceanfront building, cost them that rating. Good oceanfront location, free coffee and pastries in the lobby in the mornings where you can "talk story" with other guests. Rooms (approx. 600 sq. ft.) are $115–$245. Discounts available on their website make some rooms a good deal at certain times of the year and even a SOLID GOLD VALUE.

Kaua'i International Hostel
(808) 823–6142
4532 Lehua St.

They can accommodate 46 people in their dorms or private rooms (just a bed). Not a bad place to stay, and this is one of the cleanest hostels we've seen, with a pretty garden. They have very specific rules about who stays here. They want people who have good attitudes, are respectful of others and share in keeping the place clean. Strict 11 p.m. lights out. And they enforce those rules. There are on-site activities depending on who is staying there, from cooking to music to art. $25 for the dorm, $60–$85 for the private rooms. Laundry facilities, BBQ, shared baths (except one private room), kitchen and a pay phone. They provide the bedding, you bring the rest. 21-day maximum stay, and you must have a return ticket.

Pono Kai Resort
(800) 456–0009 or (808) 822–9831
4-1250 Kuhio Hwy
WEB REVIEW

See all Web reviews at: www.wizardpub.com

Waipouli Beach Resort & Spa
(800) 688–7444 or (808) 823–1401
(877) 838–8149 or (808) 826–9675
4-820 Kuhio Hwy

210 units, pool with keiki pool, 3 spas, free fitness room, restaurant, business

A REAL GEM center, a/c, health spa, coffee maker with free coffee daily, free room safes, free Wi-Fi. Finished in 2006, this resort has the most upscale condos on the east shore. The area is very congested and traffic into and out of the property may be an issue at times. Once you are within the grounds you won't notice that much, as most of the resort is oriented towards the pool and beach. The rooms are richly appointed and furnished. They include dark imported hardwood trim, granite countertops, over-sized Wolf ovens, etc. On the plus side, the bedrooms and baths are large. The baths have deep tubs or Jacuzzis and separate showers. On the negative side, the living area is relatively small. They didn't plan for a dining area, which is usually just a small table often shoved against a wall (an issue especially if you have more than 4 people staying in a room). We were told that the developers planned to have all the dining on the lanais, but with possible passing showers that is not always practical. The oceanfront units have the best layouts with roomy lanais and dreamy views. Second story and above are better, because first story oceanfront units have plantings in front of them that may block some of your view of the beach.

The pool is the star here. It is a saline, 2-acre, river-like pool that meanders through the entire courtyard of the property. One end it's sand-lined for the kids (since the beach is not very swimmable), and it has two waterslides. There are three spas, each with a sandy bottom, and one is suitable for kids. The pool is especially pretty at night. There are private hales for a massage by the pool.

Hotel-type rooms (325 sq.ft. with coffee maker, fridge and are closest to the road) are $255, 1/2s (824 sq.ft.) are $335–$550. 2/3s (1,155–1,414 sq. ft.) are $460–$760. The second set of phone numbers has 1 and 2 bedroom units for much less but these units don't include daily maid service or free coffee, have a 2-night minimum and charge a cleaning fee.

Kaua'i Beach at Maka'iwa
(877) 997–6667 or (808) 822–3455
650 Aleka Loop
WEB REVIEW

Plantation Hale (Best Western)
(800) 775–4253 or (808) 822–4941
4-484 Kuhio Hwy
WEB REVIEW

Islander on the Beach
(877) 997–6667 or (808) 822–7417
440 Aleka Place

See all Web reviews at: www.wizardpub.com

200 rooms, pool and spa, BBQ, coin-op laundry, poolside bar, empty refrigerator, microwave, coffee makers with free daily coffee, free room safe, hi-speed Internet access in units, free Wi-Fi in lobby. Wonderful open, plantation-style setting adjacent to Wailua Beach with very relaxing grounds. The Kaua'i and Ni'ihau buildings are fairly close to the ocean, allowing you to fall asleep to the sound of the surf. Rooms are smallish at 342 sq. ft. and go for $214–$306. Jr. Suites at 684 sq. ft. (with full kitchen) are $332. They have lots of specials, and few ever pay the price we listed (and we're assuming you won't either). Grab a beverage from the poolside bar and sip it at the adjacent beach. The resort was converted to a condotel (meaning the rooms are all individually owned), but decor is consistent and pleasing.

Kaua'i Sands Hotel
(800) 560–5553 or (808) 822–4951
420 Papaloa Rd.
WEB REVIEW

Lae Nani
(800) 688–7444 or (808) 822–4938
410 Papaloa Rd.

84 units, lighted tennis court, pool, daily maid service, coin-op laundry, free room safe. Though the resort is still a gem, it's a bit overpriced, so we're hoping that you're getting a discount. Pleasant grounds and a very nice ocean-

A REAL GEM

front location. They have a Hawaiian heiau on the premises, as well as a wonderful boulder-enclosed ocean pond for the keiki (kids). Building 5 has oceanfront units. At press time there was construction on a new housing development across the street with building 4 most affected. 1/2 units (around 900 sq. ft.) are $309–$379, 2/2 units (around 1,100 sq. ft.) are $335–$445.

Lanikai
(800) 367–5004 or (808) 822–7700
390 Papaloa Rd.
WEB REVIEW

Kapa'a Sands Resort
(800) 222–4901 or (808) 822–4901
380 Papaloa Rd.

24 units, pool, BBQ, coin-op laundry, free Wi-Fi in units and by pool. This is a very good bargain. Their small oceanfront studios **SOLID GOLD VALUE** (some have a pull down Murphy bed—these are recommended for more living space). Small, but they make good use of space for $150. For this price you are as close as 30 feet from the water on a pretty beach. Resident offshore turtles will keep you entertained at dusk. What a deal! The property feels very intimate and tropical. The aerial photo makes it look like some of the oceanfront units are blocked by trees, but the crowns of the trees are above the ocean plane. Nice staff here.

See all Web reviews at: www.wizardpub.com

At press time there was construction on a new housing development across the street. Studios (approx. 380 sq. ft.) are $120–$150 (definitely spring for the oceanfront), 2/2 units have a two-story layout (728 sq. ft.) and are $170–$205. 3- or 7-night minimum.

Wailua Bayview
(800) 367–5242
320 Papaloa Rd.
WEB REVIEW

Coco Palms Resort
4-241 Kuhio Hwy
The historic Coco Palms, where Elvis filmed "Blue Hawaii," was whacked by a hurricane in 1992 and spent the better part of a decade trying to get an insurance check, during which time Elvis had left the building. The fate of the old Coco Palms remains unknown at press time.

Aloha Beach Hotel
(888) 823–5111 or (808) 823–6000
3-5920 Kuhio Hwy
WEB REVIEW

Kaha Lani
(800) 367–5004 or (808) 822–9331
4460 Nehe Rd.

74 units, lighted tennis court, BBQ, pool, computer in office, free hi-speed Internet access in units, coin-op laundry, room safe. The buildings are on the cheap side

(and sound carries pretty efficiently), but the buildings are well-maintained, grounds are well-tended, and most of the units are reasonably decorated (though you still have lots of variation). All the units are very clean. RACK rates are on the high side, but the oceanfront units are a better deal. (Though your view might be partially blocked by trees.) One reason oceanfront units often seem better cared for is that since they need more maintenance (because the salt eats things up) and those units cost more to buy, their owners spend more money on them. Lanais aren't totally private. Adjacent to Lydgate State Park and the beach path, which may bring some unsavory characters around the property at times. 1/1 units (776 sq. ft. including lanai) are $235–$385, 2/2 units (1,100 sq. ft.) are $295–$485, 3/2 units are $385–$525.

Kaua'i Beach Villas
(800) 367–5025 or (808) 245–8841
4330 Kauai Beach Dr.
WEB REVIEW

Hilton Kaua'i Beach Resort
(888) 243–9178 or (808) 245–1955
4331 Kauai Beach Dr.

See all Web reviews at: www.wizardpub.com

350 rooms, 4 pools, 2 spas, 7 conference rooms, poolside snack bar, valet parking, room service, health spa, fitness room, a couple of shops, hi-speed Internet access in rooms, free Wi-Fi in lobby area, 3 restaurants, lounge, room service, coin-op laundry, empty refrigerator, coffee maker with free coffee daily, free laptop safe, business center. First a Hilton, then an Outrigger, then a Radisson and now a Hilton again, this resort has been through many changes. The latest owners included a $13 million upgrade to the property, pools and rooms. The resort is now a condotel (individual owners for each room). The rooms all have the same pleasant plantation style decor that was part of the 2007 upgrade.

A REAL GEM

This resort, located between Lihuʻe and Wailua, is near a pretty but relatively unswimmable beach. (A short walk farther north leads to better parts of Nukoliʻi Beach.) They've made up for it by installing a wonderful half-sand lined freshwater pool with a water slide to augment their other 3 pools complete with man-made waterfalls. We wish they had more umbrellas available for the pool chairs. Service has improved markedly, to the point that it competes with higher-end resorts, and they keep things *very* clean. The staff is warm here. Rooms are fairly small at around 360 sq. ft. If you opt for ocean view, ask for one of the ocean-facing end units in Bldg. 4.

They charge $13 per day to park your car, valet or self. Internet in your room is $13, and local calls are a buck.

Rates are $329–$439. Suites are $600–$1,500. (Most suites are simply two rooms joined at the hip.) Many good discounts and packages are available.

Tip Top Motel
(808) 245–2333
3173 Akahi St.
WEB REVIEW

Motel Lani
(808) 245–2965
4240 Rice St.

Motel Lani

8 rooms, BBQ. They claim this "was probably the first hotel on the island." It's…disheveled but reasonably clean (for the money). **SOLID GOLD VALUE** Rooms are small—most under 200 sq. ft.—and have bathrooms and fridges but no phones or TVs. Some with a/c. Best view is of the Dumpster. $55–$70. Cash only. If you stay more than two nights, the rates drop. They have a piano in the tiny lobby that you can play, but we doubt you'll find Billy Joel staying here. This is probably the cheapest place to stay on the island.

Kauaʻi Palms Hotel
(808) 246–0908
2931 Kalena St.

28 rooms, coin-op laundry, free Wi-Fi in the lobby. No phones. This is probably

See all Web reviews at: www.wizardpub.com

your best bet in Lihu'e (but it is a bit pricier). It has small, clean rooms and few amenities, but the present owner has made an effort with the decor and property. Rooms (108–260 sq. ft.) are $75–$89 (some of those $89 rooms have a kitchenette). Larger rooms with full kitchens are $100.

Kaua'i Marriott Resort & Beach Club
(800) 220–2925 or (808) 245–5050
3610 Rice St.
WEB REVIEW 💎

Garden Island Inn
(800) 648–0154 or (808) 245–7227
3445 Wilcox Rd.

21 rooms, empty refrigerator, microwave, a/c, coffee maker with free coffee daily, free hi-speed Internet access in rooms.

SOLID GOLD VALUE This pretty and colorful inn (all doors and art on the walls are original art pieces) located near Kalapaki Beach in Nawiliwili, is spotlessly clean with lots of nice touches around the place, such as fresh flowers, free use of their boogie boards, snorkel gear, beach mats and daily maid service. This is a good place to stay for those seeking a place to sleep, without the exotic grounds of a resort. The staff exudes the aloha spirit. It can be noisy on the main road, so we hope you're an early riser. The bathrooms have showers, no tubs. Rooms (approx. 225–400 sq. ft) are

$99–$180. Only wish they had some sort of laundry facilities.

Banyan Harbor
(800) 422–6926 or (808) 245–7333
(800) 767–4707 or (808) 245–4711
3411 Wilcox Rd.
WEB REVIEW

Kaua'i Inn
(800) 808–2330 or (808) 245–9000
2430 Hulemalu Rd.
WEB REVIEW

SOUTH SHORE

Grand Hyatt Kaua'i Resort & Spa
(800) 554–9288 or (808) 742–1234
1571 Poipu Rd.

602 rooms, 3 tennis courts with pro shop, golf course, 24-hour room service, 6 restaurants, Wi-Fi throughout, cocktail lounges, 8 shops, Camp Hyatt child care service,

A REAL GEM 23 conference rooms, valet parking, multiple pools and spas, 24-hour fitness center, empty refrigerator, coffee makers with free coffee daily, coin-op laundry, lu'au, complete business services and a 4,500 sq. ft. health spa. It was hard for us to review this resort without sounding like drooling sycophants. But the reality of the Hyatt is that they did almost everything right. Put simply, it's our favorite big resort on the island. As you walk into the lobby and see the ocean framed by the entrance, you realize that here they really sweated the

See all Web reviews at: www.wizardpub.com

details. The grounds are as exotic as any you will find in all the islands, complete with parrots and other birds. Their pools are incredible. Gallon for gallon, they're more fun than any we've seen on the island. The upper swimming pool seems to meander forever. It even has a slight current and hides such goodies as caves tucked behind small waterfalls (they're easy to miss). Take your time exploring as it winds through lush vegetation. At the end of the upper pool, you can take the "elevator" (a free and re-spectably fast waterslide) to the bottom. There you will find what they call the action pool complete with a volleyball net, waterfalls, spas and an area for children. An island there hides a hot tub. Above is the adult pool. Across from the lower pool are several *acres* of saltwater lagoon. If you want saltwater without the waves, here it is. The "sand" is actually gravel imported from San Juan Capistrano. (And it's hard on tender tootsies.) Inside the lagoon are several landscaped islands. The grounds are lush and very well maintained and feature a smashing waterfall below the Seaview Terrace Lounge. The resort is located on a so-so beach called Shipwreck Beach. They have covered cabanas on the beach for $100. (They're coveted, and the Hyatt could use more.) If you're lucky enough to be under one in the evening during a passing shower, it's something you will long remember. Covered chairs by the pool are $35. Cabanas by the pool are free but you have to get up early to snag one. Large hammocks and loveseat swings are scattered throughout the grounds. Their shops run the gamut from fine art to footwear. They have wedding coordinators on site, and guest services are good.

Opened in 1990, the Hyatt has matured into a fairly smooth resort. The Hyatt's an easy GEM, and their awesome grounds still keep them in a class by themselves. At press time room upgrades were underway with pleasing results.

They have an *mandatory* $18 per day resort fee covering local calls, valet parking (which can be slow at times), Internet, fitness center, room safe and some other things.

If your intention is to come to Kaua'i and never leave the resort (which we hope you *won't* do), the Hyatt is the place to come. You'll never get bored here. This is a *great* place to bring the kids, but adults will enjoy it, too. Camp Hyatt provides extensive child care service for kids age 3 (if potty-trained) to 12 for $80 per day. Anara Spa is massive and the finest spa on the island complete with couples "treatment hales," lava showers, steam and baths. So what's the catch? Well, amenities like this don't come cheap. Spacious rooms (600 sq. ft.) are $440–$1,000. Suites (866–2,463 sq. ft.) are $1,570–$5,000. Be aware they have an early departure fee if you opt to trim some days off your stay.

Makahuena
(800) 367–5004 or (808) 742–2482
(800) 367–8022 or (808) 742–7555
1661 Pe'e Rd.

78 units, small pool, spa, BBQ, free hi-

See all Web reviews at: www.wizardpub.com

speed Internet access in rooms, lighted tennis court. Every fourth day maid service with the first set of numbers. The developer seems to have spared...well, lots of expenses, actually. Like the endless concrete stairs at every turn, cheap-looking fixtures, etc. Some of the units are fairly nice inside, many are not. We've never been real warm toward Makahuena. The location out on the point will expose you to *lots* of sea spray-laden wind, so don't expect the windows to stay clean. Those winds, however, tend to keep the units cool. There are 8 different floor plans, so it's hard to say if you'll get a good one. Second floor units are better for views, whereas many first floor units are partly below ground. 2/2 units are $300–$520, 3/3 units are $380–$475. Prices are much lower at the second set of phone numbers, but the units might not be as nice.

Po'ipu Makai
(800) 325–5701 or (808) 742–2000
(800) 367–5025 or (808) 245–8841
1677 Pe'e Rd.
WEB REVIEW

Po'ipu Crater Resort
(800) 367–8020 or (808) 742–7400
2330 Hoohu Rd.

30 units, pool, sauna, BBQ, tennis court and paddle court (mini tennis). Located in the bottom of a small crater, the grounds are pleasant and well maintained, but

there is no view. (Technically speaking, you're in a hole.) When the trade winds aren't blowing, it can get pretty hot in there, and sounds bounce around in an odd way. Lots of rental agents have units here, not just the number listed (which charges for local calls). 2/2 townhouse units (1,240 sq. ft.) are a pretty good deal at $174–$213. Prices decrease if you stay longer than 7 nights.

Po'ipu Palms
(800) 742–2260 or (808) 742–2233
1697 Pe'e Rd.

Sunset Kahili
(800) 367–8022 or (808) 742–7434
1763 Pe'e Rd.

35 units, free hi-speed Internet access in rooms, free Wi-Fi in some, BBQ, pool, elevator. Built in 1968 (you'd swear it was the '50s), it's old but fairly well-kept. All units have nice ocean views, with the third floor and above being particularly good. It's very popular with seniors and long-time repeat guests. Average value. 1/1 units (780 sq. ft.) are $125–$175, 2/2 units (1,037 sq. ft.) are $250. Master bedrooms are only shut off by shoji doors, which creates less privacy. 4-night minimum. Add 3.5% for credit card payments.

See all Web reviews at: www.wizardpub.com

Po'ipu Shores
(800) 367–5004 or (808) 742–7700
1775 Pe'e Rd.

39 units, swimming pool, BBQ, free Wi-Fi by pool, free hi-speed Internet access in rooms, elevator in Building A, daily maid service. Most of the owners (not all) have been spending a lot of money on their units, and they were looking *very* nice on this visit. The grounds aren't much, but the property is well-maintained with pleasing exterior improvements done in 2008. What you're really paying for is the extraordinary proximity to, and sound of, the ocean, not the size of the rooms. This makes them a relatively decent value. The townhouse units in building C are the quietest. The one-bedroom condos are the only units without the master bedroom on the ocean side, but all units have great ocean views. 1/1 units (800–900 sq. ft.) are $295–$440, 2/2 units (912–1,322 sq. ft.) are $375–$545, 3/2s (1,225–1,280 sq. ft.) are $485–$655. They often discount. The staff here is very friendly. They charge $1 per local call (unusual for a condo). The 2,600 sq. ft. penthouse is $535–$735. It was originally built personally for the developer, is glass-walled and has one of the grandest views on the south shore. If you ask for and get a renovated unit, this property rates a REAL GEM.

Po'ipu Plantation
(800) 634–0263 or (808) 742–6757
1792 Pe'e Rd.
9 units, a/c, spa, free Wi-Fi, BBQ, coin-op laundry. Not really a condo, or a hotel. More like a plantation. (Oh…I get

¹⁄₁₀ Mile to Ocean

it!) No real views here. Grounds aren't remarkable; rooms are tidy but the appliances and bathrooms are showing their age. Many repeat guests at peak times of the year. Maid service is extra, but they will do a complimentary linen and towel service if you stay more than a week. 1/1 units (650 sq. ft.) are $135–$175, 2/2 units (900 sq. ft.) are $185–$210. 3- or 5-night minimum. Prices decrease for longer stays. The adjacent "main house" is available for weddings and as a B&B with 4 rooms.

Honu Kai Villas
(877) 595–2824
1871 Pe'e Rd.
WEB REVIEW

Nihi Kai Villas
(800) 325–5701 or (808) 742–1412
1870 Hoone Rd.

70 units, pool, keiki pool, free hi-speed

See all Web reviews at: www.wizardpub.com

Internet access in rooms, some have Wi-Fi, free room safe, 2 tennis courts and a paddle ball court (sort of mini tennis), BBQS. Well-maintained grounds. The rooms seem to vary *a lot.* The two-story townhouse units have an annoying layout, but single level 2/2 units are an acceptable value. Many of the units had been remodeled on this visit and were looking much nicer. Buildings 1, 2, 4, and some units in 8 are your best bet for a glimpse of the ocean. The rest are strictly garden views. 1/2 units (1,400 sq. ft.) are $145–$244, 2/2 units (2,100 sq. ft.) are $159–$380, 3/2 units (2,300 sq. ft.) are $300–$625. 5-night minimum.

Hideaway Cove Villas
(866) 849–2426 or (808) 635–8785
2307 Nalu Rd.

WEB REVIEW ◆

Po'ipu Kai Resort
(800) 367–8020 or (808) 742–7400
(877) 997–6667 or (808) 742–7424
1941 Poipu Rd.

Poipu Kai's 6 regions identified on larger Web site shot.

350 units, 9 tennis courts with pro shop, 6 pools (though you'll have access to only 2), 1 spa, free hi-speed Internet access, BBQS. This sprawling 70-acre resort sports lots of open ground, widely varied units and close proximity to the Hyatt, its restaurants and shops. Although many rental agents represent Po'ipu Kai, **Suite Paradise** and **Aston** have the most units.

Suite Paradise generally has better rooms at lower RACK rates, but **Aston** deals with most of the tour package companies which sometimes get good rates for you. If you book it yourself, do it through **Suite Paradise**. (Their numbers are the ones listed first, and for some reason they charge for local calls.) The resort is so varied it's hard to sum it up. Po'ipu Kai is broken into six regions with the Po'ipu Sands region having the best beach access. (Building 5 is particularly good.) In some ocean view units, the ocean is only visible if you break your neck in two places and hang it out the window. Prices are all over the place and gave us blinding headaches trying to figure it all out. In general, **Suite Paradise** 1/1 units are $168–$432, 2/2 units are $189–$492, 3/2 units are $250–$359. Price decreases if you stay more than 7 nights. **Aston** 1/1 units are $265–$440, 2/2 units are $337–$680, 3/2s are $430–$680. Daily maid service is included with Aston. **The Parrish Collection Kaua'i** (800–325–5701) also has some units. Some bedrooms at the condos (especially in the Kahala and Manualoha areas) may consist of a loft with limited privacy, so be sure and ask. One section of Po'ipu Kai, called **Regency II**, is handled in a separate review because they have a separate rental agent, and it's *sooo* different than the rest of Po'ipu Kai.

Regency II & Villas
(877) 595–2824
(800) 325–5701 or (808) 742–2000
1831 Poipu Rd. & 2387 Hoohu Rd.

WEB REVIEW ◆

Marriott's Waiohai Beach Club
(800) 845–5279 or (808) 742–4400
2249 Poipu Rd.

WEB REVIEW

See all Web reviews at: www.wizardpub.com

Ko'a Kea Hotel & Resort
(866) 806–2288 or (808) 828–8888
2251 Poipu Rd.

WEB REVIEW

Kiahuna Plantation Resort
(800) 688–7444 or (808) 742–6411
(800) 367–5004 or (808) 742–2200
2253 Poipu Rd.

WEB REVIEW

Sheraton Kaua'i Resort
(800) 782–9488 or (808) 742–1661
2440 Hoonani Rd.

394 rooms, 2 pools, keiki pool, spa, Wi-Fi, 2 shops, 2 restaurants, 3 tennis courts (2 lighted), valet parking, 8 conference rooms, coin-op laundry, coffee makers with free coffee daily, PlayStation, fitness center (with an inspiring view), 2 massage rooms. The Sheraton is the perfect complement to the Hyatt. While the Hyatt excels at gorgeous and exotic grounds, the Sheraton boldly embraces the ocean. The Ocean and Beach wings are closer to the ocean than at any other major Kaua'i hotel. The sound of the surf hitting the rocks below the Ocean Wing is soothing. Kiahuna Beach, in front of the Beach Wing, is wonderfully close and easy to access. The Garden Wing is generally lacking but is cheaper, and we're not as fond of the rooms there. All rooms are on the small side (410 sq. ft. for the garden view, 510 sq. ft. for Ocean and Beach),

A REAL GEM

were renovated in 2006 and don't feel particularly Hawaiian. But the resort makes up for it with its cozy relationship with the water. Most rooms are connected to others by a lock-off—good for families needing more than one room. Their restaurants, Naniwa and Shells, have incredible beach views. Kids (under 12) eat free with a paying adult at Shells, and they have a child care program for $50 per day. (They'll even accept kids staying at other resorts for a little extra.) Couples can enjoy a *private* oceanside dinner for $350.

The beachside pool is nice, and they have a small waterslide. Cabana chairs are $40 per day. Sheraton has a mandatory resort fee of $17 per day, which includes self-parking (a long walk), free local calls, room safe, tennis courts and a few other doodads. When picking a room, this is one of those places where it's worth the extra money to spring for an ocean view room. They have free mai tais from 5–6 p.m. Ask for an "escape rate" when you reserve. Rates are $445–$820. Suites (1,000–2,000 sq. ft.) are $1,650–$3,600.

Po'ipu Kapili
(800) 443–7714 or (808) 742–6449
2221 Kapili Rd.

60 units, 2 lighted tennis courts, elevators, free hi-speed Internet access, pool, coin-op laundry (washer/dryers in all 2/3s), maid service once a week, BBQS.

See all Web reviews at: www.wizardpub.com

Well-maintained and sculptured grounds, very spacious rooms for the money, and

A REAL GEM

a second-home atmosphere make this an easy recommendation. Buildings 1, 2, 6 and 7 (all 2/3s) have very nice ocean views and are two-story townhouses. You can pick herbs from their garden if you choose to cook. The staff is top-notch here. 1/2 units (1,120 sq. ft.) are $250–$365, 2/3 units (1,820) are $385–$500. They also have elegant 2,600 sq. ft. penthouses for $500–$625. There is a construction project on-going behind them. 3-night minimum.

Alihi Lani
(800) 742–2260 or (808) 742–2233
2564 Hoonani Rd.

Waikomo Stream Villas
(800) 325–5701 or (808) 742–7220
2721 Poipu Rd.

60 units, pool, free hi-speed Internet access, tennis court, BBQ. Pretty and well-

SOLID GOLD VALUE

kept grounds and large rooms (all garden views). Lots of privacy. Sadly, they are surrounded by large construction projects for a few years, but "construction discounts" in units in some buildings make it a great value, especially if you plan to be out of your condo all day. 1/1 units (1,050 sq. ft.) are $115–$211, the 1,500 sq. ft. 2/2 units (second bedrooms are a

loft with limited privacy) are $145–$259. 5-night minimum.

Whalers Cove
(800) 225–2683 or (808) 742–7571
2640 Puuholo Rd.

39 units, heated pool and spa, daily maid, elevator, BBQ, free daily coffee, free room

A REAL GEM

safe, free hi-speed Internet access or Wi-Fi in most in rooms and lobby. This is a lovely property and very serene. The grounds are well-manicured, and the setting for the pool is outstanding. Though individually owned and decorated, they are well-furnished with koa wood doors and even koa floor trim in the closets. In the past the units were some of the most expensively furnished we had seen. On this visit, though still lovely, the newer condos in the area are starting to make some of the furnishings feel a bit dated. The resort is very quiet, and they provide more personalized service than you will find elsewhere. (They will even do your grocery shopping before you arrive and stock your refrigerator.) Most units have Jacuzzi bathtubs, many overlooking the ocean. They ain't cheap, so do what you have to to get a discount. 1/2 units are $349–$541. (These actually have two bedrooms, but you are limited to 2 people and charged as if it were 1/2.) 2/2 units are $479–$709. Most units have 1,390 sq. ft. (plus lanai) except the deluxe, which has 2,200 sq. ft. In all, it's expensive, but worth the money if you get a deal. By the way, even at this price they have an obnoxious *mandatory* $15 resort fee. With all the services they provide, do they really have to charge an extra $15 so you can have "free" Internet, coffee and beach towels? (OK, end of rant.)

Kuhio Shores
(800) 543–9180 or (206) 938–5802
(800) 367–8022 or (808) 742–7555
5050 Lawai Rd.
WEB REVIEW

Prince Kuhio
(888) 747–2988
(800) 367–5025 or (808) 245–8841
5061 Lawai Rd.

72 units, pool, coin-op laundry (washer/dryers in *some* units), free hi-speed Internet access in some, a/c in a few. Grounds are **SOLID GOLD VALUE** very well-tended, and the pool and BBQ area are very pretty. Built in 1962, the resort's clean for its age. Located across the road from the ocean, this used to be a hotel but was converted to condos, so expect some bizarre room layouts. The ocean views here are not that great, but if you want a glimpse, get a unit above the first floor and closer to the road. Some long-term rentals here. Studios (338–450 sq. ft.) are $65–$135, 1/1 units (600–720 sq. ft.) are $110–$171. There is also a 2/1 penthouse (875 sq. ft.) with a large roof deck for $275. 3-night

minimum from first phone number, which is for a large group of owners. Prices decrease for longer stays, and because you are dealing directly with the owners, they may be more flexible with the price. The second set of numbers has more expensive rates and a 5-night minimum. Units also available from Po'ipu Connection and R & R Realty and Rentals.

Kalaheo Inn
(888) 332–6023 or (808) 332–6023
4444 Papalina Rd.
WEB REVIEW

WEST SHORE

Waimea Plantation Cottages
(877) 997–6667 or (808) 338–1625
9400 Kaumualii Hwy

Note the muddy ocean water here.

57 units, stereos, pool and keiki pool, conference room, Wi-Fi in lobby area, health spa, free room safe, coin-op laundry, BBQ (upon request), volleyball and maid service every third day. Many of these cottages were once plantation workers' homes, and each is as different as their former owner's tastes. We had a hard time coming up with adjectives to describe the rooms. They have old-style floors and furniture, just like from the plantation days. Units have been refurbished with modern amenities, but they retain the old-style feel inside, without feeling *too* old and worn. They are very

See all Web reviews at: www.wizardpub.com

clean. At this 27-acre former plantation, peace and privacy are yours—the trade-off is relative isolation given the location on the extreme west side. There is much feeling of 'ohana (family) here, and you will definitely experience the aloha spirit. With their location so close to the mouth of the very reddish Waimea River, swimming in the murky ocean water is pretty poor at this marginal beach. The coconut grove, banyan trees and hammocks scattered about add to the quiet charm of this property, and this is a good place to watch the sunset over the private island of Ni'ihau. Units vary tremendously from $220 for some 1/1 cottages, to $800 for a 5/4 oceanfront cottage Sizes range from 460–4,000 sq. ft for the oceanfront cottage. Contact them for a complete list.

PMRF Beach Cottages
(808) 335–4752
1293 Tartar Dr.

19 cottages, BBQs, free Wi-Fi and computers available at their restaurant, 1 lighted tennis court, driving range, fitness center, pool, racquetball, handball, a/c in **SOLID GOLD VALUE** bedrooms, restaurant. Adjacent to Barking Sands Beach, this place is a steal—if you're in any branch of the military or retired. (Having seen *Behind Enemy Lines* won't qualify.) It's almost worth a stint just for that perk alone. Each cottage is a self-contained 1,000 sq. ft. 2/1, and you can have 'em for only $70–$95. The newer cottages have better views and are more modern. We considered trying to bounce a quarter off the bed but thought better of it.

Koke'e Lodge
(808) 335–6061
3600 Koke'e State Park
WEB REVIEW

YWCA Camp Sloggett
(808) 245–5959
Koke'e State Park

60 beds in the bunkhouse, cottage and lodge, huge fire pit (wood available), BBQs, pay phone (bring change because your cell phone probably won't work), covered lanai with ping-pong table and other games. Built in 1925, this is a clean, no-nonsense camp with a no-nonsense attitude: "leave it as you found it." The grounds are isolated, but the scenery is quite beautiful with a small stream. It's $10 per person for tent camping, $25 for the hostel bunkhouse (bring your own bedding and towels). Community restrooms and showers for campers and bunkhouse. The two end units of the bunkhouse have a kitchen and sleep up to four people for $75–$100 per night (you still share a bath with the hostel). They have a cottage available for $85–$120 for up to four people. The lodge has a large kitchen and bath and can sleep up to 15 people for $25 per person (5 person minimum weekdays/8 weekends). Children under 5 are free. They often rent to large groups, so be sure and call two weeks in advance for availability. The cabin and lodge often are reserved a up to year or more in advance with summer being the busiest season. 2-night minimum for the cottage.

Island Dining Index on page 202, Where to Stay Index on page 232.

Island Dining Index on page 202, Where to Stay Index on page 232.

INDEX

Island Dining Index on page 202, Where to Stay Index on page 232.

Island Dining Index on page 202, Where to Stay Index on page 232.

Island Dining Index on page 202, Where to Stay Index on page 232.

Island Dining Index on page 202, Where to Stay Index on page 232.

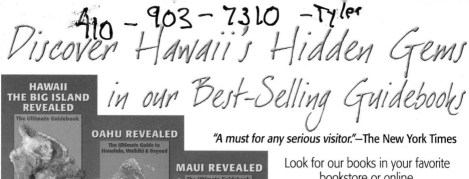